Azab Alaziz Alhashemi

Arbitration in the UAE

Azab Alaziz Alhashemi

Arbitration in the UAE

explaining the new arbitration law No. {6} for the year 2018

Noor Publishing

Imprint

Cover image: www.ingimage.com

Publisher:
Noor Publishing
is a trademark of
International Book Market Service Ltd., member of OmniScriptum Publishing Group
17 Meldrum Street, Beau Bassin 71504, Mauritius

Printed at: see last page
ISBN: 978-620-0-07285-6

The definition of arbitration in the language, legitimately and legally

Introduction:

The United Arab Emirates is in an important economic position to attract investors and capital from all over the world to develop and open the door to investment. The United Arab Emirates has sought to evolve with a distinctive and prosperous quality through the new law replacing the Civil Procedure Act No. 11 of 1992. This law was not limited to modernity but was repealed from article 203 to article 218 of the Code of Civil Procedure.

Arbitrators and international centers of practice and interest are well aware that this evolution of this law is qualitative and will have an impact on the work of international arbitration in the UAE.

Considering that the Emirian legislator has made this law subject to the provisions of Federal Act No. 11 of 1992 on the Code of Civil Procedure, Chapter IV Enforcement of Foreign Provisions, Orders and Obligations, Articles 235-238 and Chapter V Procedures for the Application of Articles 239-243.

I will try to explain this unique law in the hope that I will be able to highlight the most important documents. I would like to take this opportunity to warmly thank this special country and its wise government, which is always seeking to maintain a long international reputation and is the best representative of the Arab world through the polarization of major companies and investors from all five continents. This gigantic development and distinctive vision were not born out of anything, but the Emiratis still have the great ambition to place their country at the highest scientific and cultural level, and the Emirate government led by its leaders has proved to the world that nothing is impossible.

Arbitration can be defined as:

1- Arbitration in language:

Judgment in language: the judiciary has been sentenced to govern and govern, Arbitration in the language means delegation in the decision, it is made of the decision and convicted and the decision in its money judge who if the arbitrator (And control it) in her.

(Ocean Dictionary 988 - Dar al-Fikr for printing and publishing - Beirut, Mukhtar al-Sahah - Ministry of Education edition - p. 148).

Ibn Manzur said in his language: "Rul him among them: They have commanded him to rule among them, and it is said that we rule among ourselves.

(Ibn Manzoor's Arabic language - Dar Al Fikr for printing and publishing - Beirut - Part 12 p. 142)

In the medieval glossary - p. 190 "Decision on a decision, which ruled, He would have been convicted and convicted and convicted and convicted, And someone rule in this matter and the case: to make a judgment out of it.

2 - Arbitration in legal terminology:

And arbitration in legal terminology is: "Let the two opponents rule between them,

Any person concerned shall choose one or more persons to settle the dispute in which the arbitrator is not competent. (Footnote on the repellent on the selected edition of Dir al-Babi, Halabi, 5 p. 428 -

See also the book History of the Judiciary in Islam - Muhammad Ibn Muhammad Ibn Arnous - The Modern Egyptian Printing Press in Cairo, p. 175).

The Journal of Judicial Judgments defines arbitration in article (1790) in these terms:

The opponents took another person by their will to separate their opponents and invited them. The lawyers of positive law, Arbitration with the same advanced definition has a relevant agreement to present a given dispute, and an individual or individuals or an organization, to be tried without the competent court.

3- The legality of arbitration in Islamic law:

Arbitration - as a system for settling disputes between the parties, written in the Islamic system by book, Sunna and consensus:

As for the noble book: God says:

"If you find a schism between them, then they will bring a judgment from his family and a decision from his people, If they want a reform that will reconcile God with each other, God was an expert. (Women - 35)

It is in this verse that the Almighty grants us the right, blessed and exalted, to resort to arbitration, but he orders us to resort to him in this case.

(This part in brackets is quoted in the text of the book "Explanation of the laws of arbitration - to the consultant Abdel Fattah Mourad - 1995 edition - pages 11, 12 and 13).

He also came in the holy book says:

"And your Lord will not believe until he reigns among you among them" In the hadith "Heaven is for referees" and these are the people who own the groove.

Decision and between murder and infidelity and choosing determination on Islam with murder (Mukhtar Sahah p. 148)

4- Legitimacy of arbitration in case law, the judiciary and the law:

Egyptian case law has defined arbitration as an exceptional means of dispelling significant discounts resulting from ordinary litigation, This is at the origin of the birth of the opponents' will. Mr Ahmed Abu Al-Wafa knows that "it is the agreement to submit the dispute to a particular person or persons to separate it without the court concerned. (Abu Al Wafa - Optional and Mandatory Arbitration - 1978 Edition - Page 15)

(In this sense - Set of veto legal rules 3/1/52 - See p. 1504 - Comments on the law of procedural documents - M / Ezzeddine Dinosauri - The seventh edition - 1992)

The former Means Code No. 77 of 1949 already provided for arbitration in articles 818, 819, 821 and 822

Articles 501 and 513 of the current Code of Procedure No. 13 of 1968 correspond. The Egyptian legislator has seen a complete organization of arbitration in civil and commercial matters Law No. 27 of 1994, At the time of the publication of this Arbitration Act, it was natural that Article 3 of its Statutes provided for the repeal of Articles 501 to 513 of the Civil and Commercial Procedures Act promulgated by Act No. 13 of 1968 and any provision contrary to its provisions.

5. The most important principles concerning the arbitrary nature of arbitration:

The main principles set out by the Supreme Constitutional Court in its provisions are as follows:

1 - The original in arbitration - as settled by this court - Is to present a particular dispute between two parties to a designated arbitrator of their choice or delegation or in the light of the conditions they have indicated, This arbitrator is separated in this dispute by a decision that is free of the accused's suspicions and free of prejudice, And broke the Daber rivalry in the aspects mentioned by the parties, After giving each of them a detailed overview of the main guarantees of litigation.

2. The arbitration is carried out by the parties, in accordance with its provisions, the parties determine the extent of the rights in dispute between them, Or controversial issues that can be brought to their attention, The veto is the full authority exercised by arbitrators to decide Which are based on their arbitration agreement, their obligation to denounce and fully implement the decision in its entirety. It is decided whether or not the arbitrator is part of an agreement between two parties after the conflict, Or was waiting for a possible conflict had led them to include us a decade of contracts that the implementation of a condition allowing them to sit, The phases of arbitration are represented by the agreement on which the orbit of existence and without it does not arise at all It is inconceivable that this agreement should be implemented and, therefore, the legislator is not allowed to act contrary to its nature by imposing forced arbitration on persons who do not seek and do not seek entry.

The basis of the arbitration on the agreement is the direction of the will of the occupants and their departure to reach this path without the other and refrain from replacing the will of the legislator by this agreement, The arbitration agreement is, therefore, the original.

Accordingly, arbitration may not be mandatory and one of the parties must comply with it in accordance with a mandatory law standard that cannot be agreed upon. Is the subject of the arbitration an existing or potential dispute

5 - Arbitration is an artistic means of a judicial nature intended to settle a dispute involving a relationship of interest between the parties and a particular agreement on the basis of which the arbitrators derive their powers, And so do not assume their functions with the support of the State.

6. In this case, arbitration is considered as an alternative system to the judiciary, As it required all courts to be excluded from the consideration of matters for which they had been excluded from the exercise of their jurisdiction. Accordingly, we conclude with the following constitutional principles:

1. Arbitration according to its legal nature, originating from the agreement, the beginning, the procedures and the end of the agreement.

2. Arbitration cannot be imposed by force, even by a legal provision on the parties to the dispute, otherwise, the text will be stigmatized.

3. Any legal provision requiring the parties to the dispute to resort to arbitration, even at the initial stage before resorting to justice, is unconstitutional. I would like to highlight in the eyes of the reader the adaptation of the legal nature of arbitration as regulated by our Supreme Constitutional Court . Arbitration in investment disputes (1) is a contribution to this research.

We have already indicated that this arbitration concerns the settlement of direct investment disputes, That is, the participation of capital - whatever its nature and nationality - in the formation of a company subject to the provisions of the Investment Act, Or by increasing its capital, which is called investing in the first market to issue shares.

The jury establishes its own rules of the procedure without complying with the rules of the Code of Civil and Commercial Procedure, except as regards guarantees and the basic principles of the dispute, The Committee shall take into account the speed with which the dispute is resolved, its decisions shall be by a majority of votes and shall be final and binding on the parties and shall be enforceable, as well as the final provisions.

The arbitral tribunal shall determine who shall bear the costs of the arbitration.

The following text is noted:

1 - Arbitration has become a voluntary, voluntary and not forced choice, An agreement with the investor is necessary to resolve his disputes by arbitration, Or by virtue of the conventions mentioned in the first paragraph of the article.

2. The dispute shall be settled in accordance with the provisions of the Law on Arbitration in Civil and Commercial Matters promulgated by Law No. 27 of 1994,

Who replaced the arbitration clauses in the Code of Procedure (1, 5) to (513) It is considered as the general law of arbitration in Egypt according to the stability of the Supreme Constitutional Court, as stated in the declaration.

It should be noted that conflicts often arise between the investor and the host country for investments Or concerning any dispute that may arise between the investor and the host State in respect of his investment, between him and other legal or natural persons, public or private.

It goes without saying that the use of a means of resolving the conflict, Is the passport means optional with the agreement of the parties and therefore does not prevent an appeal by one of the parties to the competent court if it has not reached an agreement with the other party to settle the dispute in one of the most advanced ways?

Provided that none of the above-mentioned international conventions provides for the use of the means of dispute settlement provided for in the Convention, Or that there is a binding treaty text in a contract or legal instrument binding on the signatory parties, the dispute must be settled by arbitration.

Procedures and arrangements of a trial

Arbitration in the light of arbitration law

No. (6) for the year 2018 in the United Arab Emirates

Introduction:

It is necessary to assess the behavior that should prevail in society as conflicts between individuals and companies increase.

In particular in engineering work, where the judiciary decides and settles disputes, which is a burden on the judiciary.

Hence the importance of the message conveyed by specialists and academics in terms of scientific and behavioral orientation, which saves time and reduces the weight of pregnancy.

Although the subject of arbitration seems easy, a thorough study has been demonstrated

And stands by its difficulty and the legislator did not want to deprive the accused of the fundamental guarantees that surrounded them when they resorted to justice, preserving their rights, It, therefore, provides for procedures to be followed when arbitration is used.

In the modern era, there have been many disputes and disagreements between individuals and companies, particularly in engineering.

It was natural for the judiciary to deal with and resolve them, which would increase the burden of justice in countries.

It was necessary to address the deterioration of human behavior in general and the situation of the geological environment in particular,

That specialists and managers aspire to establish rules of good conduct that should prevail in society to ensure stability and development,

In support of the movement for progress and prosperity and the streamlining of work on the judicial system, It can, therefore, be said that arbitration is a kind of private judicial power whose existence derives from the will of the opponents, Whether the fuqaha' differs by its nature or not.

Free arbitration and institutional arbitration

1. Free arbitration: Arbitration AD HOC:

Free arbitration means that the parties to the dispute agree to choose one or more arbitrators to settle the dispute between them, In accordance with the arbitration clause included in their initial contract, Or by a subsequent agreement between the arbitration agreement after the dispute has arisen The clause or agreement of free arbitration shall provide for the choice of the arbitrator or arbitral tribunal, procedural law and substantive law to be applied to the dispute, And on the issues in which arbitration is judged.

Institutional Arbitration

What it means: Institutional arbitration means that the parties choose the arbitral procedure in accordance with the rules of a particular arbitral institution and must be the subject of an explicit, correct and complete agreement. If the dispute is submitted to arbitration in accordance with the rules of one of these institutions,

These rules apply to the arbitration process And committed by the parties even if they did not see them in advance as having been committed by the arbitral tribunal after its formation, Even the Arbitration Foundation can also say in this case:

The arbitration rules have become a contract or part of a multilateral contract to which each party is bound by arbitration in accordance with these rules.

In the relationship between the two parties, The simple assignment in the arbitration agreement to the rules of a particular institution, these rules become an integral part of the agreement.

- The parties expect the arbitration institution to provide certain services related to the organization of the arbitral proceedings And supervise them.

- It should be noted that not all arbitration institutions provide the same service.

- Some arbitral institutions may provide only a set of rules and guidelines

Without providing arbitration services such as the London Association of Maritime Arbitrators (LMAA).

- There are other arbitration institutions. Establishes its own arbitration rules and maintains a list of arbitrators.

As it does not interfere with the appointment of arbitrators nor does it manage cases such as the Association of Maritime Arbitrators in New York.

- A range of arbitration institutions assist in the management of the arbitration process

In particular the appointment or assistance of arbitrators.

- Finally, some arbitral institutions control the entire arbitration process from the notification of the claimant to the request for arbitration submitted by the claimant until the arbitral award is notified to parties such as the International Court of Arbitration of the International Chamber of Commerce.

Mixing the rules of procedure

The parties to the dispute may adopt the rules of an arbitral institution or some of them, as the case may be.

Or mixing some of the rules of one institution with the rules of another institution,

Without arbitration being institutionalized, but in the context of free arbitration, although rarely in practice.

The main arbitration institutions in the world

- International Court of Arbitration of the International Chamber of Commerce (ICC)

- Founded in 1923 in Paris, it organizes the annual arbitration of the International Chamber of Commerce in about 35 different countries.

The role of the 80 members of the Court from 70 different States is to examine and ratify arbitral awards in the form of draft judgments.

In 2000 alone, the Court handled approximately 550 cases involving parties from some 100 countries.

International Centre for the Settlement of Investment Disputes (ICSID)

The Centre was established by the 1965 Washington Convention to settle investment disputes between governments and nationals of other countries.

The agreement has been ratified by 135 countries and there is no need to hold an arbitration procedure at Washington headquarters, and by 2010, the Centre had completed about 51 cases.

CIEIAC - China International Economic and Commercial Arbitration Commission

The Committee was established in 1954 to resolve disputes between foreign and Chinese companies and in 1998, the Commission amended its arbitration rules to allow it to hear local disputes.

American Arbitration Association (AAA) International Dispute Resolution Center

The American Arbitration Association was founded in 1926 and provides education and training

In 1999, the United States administered more than 140,000 cases.

In 1996, the American Arbitration Association established the International Dispute Resolution Center in New York.

Arbitration Centre of the Stockholm Chamber

The institute was founded in 1917. In the 1970s, the United States and the Soviet Union accepted this institute as a neutral institute for the resolution of trade disputes between East and West.

The Institute has managed cases involving parties from more than 40 countries and in 1999, it managed 135 cases.

LCIA International Court of Arbitration

Created in 1985, one of the most important functions is the appointment of arbitral tribunals.

And the dismissal of arbitrators and the control of expenses and arbitral judgments are not examined and the annual number of cases 70 cases per year at the end of 1999.

Kuala Lumpur Regional Arbitration Centre

The Centre was established in 1978 (under the auspices of the Asian and African Legal Advisory Committee) with the assistance of the Government of Malaysia.

The Centre applies the 1976 UNCITRAL rules

The center offers facilities such as conference rooms and toilets for referees, the library and the auxiliary secretariat.

The number of cases in 2000 was about 35.

Cairo International Centre for International Commercial Arbitration (CRCICA)

The Centre was established in 1978 under the auspices of the Asian-African Legal Consultative Organization, with the assistance of the Government of the Arab Republic of Egypt.

The Centre's main activity is the management of national and international arbitration cases.

International Commercial Arbitration Court of the Chamber of Commerce and Industry of the Russian Federation

The Court has extensive experience as a leading arbitration institution and, in 1998, there were approximately 415 pending cases involving parties from 59 countries.

WIPO Arbitration and Mediation Center (WIPO)

The center is located in Geneva, Switzerland

The center has been specially designed to resolve intellectual and technological conflicts

Since 1999, the Centre has become one of the leading providers of dispute resolution services for the registration of domain names on the Internet.

OHADA Permanent Court of Justice and Arbitration

Is one of the institutions of the 1993 Convention of the African Organization for the Coordination of Business Law (OHADA)

It is located in Abidjan. Côte d'Ivoire In 1998, the Arbitration Act of OHADA entered into force with the Arbitration Rules of the Permanent Court.

One of its tasks is to manage arbitral cases and review draft judgments.

The requirement of institutional arbitration

The parties, if they wish to resort to institutional arbitration, must formulate the arbitration clause as close as possible to the model clause proposed by the arbitral institution.

Arbitration in accordance with UNCITRAL rules:

The United Nations Commission on International Trade Law (UNCITRAL) Rules were adopted on 28 April 1976 as special arbitration rules to settle disputes arising out of international commercial relations.

The UNCITRAL rules stipulate that if the parties do not agree on the method of appointment of arbitrators,

(Or if the Appointing Authority refuses to appoint an arbitrator), either party to the dispute may request the Secretary-General of the Permanent Court of Arbitration in The Hague (Netherlands) to determine the Appointing Authority.

Advantages of institutional arbitration:

1- The institutional arbitration of opponents provides many guarantees with its technical and human resources capable of following the arbitration file at all stages.

2 - Transparency of the appointment of arbitrators: where the centre, if it is responsible for selecting arbitrators according to their competence, takes into account the nature of the dispute submitted.

3. Retention of the files on which the dispute has been settled: it is kept in the Centre's archives for several years in order to allow the parties to the conflict to find their supporters or to review the judgments rendered.

Or obtain copies of expert reports. These services are not provided by free arbitration, as the task of arbitrators in this type of arbitration ends with the publication of the judgment.

4. Arbitrators may be required to make interim or preliminary decisions depending on the nature of the dispute and the requests of the parties.

These transitional provisions must be included because they are subject to appeal or suspension and these services are easily provided by institutional arbitration.

Because, as we have mentioned, it benefits from integrated management to guarantee these rights.

5. Institutional arbitration helps to assist the parties to the dispute before it is submitted to the Centre.

By establishing the typical conditions of the arbitration clause: for the parties to be included in their contracts in order to avoid the existence of vague arbitrary clauses, generally subject to invalidity.

6. In the case of institutional arbitration, avoidance or side effects resulting from free arbitration should be avoided at the outset.

Examples of refusal by a party to a dispute to appoint a tribunal or defame arbitrators or failure of an arbitrator to perform his or her duties or to withdraw from the proceedings. Among the problems of institutional arbitration:

However, the reference to institutional arbitration poses a significant practical problem if such an assignment is made in the form of an arbitration clause.

The seriousness of this situation is sometimes reflected in institutional arbitration, where the parties agree on a foreign institution that is foreign to them.

This may lead to the appointment of an arbitral tribunal, or one of its members, by persons who are not familiar with the legal regime applicable to the dispute. They may not even know the language of the arbitration.

Therefore, we believe that the wording of the arbitration clause in such circumstances must give them the necessary importance, so as to ensure that the arbitral tribunal is constituted in a reasonable manner and consistent with the nature and circumstances of the dispute.

It may also be important that the arbitration clause specify the specifications of the arbitrator who will review the dispute.

In such cases, the arbitration institution concerned shall comply with the wishes of the parties,

Otherwise, the formation of the body is defective, which opens the way for an appeal against the arbitral award, which constitutes a valid reason to contest it.

Effects of institutional arbitration:

The institution assigned to the dispute has jurisdiction only for the examination of the dispute and its settlement by arbitration only.

If one of the parties submits a request for arbitration to another institution, the other party may respond to it after jurisdiction or not.

If we assume that it has always been submitted to arbitration, arbitration is subject to recourse to the courts, nullity, appeal or otherwise, as provided by State law.

If arbitration is institutionalized, the arbitration system applicable to the arbitration institution must be respected and no derogation from this system shall be permitted, except to the extent authorized by the system itself, if so authorized.

On the other hand, institutional arbitration confers on the arbitral institution in charge of the dispute certain powers, before and during the dispute, to be examined by the arbitral tribunal, as provided for in its rules.

The institution is then the holder of the power within the limits provided by these rules.

However, in the event of a conflict of jurisdiction over a particular matter between the national judiciary and the arbitration institution,

It was a matter of public policy: it was not permissible to disqualify the national judiciary, to entrust it to the arbitral institution, and any agreement was null and void.

Disability is only partial in this question.

A comparative study of the rules of the main arbitration institutions and organizations

(1) American Chamber of Arbitration AIA

Selection of arbitrators:

If the arbitration agreement provides for the appointment of the parties to the arbitrator or the method of selection of arbitrators, this choice shall be followed

If the arbitration agreement does not specify the number of arbitrators, the dispute shall be submitted to a sole arbitrator for adjudication, unless the American Arbitration Association decides that the matter requires the appointment of a number of arbitrators.

B- If the parties have not appointed an arbitrator or have not submitted any method of appointment, the arbitrator shall appoint from the American Arbitration Association's list of arbitrators, at the same time, each of the parties to the dispute shall appoint a copy identical to the names of the persons selected from the list.

The American Arbitration Association invites persons who have been approved in order of priority by both lists to accept the assignment as arbitrators or arbitrators to rule on the dispute.

If the parties knowingly select the arbitrators or if the arbitrators are appointed and the parties authorize them to appoint a neutral arbitrator within a specified period of time and no such appointment has been made, the American Arbitration Association may appoint a neutral arbitrator to chair the arbitral tribunal.

If the parties are national or resident in different countries, the neutral arbitrator shall be appointed at the request of one of the parties, whether a national of the State Party or of the State Party.

The request must be made well in advance or within the time limits for the appointment of the arbitrator as agreed by the parties (rule 16).

Evidence and pleadings:

The same American system that can follow the procedure that arbitrators can modify (rule 28)

Suspicious witnesses:

Applicable law:

There is no provision concerning the applicable law (a text may be added to the agreement): the arbitrators are separated in accordance with the terms of the contract, taking into account the application of commercial practices.

Arbitral Award

Arbitral awards shall be made by a majority of the arbitrators by a brief decision, without reason

Administrative services:

The American Arbitration Association offers comprehensive administrative services

Forms of the arbitration clause in the American Arbitration Chamber

If the parties agree to arbitrate under the UNCITRAL Arbitration Rules and the American Arbitration Association is the appointing authority and provides its administrative services, it may add this condition:

Any dispute, controversy or claim arising out of, relating to or relating to this contract or its breach, termination or invalidity shall be settled in accordance with the UNCITRAL Arbitration Rules in force on the date of the contract.

The appointing authority is the American Arbitration Association.

Note:

Parties may wish to add:

(A) The arbitrators shall be (one or three).

(B) The place of arbitration shall be (city or country).

C) The language (or languages) used in the arbitral proceedings is

The arbitration is administered by the American Arbitration Association in accordance with its rules and procedures, in accordance with the UNCITRAL Arbitration Rules.

The arbitration clause in accordance with the UNCITRAL rules on mixed enterprises:

Any dispute or claim concerning or relating to this Agreement, or the violation of its provisions, shall be settled by arbitration held on...

In accordance with the arbitration rules of the United Nations International Commercial Arbitration Commission in force at the time of conclusion of this Agreement. The arbitration shall be conducted by a single person chosen by him.

The arbitrator shall be settled in accordance with the principles of conciliation. All arbitral proceedings must be carried out, including identifiers and memoranda (language). The arbitrator has the right to accept evidence directly from witnesses and documents submitted by the parties. All witnesses are allowed to be questioned:

The arbitrator must render his decision in writing, stating the reasons for the decision, namely that the decision must be rendered within a period of... months from the date of the request for arbitration. The judgment is final and binding on both parties.

Payment of amounts allocated by the judgment rendered by the arbitrator (arbitrators) must be filed with the competent court... or by the application for final authorization and the order to enforce the judgment of the court... In accordance with the law of the State in which the Court is located.

The parties to the arbitration shall be responsible for the costs of the arbitration as determined by the arbitrators, provided that each party pays the costs of the experts, evidence and lawyers.

The court cannot decide that a provision can be made for the absence of a legal provision governing the case and the ambiguity of the law.

The texts of the first and second paragraphs shall not affect the right of the Court to rule on the dispute in accordance with the rules of conciliation if the parties have so agreed (Art. 42).

Decision on the arbitration:

The Court shall decide all questions by a majority of the votes of its members.

- The decision of the Tribunal shall be in writing and signed by the members of the Tribunal who voted in favor, the arbitral award shall be decided on all questions submitted to the Tribunal, indicating the reasons on which it is based.

Administrative services:

- Full administrative services

Models of the Dispute Resolution Centre's International Arbitration Clause

Investment in Washington

The above-mentioned parties shall accept the submission of any dispute arising out of or relating to this Agreement to the International Centre for Settlement of Investment Disputes.

To be settled by conciliation or arbitration in accordance with the Convention on the Settlement of Investment Disputes between States and Nationals of Other States.

(5) Model international arbitration clauses

From the London Court of International Commercial Arbitration

By virtue of the validity, interpretation and application of the law

Any dispute arising out of or relating to this contract, including its validity, amendment or performance, shall be settled in accordance with the rules of the London Court of International Arbitration in force at that time.

The arbitration rules of the United Nations Commission on International Trade Law (UNCITRAL) are applicable to the regulation of certain matters

The parties agree that all statements of arbitration sent to the addresses mentioned in the contract (or subsequently considered in writing) are true and sufficient.

- Selection of some typical arbitration terms:

1. International Chamber of Commerce ICC

All disputes arising out of or in connection with this contract shall be settled in accordance with the Rules of Arbitration of the International Chamber of Commerce by an arbitrator or arbitrators appointed in accordance with these Rules.

2. American Arbitration Association (AAA) International Dispute Resolution Center

Any dispute or controversy arising out of or relating to this contract shall be settled by arbitration in accordance with the International Arbitration Rules of the American Arbitration Association and the parties may wish to add the following information:

A) The number of arbitrators shall be one or three.

B) The place of arbitration shall be (city or state).

C) The languages of arbitration shall be.....

Cairo International Centre for International Commercial Arbitration (CRCICA)

Any dispute, controversy or claim arising out of or in violation of this contract, or in breach of its provisions, dissolution or invalidity, shall be settled by arbitration in accordance with the Arbitration Rules of the Regional Centre for International Commercial Arbitration in Cairo.

Parties may wish to add the following data:

A) The appointing authority... (name of the organization or person)

B) The number of arbitrators (one or three arbitrators)

(C) The place of arbitration shall be... (city or country)

(D) The language or languages used in the arbitration proceedings shall be...

E) The number and modalities of appointment of arbitrators in multilateral arbitration shall be...

If the parties do not agree, the amended rules shall apply from the Cairo Regional Centre for International Commercial Arbitration and shall be executed by the Centre.

In accordance with Article 8 bis of the appointment of all arbitrators

Among them, it will be determined who will preside over the arbitral tribunal

Note:

But not necessarily as stated in the letter, as the parties may use other terms at their convenience,

But with a clear reference to the organization of arbitration through the institution concerned.

Principles of arbitration in the event of a dispute:

It is important that both the public and private sectors recognize that this legal system was created as a result of enormous economic development.

This is progressing very quickly due to the rigidity of procedural structures and its inability to pursue development with solutions appropriate to the spirit of the times.

And solve the difficult equation instead of using the old legal structures and try to adapt them to the spirit of the times.

If the legislator has put arbitration in order to exempt litigants from resorting to justice, it is nevertheless necessary to establish rules to be followed by arbitrators.

Therefore, if the latter rules do not constitute a clear, simple and valid court, in order to avoid any dispute over the enforcement of judgments, arbitration is a reason for the complexity and complexity of cases rather than their facilitation.

The arbitration system involves the various sectors of industry and commerce at all levels, international and local.

Because it helps to solve many of the delicate technical problems that are the common denominator in most modern conflicts

There is no doubt that the jurisdiction of the judiciary over these issues will hamper economic growth,

Due to the length and high cost of regular litigation, potentially leading to a loss of interest in such litigation.

This arbitration has appeared since antiquity and has extended to a greater number of disputes

Aristotle says that parties may prefer arbitration to courts

Since the arbitrator considers justice while the judge only considers the law".

Definition of arbitration:

On the basis of the above, arbitration can be defined as an agreement to submit the dispute to a particular person or persons for the decision, without recourse to the competent court.

In this arbitration, the parties to the dispute waive recourse to the courts, which are required to refer the dispute to one or more arbitrators in order to be separated by a binding judgment of the parties,

Such an agreement may be consistent with a particular contract in which the transaction is called an arbitration clause

This may be in connection with a particular dispute already existing between the opponents and, in this case, the partner or arbitration agreement is called.

States allow arbitration in order to facilitate dialogue between the parties and until the dispute is resolved by a technical body in order to avoid hearings and judicial proceedings, while saving time and effort in all cases.

Arbitration is based on two principles: the will of the opponents and the approval of this will by the legislator.

By arbitration agreement, the arbitrator gives him or her the power to decide the dispute rather than the court initially competent to hear it,

The arbitrator's will in the arbitration contract is limited to the simple replacement of the arbitrator by the arbitrator in the dispute so that if the arbitration contract has not been performed for any reason, the power of judgment has been transferred to the court.

There is a link between arbitration and judicial patrimony, which begins with a contract

And ends by virtue of or is subject to the rules of civil law as regards its convening - which in this case is subject to procedural law in terms of effects, access and procedures.

Arbitration is annulled by the invalidation of contracts and its judgment is contested, as it contests judgments and is executed as the provisions are applied.

Effects of arbitration:

The effects of arbitration are subject to the will of the parties on the one hand and the will of the law on the other.

We present here the study of the arbitration system in three areas:

1. Arbitration agreement

2. Arbitration procedure

3. The arbitrator's judgment

Section I Arbitration Agreement

Introduction:

1. The arbitration agreement constitutes the legal basis of the arbitration and its constitution, which defines its scope and extent,

The dispute arises from the jurisdiction of the judiciary and the competence of the arbitrators,

Arbitration legislation concerned the drafting of the rules governing the arbitration agreement, the United Arab Emirates Arbitration Act of 2018, the Model Arbitration Act (UNCITRAL).

Where almost none of its articles mention the agreement of the parties to the arbitration and its procedures.

If it is the importance of the arbitration agreement, one must be very careful in formulating its terms. The disadvantages of such wording often lead to serious consequences, such as extending the duration of the proceedings, increasing their complexity, delaying the settlement of disputes, and problems in applying the judgment given, The disadvantages of drafting can sometimes lead to the loss of the disputed right and, in some cases, to surprises that should not occur among the parties to the conflict,

Although the quality and precision of the formulation avoids many problems, inconveniences and surprises

On the contrary, the quality of the wording and its provisions often deters the ill-intentioned party who intends to violate its contractual obligations,

And forces them to respect them and then the need to resort to arbitration in the original.

An arbitration agreement may be concluded before the dispute arises and in this case (1) the arbitration clause Compromise Clause is called

It may then be contained in a contract and terminated by an independent agreement, which is concluded on the basis of independence and after the dispute arises, concerns the compromise.

In any case, the arbitration agreement - like any agreement.

Is it an expression of the convergence of two wills on the choice of arbitration as a means of resolving existing or potential disputes, and must, therefore, meet the formal requirements imposed by law -

When both conditions are met, the arbitration agreement arranges its legal effects, so we consider that the arbitration agreement is treated in three parts:

The first: the individual to the conditions of his health.

Secondly: dedicate it to its effects.

Thirdly, we present the essential data to be taken into account when drafting this agreement.

Section I

Conditions for the validity of the arbitration agreement

2. While, as a general rule, the Arbitration Act treats the arbitration clause and its parity equally, it is imperative that the proposal be valid to indicate in substance the subject matter of the dispute to be resolved by arbitration.

The arbitration clause is contained in the terms of a contract and it is not possible for the parties to predict the type of dispute that may arise between them,

This condition is then generally stated and concerns certain types of disputes. If a dispute arises later than in them, the subject matter of the dispute shall be determined in the declaration of arbitration.

Whether the arbitration agreement takes the form of a condition or a partnership form, it is subject to certain conditions, including what is objective and what is formal.

3. Substantive conditions:

It does not go beyond what has already been studied in the theory of contract, namely the conditions related to shop satisfaction and motive

The arbitration agreement must be concluded on the basis of valid consent and must be possible and appalling.

And all this for a reason not contrary to public order and morality.

4. Satisfaction:

The convergence of the two free will to use arbitration to resolve the dispute, current or potential, And arrange all its legal effects because it is necessary to free this satisfaction from defects that can be distorted such as stress, error, fraud, etc.

In addition, the Arbitration Act stipulated that the party to the agreement must be able to exercise its rights.

Whether the parties to the UAE arbitration must have the capacity to dispose of their rights in accordance with UAE law,

As far as foreigners are concerned, their eligibility to their personal right is subject to the law of nationality or domicile.

As for the New York Convention, it only satisfies the eligibility of the parties, either under the law of the contract or the law of the State in which the arbitration takes place.

5- The shop:

The arbitration agreement is the substantive relationship in which the dispute must be settled and the Arbitration Act

And to broaden the scope of legal disputes suitable for arbitration, whether contractual or non-contractual, Public or private, civil or commercial,

Even in matters of a tort, the arbitration agreement may be the subject of an arbitration agreement, unless it is a violation of public policy

(Such as an arbitration agreement to determine criminal liability for an offence)

Although arbitration in the matter of compensation for damage caused can be a crime.

However, it is not permitted to arbitrate in cases where it is not permitted to settle

Personal status or public order issues are not guaranteed but the financial interests of the personal situation can be settled or resulting from the commission of an offence.

Consequently, it is not permissible to agree on arbitration in matters of eligibility, validity or invalidity of marriage, proof of proportion or acknowledgement of paternity, etc., as well as on arbitration of murder, theft, waste, etc.

The prohibition extends to public policy, such as arbitration in an illegal relationship, gambling, etc.

It should be noted that the concept of public policy is flexible and its content varies according to time, place and subject.

Domestic public policy is not necessarily the general system of international commercial arbitration - Nor is there a direct relationship between the idea of jus cogens, the idea of international public order - French law is almost identical to Egyptian law, but it differs with regard to the prohibition of arbitration in civil matters unless the law provides otherwise,

The prohibition of arbitration for public persons, except where it concerns persons of a general industrial or commercial nature, may be authorized by arbitration.

It should be noted that the prohibition of arbitration for public persons and the prohibition of arbitration in civil matters do not apply to international arbitration.

6. Reason:

The reason for the arbitration agreement is the choice of the parties to prevent the dispute from being submitted to justice and to submit it to arbitrators who authorize them to resolve it.

This is legitimate because the law is recognized and regulated by provisions that are often complementary to the administration of the parties to the arbitration. The reason is illegal if the cases of fraud are covered by the law. As if arbitration had been used to escape the law that should have been applied if the dispute had been brought before the courts. In view of the restrictions or obligations of this law from which it is intended to derogate:

As if arbitration was intended to escape the legal rules of proving ownership of real estate or to circumvent the law by collusion in order to deprive others of their rights...

For example, an agreement on arbitral proceedings between the parties, some of which are supposed to be the property of an estate, and in arbitration, the other party assigns its claims to the defendant as a result of their collusion,

The defendant obtains an arbitral award - by fraud - then files it at the registry of the competent court and may add it to the executive form and use it to deprive, pressure or blackmail the rights of others.

7. Formalities:

Article 12 of the Arbitration Act stipulates that "the arbitration agreement must be in writing and not void...

"Thus, writing in accordance with the said law became a condition for the arbitration agreement and its existence. The nullity of the writing does not result and writing, as in the case of the repealed trial law, is no longer a condition for proving agreement. However, the legislator has relaxed the type of writing required, simply by exchanging letters by fax, telex, mail or any other means having a written effect allowing the arbitration contract to be concluded.

As such, it is not necessary for all parties to sign or sign the same document at the same time.

(1) circumvent the publication fee rules for the validity of the newspaper and the effectiveness of the sale of the property

An agent may enter into an arbitration agreement but the agency must be in writing. And be a private agency. Therefore, the Attorney General's power of attorney does not give him the power to enter into the arbitration agreement but requires special authorization. In accordance with section 6 of the Arbitration Act, the written obligation to provide in the original contract for assignment to a document containing an arbitration clause may be satisfied,

As in the case of an assignment to a standard contract in the field of maritime transport, the sale of goods or a construction contract, such as the contracts of the International Grain Commission in London, commodity market models or Hamburg contract forms

General conditions established by the International Federation of Consulting Engineers (FIDIC) or forms of maritime transport and insurance contracts. It should be noted that, in such cases, the assignment of the arbitration clause contained in the document to which it refers must be clear and explicit. If the assignment is public or public, it is clear that a party is unaware or unaware of the existence of an arbitration clause in the document submitted to it

In this case, it cannot be said that there are an agreement and written consent to the arbitration clause (Art. 10.3 of the Arbitration Act).

11. In France, the internal arbitration clause must be written and not null and void -

The entry must be provided by providing for this condition in the original contract or in a document to which this contract refers.

It is further stipulated that the arbitration clause must include the determination of the arbitrator or arbitrators or the manner in which they are appointed, and that the requirement to appoint arbitrators is not limited to domestic arbitration without international arbitration.

As for international arbitration, writing is a means of proof and not a condition of convocation.

Participants must include a statement of the issues in dispute and the agreement has not been cancelled - even under French law,

If it is further stipulated that the nominee must include the appointment of the arbitrator or arbitrators or the manner in which they are appointed.

Section II

Implications of the arbitration agreement

12. If the formal and objective conditions for the validity of the arbitration agreement are met, it shall have effect

These effects can be grouped into three categories: effects on persons, effects on the subject and special effects on the authority competent to deal with the dispute.

13. Effects of the arbitration agreement on persons:

These effects govern the relative effect of contracts and are subject to the general rules of civil law in this regard.

However, in some cases, the case is heard, for example, in the case of a hawala, the arbitration clause contained in the contract is not binding on the transferee until the transfer is applicable to him - As well as in a lawsuit brought by one of the persons affected by the Libyan aircraft accident that was dropped in the Sinai in 1973 against Libyan Aviation Corporation, which entered the company in charge of the operation until the case was tried, the latter being open to trial by Libyan society. The operator has settled the arbitration clause between him and the Libyan institution and cannot be prosecuted, the Court of Cassation has approved the arbitration clause between the company and the institution.

The same happened in the case of the Al-Ahram plateau in Egypt in the dispute between Egot and the Ministry of Tourism and a foreign investor. The Arbitration Tribunal of the International Chamber of Commerce has ordered the Egyptian government to pay compensation.

However, the Egyptian government challenged the arbitration decision before the Paris Court of Appeal, which was invalidated and supported by the French Court of Cassation on the grounds that the Ministry of Tourism was not a party to the contract, which included the arbitration clause.

And that the Minister's role was limited to the adoption of the agreement between Egot and the foreign investor (1) also occurred in the case of the Arab Industrialization Organization of Egypt. As it had contracted with an English company to manufacture a helicopter in the Commission's factories. After reconciliation with Israel, the participating countries withdrew

The Commission was unable to complete the implementation of the contract,

Here, the company has sought compensation from the English-speaking member countries of the Commission and it appears that the dispute has put an end to reconciliation.

14. The arbitration agreement on the subject was raised:

The effects of the arbitration agreement are determined in terms of matters in accordance with the terms of the agreement concluded by the parties themselves,

Therefore, the drafting of the arbitration agreement - a condition that was or was of interest - was of great importance and we will, therefore, assign a separate section to this wording.

It is sufficient to mention the precision required in the choice of terms and wording of the arbitration agreement. The provision that arbitration in the event of a dispute is linked to the interpretation of the contract, arbitration limits the interpretation of the contract only in the absence of disputes relating to its performance,

There is also a difference between the term "arbitration" in disputes arising from the contract arising from the scope of arbitration and disputes relating to the performance of the contract after its conclusion: non-performance, delay or violation of the agreed terms of reference, etc.

Not to include disputes relating to the formation of the contract in terms of validity or invalidity.

The expression "disputes with or relating to the contract" in connection with "is more important and more complete insofar as all contract disputes involve validity, invalidity, interpretation, implementation and expiry

Moreover, if the arbitration agreement concerns the accounting of the company's accounts, the arbitration does not extend to the examination of the validity of the company's contract or to the invalidation....,

---

1) The dispute was then referred to the Center for the Settlement of Investment Disputes in Washington and the foreign investor received compensation from the Egyptian government.

The importance of careful consideration of the drafting of the arbitration agreement is that international arbitration is an exception to jurisdiction (the competence of the State) and its general mandate. The arbitration agreement must, therefore, be interpreted narrowly,

On the other hand, the arbitration agreement is its constitution and its reference base, which determines the powers of the arbitrators so that the arbitrators' judgment is null and void in matters that do not fall within the scope of the subject defined by the parties and that the veto or ambiguity opens the door to disagreement and problems

It also presents the parties with unspeakable surprises as to the conduct of the arbitration proceedings and, consequently, what will be demonstrated in due course.

15. The arbitration agreement concerning the jurisdiction of the dispute raised the dispute:

1. The court seized of a dispute shall be subject to an arbitration agreement enabling it to rule on the inadmissibility of the case if the defendant so requests or defends it in the proceedings prior to its execution.

2. The action referred to in the previous period shall not prevent the commencement or continuation of an arbitration procedure or arbitral award.

This means that the arbitration agreement prevents the courts from considering the dispute in question. The so-called adverse effect of the arbitration agreement, if a court reviewing a dispute that is the subject of an arbitration agreement is required to rule that the claim is inadmissible.

However, the Court did not have the effect per se, but the defendant must adhere to the arbitration agreement before making a claim or defense.

Moreover, the filing of a complaint before the courts does not prevent the opposing party from initiating arbitration proceedings,

In addition, if such proceedings are initiated, the filing of the case before the courts does not prevent the continuation of the arbitral proceedings and the adoption of a judgment,

After allowing the other party to express its defense and notify it of its submission within the agreed time frame. But what is the solution if the judge is refused acceptance of the thesis that an arbitration agreement exists while the other party to the nullity of this agreement?

Or if the judge considers that the arbitration agreement is invalid because the number of arbitrators is my husband, for example, or because he does not specify the issues that are the subject of arbitration in the arbitration partner or because the place of the arbitration agreement is not arbitral. If the court definitively decided that the arbitration agreement was null and void or unenforceable before the award, the arbitral tribunal had to terminate the proceedings.

The action does not prevent the continuation of the arbitration procedure because of the person concerned by the decision not to accept the case - for the existence of an arbitration agreement - Is it the existence of a true arbitration agreement and not simply the physical presence of a publisher who understands such an agreement.

Decided that the courts were not in a position to consider the dispute - where the arbitration clause existed. The arbitral tribunal shall decide on the defenses based on its lack of jurisdiction, including those invoked in the event of the absence, nullity or invalidity of an arbitration contract or lack of understanding of the subject matter of the dispute", insofar as this provision setting out the principle of jurisdiction does not deprive the courts of its jurisdiction to rule on the defenses contained in this provision if it is raised at the time of a party's accession to the arbitration contract, and the other party to invalidate this agreement, as the prosecution judge is the payments judge. It is inconceivable that the judge should be obliged to rule on the inadmissibility of a case based on the accession of one of the parties to an arbitration agreement that he considers invalid.

Secondly, the competence of the arbitral tribunal to rule on the defenses relating to the arbitration agreement will be subject to the control of the invalidity tribunal once the award has been made.

17. In France, the draft law distinguishes between the first two proposals concerning the filing of a complaint in court after the arbitration procedure has begun

In such cases, the judge must rule against his or her jurisdiction and the second judge must rule against his or her jurisdiction.

In this case, the dispute has not yet been submitted to the arbitral tribunal, in which case the judge shall also rule on its jurisdiction, provided that the arbitration agreement is not null and void.

In all cases, the State courts have no jurisdiction over their own jurisdiction.

The French legislator finds justification in the fact that the arbitral tribunal, after having contacted the dispute, has a monopoly on the consideration or invalidity of the arbitration agreement,

The determination of the principle of jurisdictional competence having been initiated, it must not disrupt the arbitration process,

The arbitral tribunal shall not suspend the proceedings until the case has been brought before the court,

But would continue to examine the dispute if it considered that the defenses were intended to postpone and prolong the conflict without justification. (2)

However, we do not consider that such justifications prevent the judge from verifying or invalidating the arbitration agreement, quite the contrary, from justifying his authority in dealing with the validity of the arbitration agreement,

Especially since the lifting of the order does not result in a suspension of the arbitration process,

The termination of the arbitration agreement and its response to the question of the dispute and its final judgment will make the continuation of the arbitral proceedings the latter if it is not enforceable.

The issuance of an arbitral award prior to the judgment of the court of dispute shall have the authority of the order

And making the case before the courts is not unfair to the previous chapter in the arbitration of matters

It should be noted that article 8/1 of the UNCITRAL Model Law gives the judge the power to deal with the subject matter of the dispute that is the subject of an arbitration contract if it is declared null, void, ineffective or unenforceable -

The same provision is also contained in article 2/3 of the 1958 New York Convention on the Recognition and Enforcement of the Provisions of Foreign Arbitrators.

Finally, it should be noted that if the arbitration agreement is void or voidable or has expired

This will result in the invalidation of the award that may be made by the arbitral tribunal under section 35 / 1a of the Arbitration Act.

18. Principle of independence of the arbitration clause:

This important principle of new subjects introduced by arbitration, although it has long been decided in French law on issues related to international trade - this principle means two things:

First, if the arbitration clause was null and void, it would have no effect on the original contract it contained, and second, that the contract itself was null and void did not affect the arbitration agreement.

The arbitration clause is deemed to constitute an agreement independent of the other clauses of the contract and the nullity, copying or termination of the contract has no effect on the arbitration clause it contains if this condition is in itself true".

In France, the principle of international commercial arbitration was abolished even though there was no explicit legislative provision to be adopted.

It should be noted that the decision of the arbitral tribunal cannot be challenged by refusing to pay independently for the invalidity, annulment or termination, so that the chapter on arbitration proceedings

But even the publication of the final judgment of the dispute of the said body,

Then, the stakeholder can withhold this payment by submitting a request for the sentence to be invalidated.

Section III

Draft arbitration agreement

19. The arbitration agreement constitutes the direct legal basis for extracting a dispute from the jurisdiction of the courts of the State of general jurisdiction,

What is the source of the arbitrators' powers and, therefore, particular attention to its formulation is of great importance for the determination of all aspects of arbitral proceedings from beginning to end,

The shortcomings that can have such wording often lead to serious consequences that the parties to the conflict have not taken into account,

Although good wording avoids many problems and surprises and contributes significantly to the smooth running of the arbitration process and the desired objective,

But may deter a Contracting Party from violating its contractual obligations without having to arbitrate itself.

The first is that the arbitration agreement should include express and complete authorization allowing the arbitrator or arbitrators to rule on the dispute submitted to arbitration,

The second condition is that the arbitration agreement includes the basic elements that make it a complete agreement that enjoys self-sufficiency and avoids the use of third parties to remedy the default.

20- First: Delegation of arbitrators to rule on the dispute:

The delegation of arbitrators to the dispute being arbitrated must be explicit and unequivocal: the choice of the parties to the arbitration is the only way to resolve the dispute outside the courts of the State.

It is therefore important to avoid ambiguities and other shortcomings that may result from the drafting of the project, the most important of which are as follows:

1 - The text of the contract on the competence of arbitration and judicial settlement of disputes,

The contract contains a clause providing for arbitration and another provision on the jurisdiction of a State to rule on disputes that may arise under the contract,

This contradiction poses problems and one of the two texts must prevail. The jurisdiction of the general court is often privileged.

2. The lack of precision and determination in the formulation of the condition, as the reference to arbitration may take the form of a lawfulness. For example, "disputes arising from the contract may be submitted to arbitration,

This opens the door to disagreement on the interpretation of the clause and whether it allows the parties to choose between arbitration or justice and whether they should agree to arbitrate any dispute again.

3. Preventive arbitration agreement: as if the agreement provided that the State courts have jurisdiction to rule on disputes with the possibility of settling them as a subsidiary by arbitration abroad.

4 - The provision allowing certain disputes to be resolved by conciliation and others by arbitration.

5 - The provision on the referral of disputes to arbitration in the settlement of disputes before the courts raises the issue of the distinction between dispute and conflict and how to do so

6 - The possibility of resorting to justice if the arbitration does not resolve the dispute.

This creates the problem of determining what is meant by failed arbitration and when.

7. Provide for the referral of technical disputes to experts,

And the referral of legal disputes to arbitration. It is not difficult to define what is technical and what is legal,

So what is the legal status of experts as arbitrators?! What are the guarantees of their work?

21. Determination of the power of arbitrators: In addition to avoiding any ambiguity in the drafting of an arbitration agreement, this agreement must include a clear definition of the arbitrators' role.

And that these powers be as broad as possible to resolve all disputes related to the contract, including the interpretation, performance, nullity, cancellation or annulment of the contract, as well as the liability of the parties, both contractual and declaratory.

The best wording would be "all disputes arising out of or in connection with the contract". It would be superfluous to state that "disputes relating to the interpretation or performance of a contract" are not sufficient for disputes that may arise concerning the nullity or termination of the contract.

22. Limitation of the scope of third party intervention in arbitral proceedings: (self-sufficiency)

By agreeing on all matters necessary for the unimpeded conduct of such procedures.

Determining the method of appointment of arbitrators and appointing them accurately and unequivocally facilitates the appointment procedures in the event of non-appointment by one of the parties.

The text also provides that the arbitral award shall be final and binding on the parties.

It also improves the provision for prior waiver of the means of challenging the arbitral award to the extent permitted by law.

Similarly, if the law allows appeals against arbitrators' appeals,

With regard to contesting nullity, most laws do not allow for a waiver before the arbitral award is made, although the law allows it. Provided that the waiver is as explicit as under Swiss law.

It goes without saying that it is not possible to accept to exclude grounds for appeal from public policy.

23. Secondly: the requirement of self-sufficiency:

To achieve the objective of choosing arbitration as a means of settling disputes, the arbitration agreement must include all aspects of the arbitration, from its beginning to its end.

This agreement must include several basic elements, the most important of which is how to constitute an arbitral tribunal, the number of its members, the power to choose and determine the place of arbitration and the law applicable to proceedings and objects.

The language in which the arbitration proceedings are conducted and their duration

And the determination of the issues covered by the arbitration in the arbitration partnership, otherwise it was annulled that any gap or lack of data in the arbitration agreement

Such a veto could be supplemented by decisions taken by non-parties to the arbitration, which could have unexpected surprises.

24. Designation of the place of arbitration:

If the parties do not specify or agree on the place of arbitration, the decision shall be taken by the decision of the arbitration center or institution.

Which takes place in accordance with its system in the event of institutional arbitration,

And by a decision of the arbitral tribunal itself in the case of free or non-institutional arbitration. Often, a place of arbitration that has not been notified to the parties -

The parties to the arbitration shall agree on the place of arbitration, taking into account the circumstances of the case and the suitability of the place for the parties.

This shall be without prejudice to the competence of the arbitral tribunal to meet at any place it considers appropriate for the conduct of arbitral proceedings. Such as hearing the parties to the dispute, witnesses or experts, accessing documents or inspecting property or funds, or conducting deliberations among its members or otherwise. The court will determine the place of arbitration if the parties disagree.

The arbitral tribunal may hold meetings and meetings at any other place it considers appropriate, after consultation with the parties, unless the parties have agreed otherwise. The arbitral tribunal may deliberate at any place it deems appropriate. "The rules of the London Court of International Arbitration provide in Article 16 that:

1. The parties may agree in writing on the seat of the arbitration.

In the absence of such a choice, the place of arbitration shall be London, unless the LCIA decides that another place is appropriate for arbitration. Taking into account all the circumstances and after giving the parties the opportunity to submit a written comment.

2. The arbitral tribunal may hold meetings, meetings and deliberations in any geographical location, as the case may be.

3. The law applicable to the arbitration (if any) is the law of the arbitral tribunal. Unless the parties have expressly and in writing consented to the application of another law and to the extent that such an agreement is not reviewed under the law of the arbitral tribunal.

25. Importance of designating the place of arbitration:

The location of the arbitrators is particularly important:

1. An arbitral award is deemed to have been made at the place of arbitration and is therefore considered a foreign judgment if it is made abroad with such enforcement difficulties,

It should, therefore, be noted that a State party to the 1958 New York Convention should recognize and apply the provisions of foreign arbitrators.

2. An appeal for the annulment of an arbitral award shall be submitted to the courts of the State in which the place of arbitration is located and on the grounds provided for by the law of that State.

It should be noted that the grounds for challenging the invalidity of arbitral awards differ from one State to another, whether narrow or broad,

The legislation of some countries also allows the prior agreement to cancel the nullity (Swiss law)

It is therefore in the interest of avoiding choosing the place of arbitration in States whose legislation allows for an appeal.

3. Arbitration proceedings shall be governed by the law of the State of the place of arbitration, including its rules of procedure.

If, for example, the law of the place of arbitration allows the arbitral award to be made without just cause, its implementation will encounter difficulties in other States.

4. Poor management of the place of arbitration can lead to a total loss of rights, as the legislation of some States considers that the limitation period is procedural rather than substantive.

If these States were to submit to arbitration and if the arbitral proceedings were subject to the law of the State of the place of arbitration,

In this case, the limitation period specified in the law of the State of the place of arbitration applies to the rights in dispute in the arbitration as a procedural matter.

This may result in the loss of these rights within the short period of time provided for by that law, even if the limitation period provided for by the law governing the subject matter of the dispute is much longer,

Although the limitation under the latter law is often considered a substantive rather than a procedural matter. Therefore, such results should be avoided. It follows from all the above that the parties must explicitly agree on the place of arbitration and not allow any other authority to choose,

And to examine the choice of this location after study and in the light of the considerations mentioned above and the consequences that may result,

And that the choice of the place of arbitration should not be based solely on its proximity to one of the parties to the dispute, on considerations of personal mood or on that place of considerations, It was stated that arbitration procedures should verify and examine certain things with the greatest precision, as follows:

1. Verification whether the State of the place of arbitration has legal rules that are incompatible with the rules of procedure agreed between the parties, and if there are rules in the law of that State that contradict the rules of that procedure.

2. Are there any binding conditions relating to the form or validity of the arbitration agreement in the law of the country of arbitration.

3. Are there any special conditions that arbitrators must meet? States using an arbitrator of a particular nationality or profession.

4. Are there any restrictions on the parties' freedom to agree on arbitral proceedings and are there any mandatory standards in this regard?

5. Does the law of the country of arbitration contain provisions concerning the cooperation of the courts of that country with the arbitral tribunals in its proceedings?

6. Are there any legal restrictions on the freedom of the parties to choose the law applicable to the subject matter of the dispute?

7. Are there any limits or limits to the power of judicial arbitrators to settle or be authorized to settle?

8. Does state law allow the offence?

9. What are the limits of public policy in the law of the country of arbitration? Does this law define the distinction between international public policy and national public policy?

10. What happens after the award has been declared void, in accordance with the law of the country of arbitration, is the arbitration case referred to state courts (such as Taiwanese law)? or referred to an arbitral tribunal that rendered the judgment for annulment.

Or arbitration before the arbitral tribunal other than the body that rendered the judgment?!

Or the invalidity court rules on the subject matter of the dispute within the limits of the arbitrators' specific task (as in the case of domestic arbitration in France).

11. Are there any legal or political restrictions on the granting of visas? Check that there is nothing to prevent the entry of arbitrators, witnesses, parties, advocates and experts into the country of the place of arbitration.

12. Are there any restrictions on the free transfer of funds to and from the place of arbitration?

13. Does the political climate allow for free arbitration procedures and the absence of influence on the quality and independence of arbitrators, their impartiality and their access to the territory throughout the arbitration procedure?

14. Economic considerations must also be taken into account

In terms of accommodation, travel, translation costs, etc.

27. Designation of the applicable law:

The arbitration agreement shall include the law applicable to the subject matter of the dispute,

Because if the agreement were to remain silent, it would be appointed by the arbitral tribunal

By applying such conflict of laws rules as it deems appropriate (Article 28 of the Rules of the Gulf Arbitration Centre in Bahrain,

With regard to the direct choice of the law which it considers most relevant to the dispute (Article 39/2) of the Egyptian Arbitration Law or which it considers appropriate (Article 17 of the ICC Rules). The choice of law applicable to the subject matter of the dispute must be considered. In addition, that this choice is based on a meticulous and precise study. The national legislation of a party is not necessarily the best,

The choice of a foreign law must be based on a careful examination of its provisions. The parties may agree on the law of a given State at the time the agreement is concluded in order to avoid future surprises if there is an amendment to this law,

In this case, the freezing of the applicable law should be subject to an explicit and explicit agreement. Nor should we run after rules that are supposed to be more advanced or free of laws. For example, the acceptance to subject the contract to the basic rules of international law. Rules adopted by civilized nations, common principles of Arab or European law or international trade law Lex mercatoria. Alternatively, the traditional rules governing international contracts or the general principles of law applied in Europe.

Such rules are not unanimous or agreed upon as to their content and thus open the door to the possibility for arbitrators to judge and dictate their personal opinions to the parties,

However, there are combinations between the international rules of certain contracts and we see no reason to agree on their application, such as the Vienna Convention on the International Sale of Goods, and the rules for the verification of international credentials. This was decided by the International Chamber of Commerce in Paris.

28. Language of the arbitration:

The arbitration agreement shall include the designation of the language in which the arbitration is conducted and the arbitral tribunal,

The choice of the appropriate arbitrator depends on the language of the arbitration and the extent of its control.

Translation also wastes time and money, especially in major disputes,

This is in addition to the risk of translation in terms of errors or inaccuracies that can result in technical terms that are difficult to translate into another language.

In addition, the omission of the text on the language of the arbitration renders the arbitral tribunal competent. He may choose the inappropriate language or cause undue damage or difficulty.

Difference between arbitration and reconciliation:

The two systems of arbitration and reconciliation are distinct. In conciliation, the parties to the dispute are willing to agree to reciprocal waivers, each waiving some of its rights in exchange for the other to do something similar. In order to resolve the dispute that may exist between them, In fact, in the legal system of reconciliation, the parties to the conflict are separated,

In arbitration, the parties are present as opponents in a case whose proceedings are before the arbitrator who is another person.

On the other hand, in reconciliation, we find mutual concessions on both sides on some of its rights. In arbitration, one party can win the entire case. Persons in conflict approach one or more non-combatants to find a solution to their dispute and the solution to which such interests can be accepted can be accepted by these persons and thus serve as a basis for the next step of reconciliation;

The use of interest is in fact without procedural or substantive rules despite this illegal ownership of this type of social solution. However, it is considered a limited system in the legal field.

These persons are not considered to be arbitrators or conciliation arbitrators for a clear reason, Does the decision or solution they reach not have binding force for those who use this method, but accepts most specialists.

Therefore, what the interests of the parties must be an introduction or a proposal for a direct settlement between the opponents, i.e. the contribution of the interests to this process is nothing more than an event of moral value for the opponents in order to achieve the expected rapprochement.

Problem 2: Reference to a document containing the arbitration clause

The arbitration clause may not be reflected in the original contract but in another document which may be another contract or otherwise

However, the initial contract contains an assignment containing the terms of the arbitration in order to apply the provisions of this document to the relations between the parties to the initial contract for all matters not provided for in this contract.

To clarify this issue, we assume that there is a contract of carriage between carrier A and shipper b for the carriage of goods by sea.

The bill of lading provides for the application of the ship lease agreement between (a) and (c) to the relationship between (a) and (b) in all matters not provided for in the bill of lading.

The shipping document generally does not contain an arbitration clause, whereas the ship's lease agreement contains such a condition.

The conclusion of a subcontract between the main contractor (d) and the subcontractor (e) is another example frequently applied in practical life.

Does not include an arbitration clause and provides for the application of the main contract between the main contractor (d) and the employer (g), which includes an arbitration clause

The question in both cases is whether the arbitration clause between a) and c) applies to b) in the first example or between d) and g) applies to e) in the second example.

It can be said that the general rules require that the arbitration clause in force in this case be applied in accordance with the contractual rule of contract law and that the contractual conditions must be fulfilled as long as they are not contrary to public policy.

However, given the seriousness of the arbitration and the resulting loss of jurisdiction, the reference or reference to the arbitration clause must be so clear that the other party to the contract (the shipper in the contract of carriage and the subcontractor), for example in the bill of lading,

Including an arbitration clause or any other such term 2, this is what is indicated in modern arbitration laws.

(1) The Dubai Court of Cassation ruled that the assignment of the contract to Fidek's general conditions relating to the settlement of the dispute was sufficient to bind the parties to the arbitration agreement (Appeal 462/2002, 2 March 2003, No 14, p. 251).

The same court ruled that if the bill of lading referred to the ship's concrete and the participants included an arbitration clause

This condition applies to the consignee under the bill of lading (call 51 of 18/5/2003 No. 14 p. 611)

In this respect, too, a judgment delivered by Germany on 14 September 2000 (CLOUT, case 443).

(2) Compare a case in Hong Kong on August 18, 1994 where there was a contract with an arbitration clause and a subcontract with no arbitration clause, but the last contract providing for the application of the main contract back to back proportionally.

A copy of the main contract had been given to the subcontractor well before the court decided that the arbitration clause of the main contract applied to the relationship between the main contractor and the subcontractor (see CLOUT case No. 78). For example, article 7/2 of the model law. In the United Arab Emirates, the Federal Code of Civil Procedure No. 11 of 1992 (articles 203 to 218)

Then the Arbitration Act No. 6 of 2018 was promulgated. In this article, we will discuss arbitration under these two laws. In Bahrain, arbitration was organized into two laws, the first on international commercial arbitration, Legislative Decree No. 9 of 1994, and the second on national or domestic arbitration.

Decree-Law No. 12 of 1971, including the Code of Civil and Commercial Procedure (articles 233 to 243).

This study focuses on the most important provisions of the above-mentioned laws, which are frequently applied, and on the problems surrounding them in working life.

2/1 This Bahraini law is the law of national or domestic arbitration without international arbitration.

These are the arbitration rules set out in Act No. 12 of 1971 on civil and commercial proceedings and not in Decree No. 9 of 1994 on international commercial arbitration.

2.2 In Lebanon, the legislator devotes a special chapter to international arbitration (articles 809 to 821), including the implementation of foreign arbitral awards rendered abroad, their recourse and the provisions relating to international arbitration enacted in Lebanon. And excluded from many of the rules that apply to domestic arbitration. Our study will be limited to the majority of the provisions relating to domestic arbitration contained in articles 762 to 808, with reference to certain provisions relating to international arbitration where the study so requires.

2.3 It should be noted that the legislator in the Arab countries, with the exception of Saudi Arabia, governs the provisions relating to arbitration in the context of civil or commercial procedural law and not by law itself.

In Saudi Arabia, arbitration was governed by a special law, the Saudi arbitration system mentioned.

2/4 The reference to Arab laws in this study refers to the laws mentioned above without any other Arab countries. As well as the reference to the law of one of the States mentioned in this study. Unless the context of the speech indicates that another law is being considered in that State and the arbitration rules of all those States apply to domestic and international arbitration.

Without a distinction between them, with the exception of Bahrain and Lebanon, which are making progress.

The third problem: the separate agreement

Article (203/1) of the United Arab Emirates Act provides that the agreement on pre-dispute arbitration may take the form of a subsequent agreement relating to the original contract.

Not only in the form of an arbitration clause and, therefore, but the prior arbitration agreement for the settlement of the dispute also cannot be contained in the form of an arbitration clause in the original contract, as mentioned above.

But rather in the form of a separate agreement for this contract so that such an agreement does not form part of it, for example, the contract does not contain an arbitration clause

However, the parties shall conclude a separate agreement to submit their future disputes concerning the original contract to arbitration, such an agreement may be attached to the contract and attached to it (1)

It may be concluded later, but before the dispute and in the same way as the arbitration clause, no specific wording is required in the author's agreement.

(1) It should be noted that there is no difference between the arbitration clause and the separate agreement before the dispute begins, both of which are admissible and should be applied to future disputes submitted to arbitration.

In Dubai, it held that it was sufficient for the validity of the arbitration clause to be approved in principle without any further details that could be agreed at a later stage.

Especially since the dispute did not exist on the date of the agreement on the arbitration clause (Appeal 91/92 of 21 November 1992 No. 3, p. 778).

Question 4: Arbitration clause and separate agreement together

The arbitration clause may be in accordance with the subsequent arbitration agreement

But before the conflict broke out, we are faced with an arbitration clause,

As well as an arbitration agreement, for example, an arbitration clause must be included in the contract. After the conclusion of the contract, the parties agree on the terms and conditions of the arbitration based mainly on this condition,

Such that the place and language of the arbitration, its proceedings and the names of the arbitrators and of course the parties are not obliged to conclude a new arbitration contract as such they may also agree in the original contract, for example in the arbitration clause, that their contractual disputes shall be submitted to arbitration in accordance with conditions to be determined later.

If they so agree, this Agreement shall apply to them. If they do not agree, the arbitration clause shall not be null and void, but shall remain valid and enforceable

In this case, the arbitration clause is fulfilled by the provisions of the law entrusted to it, such as the appointment of arbitrators and the procedure before the arbitral tribunal and the terms of the arbitral award. And other provisions of all this unless the will of the parties shows that the application of the arbitration clause is linked to the conclusion of a subsequent detailed agreement.

In this case, failure to comply with this agreement results in the failure of the arbitration clause and the loss of the result.

If the separate arbitration agreement complies with the arbitration clause as such and the first is based on its existence at the second

It follows that the separate arbitration agreement follows the arbitration clause in terms of nullity rather than existence in the sense that if the arbitration clause is null or terminated for a reason such as a treaty annulment,

But the opposite is not true in the sense that the arbitration clause may be valid and enforceable while the separate arbitration agreement is void, each party may be fully qualified at the conclusion of the arbitration clause.

While one becomes incompetent at the conclusion of the subsequent arbitration agreement for this loan, the first is true

While the second is null and void and does not affect the arbitration clause because it follows this condition and not the other way around

However, it can be argued that the relationship between the arbitration clause and the subsequent arbitration agreement is a matter of interpreting the will of the parties, depending on the party.

The subsequent agreement may be intended to follow the arbitration requirement set out and the parties may intend to terminate the arbitration clause and replace it with the new agreement.

In the latter case, the arbitration clause shall be considered terminated as long as the arbitration agreement is in force. Arbitration is then based on the latter rather than the former.

Section II: Images of the post-conflict agreement

The arbitration agreement must be concluded after the dispute in different forms, the most important being the arbitration committee.

Including the so-called arbitrator's task document, which is frequently applied in professional life But are mandatory under ICC rules In addition to this arbitration agreement before the Court in the context of a dispute it is considering.

The first issue: the Arbitration Committee

First: it is a marshmallow

The arbitration agreement may be subsequent to the creation of the dispute when the parties agree to submit the signed dispute to arbitration.

This type of agreement is generally referred to as an arbitration partner, to distinguish it from the arbitration clause.

Thus, the difference between the arbitration clause and other arbitration agreements is that the arbitration agreement was concluded before or after the dispute.

In the latter case, we are within the scope of the arbitration agreement and only within the scope of other arbitration agreements (1)

Second: the distinction between participants and the arbitration clause

The distinction between an arbitration clause and an arbitration clause is very important: the laws of Bahrain and Bahrain require that the subject matter of the dispute be determined in the arbitration instrument.

Arbitration clause

Relating to potential future conflicts that are not known in advance and therefore impossible to resolve in the arbitration clause before they occur.

However, the laws of Bahrain, Qatar and the United Arab Emirates added that if the subject of the conflict was not identified in the area

It must be determined during the pleadings and is intended to plead before the arbitral tribunal, which is self-evident because it is unreasonable to submit one of the parties to arbitral pleadings without specifying the subject matter of the dispute.

It is also impossible for the Commission to examine and resolve a dispute without the conflict being specific and clear to it.

Otherwise, the arbitration process would be invalid under the various laws if the parties included the dispute

What was caused by the parties during the pleading is only the elaboration and elaboration of this already determined dispute.

(1) In the arbitration panel, see generally Fouchard para 356 Chapter Hunter

(1) Article (203) Emirati Article (233) The law of Bahrain, Kuwait and Kuwait has been informed of the duration of the arbitration contract (Article 173).

Example of an arbitration clause:

Any dispute arising from this contract that cannot be settled amicably shall be submitted to arbitration.

The arbitrator shall notify the other party of his request on behalf of the court and the subject matter of the dispute and the other party shall choose a court within fifteen days of notification of the request for arbitration.

The two arbitrators appointed by the parties shall be appointed within fifteen days of the appointment of the second of them as a possible arbitrator, who shall preside over the arbitral tribunal.

If one of the arbitrators is not selected in time, any interested party may request the Arab Arbitration Centre to appoint him or her.

Arbitration sessions shall be held at the seat of the Centre or at the seat determined by the Arbitral Tribunal and the dispute shall be governed by Egyptian law.

The arbitration shall be conducted in Arabic and the arbitrators shall be allowed to reconcile.

Form for arbitration contract or arbitration contract:

Arbitration contract

For Gentlemen.

An agreement and an agreement have been concluded between:

(1) Mr. ....

No.. in the region.

As a..

(First part)

(2) Mr. ....

No.. in the region.

As a...

(second party)

Introduction or indentation of the contract

The contract and its stages and the stages of disagreement and the subject of the dispute

Article 1: The two parties to this contract wishing to resolve the dispute between them by arbitration,

With the authorization of the arbitrator (or not delegated)

They agreed to choose.. on the street.

The second subject is the arbitrator

Power of the arbitrator:

The arbitrator shall have jurisdiction only in respect of the dispute relating to the arbitration agreed upon and between its parties only.

And has no power to govern in another conflict if it was related to that dispute only with the explicit consent of the opponents and included. He also has no power among others, except with their consent.

The power granted to the arbitrator shall in no case exceed the civil or commercial aspect of the dispute. Thus, he has no right to sign a criminal sanction or fine in favor of the State, even if this is provided for in the procedural code.

If there is a dispute between the parties to the dispute concerning the arbitration in terms of validity, admissibility, scope or order in general - because of its power or scope in the judgment, it cannot decide. But immediately refrains from looking at this dispute, which is the ordinary judicial power, contrary to the scope of his authority within the government so as not to exceed them, will invalidate his power. It should be noted that, while the arbitration agreement is clear, it is nevertheless valid.

The referee can go, the judiciary will then have the final say in appealing its decision or granting the application for invalidation, as the case may be.

The arbitrator shall not be entitled to appoint another person, even for his or her assistance, unless this is based on the agreement of the parties.

But of course, must call on an expert to consult him on technical issues. He also has a secretary to write the minutes of the meeting, even without the permission of the opponents. The arbitrator's judgment rendered in a manner not assigned to him or her shall not be taken into account.

The arbitrator's responsibility:

An example of an arbitrator's error is that he or she cannot rule without an acceptable excuse or exceed the time limit, or have his or her judgment set aside due to negligence or error, which can result in a loss of time and effort.

If the arbitrator's judgment is set aside and he has no income in this disability, he will not be liable for compensation

The arbitrator is also asked whether he or she charges significant amounts of money for investigations that do not reflect the value of the dispute,

He asked whether one of the opponents had concealed his solid relationship with the other party or his proximity to him.

This results in the arbitrator's response and the loss of time, effort and money and causes his or her rule of negligence and misconduct.

If, by virtue of the agreement of the opponents, he must appoint other arbitrators with him,

And he had the power to determine the number, he had to take into account the law and respect for the determination of the number and for the right choice and validity. It does not appoint any prisoners, minors or criminals, etc.

Fees and expenses of the arbitrator:

Certainly the arbitrator who has completed his work to claim his fees and honoraria, unless he has accepted the task without charge,

Expenses include travel expenses from home to the place of dispute, if necessary, full accommodation costs in that place, the costs of the writer who assists him in taking minutes of meetings, transfer costs for filing judgments, etc.

The fees are limited to compensation for the efforts made by the arbitrator during the examination of the dispute on the basis of the duration of the arbitration. The difficulties and efforts he has made, the value of the case and the status of the social and financial arbitrator, with regard to current custom if there is a custom in this regard.

And he is entitled to fees in exchange for the effort and time devoted to the task and often accepted in bringing the arbitration closer together, provided that the arbitrator's costs and fees are shared equally between the parties.

If the arbitrator's judgment is set aside for a reason due to negligence or error, he or she is not entitled to claim the fees, as it may have caused the loss of opponents' time and effort, but in vain, regardless of what has been lost

But he is entitled to a penalty if he is found disabled for a reason beyond his control or not, and it is not his duty to check his availability,

For example, he is not entitled to a penalty if he is found guilty of quashing his judgment for having rendered a minor when the circumstances of the case and the appearance of the opponent interrupts the fact that he does not exceed the age of majority.

Especially if he is not asked to present his birth certificate... etc.

The parties may authorize the arbitrator to assess his fees and determine them in this case after the judgment in this matter.

In estimating the costs of the case and determining the discount allocated to it, the parties may, with the authorization of the arbitrator in assessing his fees, grant him the power to assign the share borne by each opponent or by the opponent who bears it alone.

Rather, it is said that the arbitrator has the determination of the reduction that supports the sole commission, even without the authorization of the parties in this regard. The arbitrator's report to the clerk is subject to review by the court that has amended it. The jurisdiction of the court before which the dispute is to be decided shall be determined in accordance with the general rules of jurisdiction and jurisdiction.

It may be agreed in advance and before the dispute to determine the arbitrator's fees. And the part that each opponent must play,

Here the opponents and the referee have committed themselves to this determination

This or those that can only be modified for reasons that are then found, and if the arbitrator is invited to settle another dispute in which he accepts arbitration or concludes other opponents with their consent.

Either the court has exhausted an effort that was not expected in any way when determining the first fees or if the arbitrator withdraws from a part of the dispute,

Or the rest of the dispute between the parties was settled directly.

If it is agreed in advance to determine the fees and the arbitration is completed for any reason before the dispute is considered,

The arbitrator is not entitled to any fee unless the case file has been submitted for consideration and the arbitrator has not exhausted the efforts and time available in this regard.

It should be noted that if the parties do not expressly agree to allow the arbitrator to assess his fees. Under no circumstances does he have an estimate because it exceeds the limits of the assigned task. In addition, let it be both rival and judgmental. Jurors realize that the arbitrator does not have custody of the litigants' documents and their papers until he has received his fees from the plaintiffs. Finally, it should be noted that even if the arbitrator's judgment is set aside. He must be reimbursed for expenses actually incurred in connection with his mission, such as travel expenses and expenses for full residence in his country of origin... etc.

Unless it is malicious, i.e. it deliberately causes the nullity of its judgment or the previous actions on which it was built.

Expiry of the arbitrator's duties and effects - the death of the arbitrator

The arbitrator's task ends with the judgment on the subject matter of the dispute,

This is the natural result of the situation and may terminate the arbitrator's task because of his or her inability to work or his or her response, incompetence or isolation due to the agreement of the parties. Even if appointed by the Court (in the legislation authorizing it).

His mission expires because of his death, loss of eligibility, bankruptcy judgment, criminal sanction, etc. As his mission ends with the verdict on the subject of the dispute and then declared null and void for any reason. The parties again agree to arbitration and there is no reason to prevent the appointment of the same first arbitrator reinstated until the disability has been adjudicated as a result of contact with that arbitrator.

End of the arbitrator's work

The original is that the arbitrator is obliged to fulfil his mission and follow it to the end.

In fulfilment of its obligations arising from the acceptance of the written arbitration

The so-called mission acceptance document, which is usually signed by the arbitrator after the dispute has arisen and once he or she has been selected as an arbitrator.

In signing the deed of assignment, the arbitrator shall refrain from withdrawing from the arbitral tribunal or abandoning his or her duties,

Unless there are strong grounds for doing so, an act without cause of this type and the resulting damage shall be compensated for such damage.

This was determined by the Lebanese Code of Civil Procedure of 1985, that after the acceptance of the mission, the arbitrator cannot withdraw without serious justification,

Otherwise, he will be liable for damages in favor of the injured party.

However, circumstances and reasons may arise between the arbitrator and the performance of his obligations to carry out his mission.

This threatens not only to disrupt the arbitration process but also to defeat the entire arbitration dispute.

These circumstances and reasons may be voluntary or involuntary and all of them result in the arbitrator's seat being vacant.

In view of these circumstances and reasons, it is conceivable that the arbitrator may voluntarily withdraw from the dispute if he or she does not wish to do so.

Although this may result in delays and the disqualification of the arbitral proceedings, it may be challenged and rejected either by agreement of the parties or by the decision of the competent court.

As a general rule, it is often difficult for the parties to the dispute to agree to dismiss the arbitrator, even when there are serious grounds for excluding him or her from the consideration of the dispute.

There is no escape from the use of justice to terminate the arbitrator's task.

"If the arbitrator is unable to perform his duties or fails to perform them or is prevented from performing them, resulting in an undue delay in the arbitral proceedings

If the parties do not accept its transfer, the court may order the termination of its mission at the request of either party. "

The application of this provision, the Court's intervention to terminate its mandate, requires several conditions:

First condition: there are reasons to justify the termination of the arbitrator's work, including the impossibility of carrying out his or her mission, the absence of direct or non-functional control for health or social reasons or the existence of a legal or real obstacle preventing him or her from working.

The second condition: the parties do not agree to isolate the arbitrator despite the availability of isolation obligations,

As if a party clings to its survival thinking that the reasons for the prosecution do not justify its isolation,

While the other party opposes the existence of such an arbitrator and insists that he be dismissed.

Third condition: the failure of the arbitrator to carry out his or her duties constitutes an undue delay in the arbitral proceedings, in a manner likely to prejudice the interests of the parties,

The assessment of the extent of this delay is the responsibility of the competent court.

The fourth condition: that the arbitrator refuses to withdraw and leaves his place of choice despite the availability of reasons,

This is arbitrarily arbitrary.

The fifth condition: that of the parties,

Of course, it is the party who opposes the arbitrator of the arbitral tribunal being retained by the competent court to refer him.

If these conditions are met and the court has determined, objectively and in good faith, that it is not in the interest of its opponents to the arbitration to appeal to the arbitrator, it has decided to refer him back.

The vacancy of the arbitrator's place and the need to appoint another arbitrator:

The vacancy of the place of the arbitrator by the end of his mission: from the previous presentation that the end of the task of the position of the arbitrator vacant, which requires filling this vacuum before the arbitral tribunal,

By appointing another arbitrator for this task.

The termination of the arbitrator's task, even if this results in a disruption of the dispute in arbitration,

This does not result in the expiry of the arbitration agreement, which requires the appointment of another arbitrator.

Define the alternative arbitrator:

Arbitration legislation and rules agree on the need to appoint another arbitrator for the arbitrator who replaced him.

If the arbitrator's task ends with a judgment of revocation, revocation, revocation or any other cause,

An alternate shall be appointed in accordance with the procedures followed for the selection of the arbitrator who has fulfilled his or her duties. "

This text is based on the provisions of the 1985 (XV) Model Law of the United Nations Commission on International Trade Law on International Commercial Arbitration and the 1976 UNCITRAL Rules (P.13).

And the 1965 Washington Convention on the Settlement of Investment Disputes between States and Nationals of Other States.

The substitute arbitrator must have the necessary conditions and qualifications in arbitrators in general,

The substitute arbitrator has the power to assess the continuation of the former arbitrator's investigation or prosecution or to reopen all arbitral proceedings.

If the arbitrator is unable to perform his or her duties or fails to perform them or is prevented from performing them, which would result in an undue delay in the arbitration proceedings

The Tribunal may order the termination of its functions at the request of either party, which means that the parties to the arbitration must have recourse to the Court to terminate its mission if there are grounds to do so and to ensure that the arbitration can delay the arbitration.

As was the case and the court had the right to examine the documents that the second defendant (the arbitrator was required to terminate his mission), the defendant's arbitrator against him ceased to carry out his mission without a valid excuse.

This is contrary to the characteristics of the arbitration procedure, which requires a prompt referral, obliging the court to terminate its mission.

This does not prejudge what the second applicant wrote in his brief, as what is stated in it does not constitute a reason not to attend the hearings.

If he is required to attend meetings and show what he has to record his meetings, but he has not done so and has been interrupted,

This resulted in the disqualification of the proceedings between the two arbitrators, which ends with the Court's previous decision, which will follow up on the action.

Since the Prosecutor had requested the appointment of another arbitrator, he would be ordered to dismiss or dismiss him or her or challenge him or her if the Court's work was completed.

Or for any other reason, an alternate shall be appointed in accordance with the procedures followed for the selection of the arbitrator who has completed his or her term.

The third topic concerns opponents of arbitration

- How does a dispute arise in arbitration?

The dispute arises in arbitration as soon as the parties appear before the arbitrator or by declaration, whatever its image.

- In their presence, even by mail, and it is presumed that this declaration will be made by one of the parties to the dispute before the other party

Or by a member of a party against the rest of his opponents and of course, it is not necessary to have a lawyer sign the case before the arbitrator.

Respect the deadlines for filing the complaint:

If the parties agree to a time limit for bringing the matter before the arbitrator, the arbitrator must respect this time limit on his or her own initiative.

For example, if the parties agree that the action must be brought within two months, for example, it must respect that date.

Advocacy language:

The original must be heard and the judgment must be written in the language of the country unless the parties agree that the procedural document must be in another language.

In all cases, the judgment shall be rendered in the language of the country where the meetings are held at the time of their convening.

It is not necessary for the arbitration to take place in a particular location and not all meetings should be held in the same location.

Arbitration sessions:

The law does not require the presence of the arbitrator's clerk to write the minutes of meetings and does not require the arbitrators' signature on their judgment.

The first meeting of the arbitrators is not necessary in the presence of the parties, but all hearings may take place in the absence of the parties.

All that is needed in this regard is that they can make other demands and defend themselves.

They should also be able to see all the demands of their opponents and their defense so that action can be taken against them.

The arbitrators' decision invalidates the decisions they make if one of the parties to the dispute is invited without inviting the other party

Or when you only hear the defense of the first party and the arbitrators' sessions are held in public, but the origin is the non-attendance of non-adversers at these meetings and their decision is not made in public meetings.

What must be taken into account to trigger the rivalry?

The arbitrator shall determine in the first few minutes of his meetings the day on which the dispute was submitted to him until the date provided for in the agreement or the beginning of the law to render his judgment.

It must also check its own attributes of opponents and the availability of their full capacity to avoid conducting invalid procedures.

And on its own initiative to stop the conduct of the dispute if this was caused by one of the reasons for the interruption in accordance with the rules that have been studied.

Presence and absence of the parties and presentation of their requests and documents:

On the day appointed for the consideration of the matter in arbitration, the parties shall introduce themselves or call upon their counsel by virtue of a special non-public power.

The power of attorney must be formal and if the litigant(s) or one of them does not appear before the arbitrator, he or she will not apply the rules and procedures established in the absence of litigants in the law of procedural acts.

And if the absence of the parties before the court may lead to the inadmissibility of the counterparty or to the disappearance without the provision in force in certain cases

Or that the judgment rendered in absentia is questionable in some cases or if the absence of the pleader before the arbitrator does not lead to an advanced result, the judge may consider the matter even if the absence of the litigants is affected

It has no power to judge the dispute as if it were not so, and the absenteeism rule it lays down does not accept the opposition.

If the parties do not appear before him, he has no right to close the case but to postpone the hearing to another session.

If litigants file their notes and documents, the arbitrator does not suspend the judgment subject to their presence.

For example, if he has not been ordered to do so to question him, for example, if he does not appear before the arbitrator who issued the invitation to appear before him

The arbitrator is nevertheless entitled to consider the case in his or her absence because the presence of the defendant at the first hearing before the arbitrator is not considered a case.

If the defendant fails to attend the first session. If he has not submitted a defense, the arbitrator must adjourn the trial to a hearing to be determined and declare absent by himself or by the prosecutor, even by mail. If the applicant does not attend the rehearing and if he or she has not submitted a statement of defense, the judge may consider the matter after verifying the validity of his or her statement.

The requirement of the origin of the declaration by registration or under the arrival flag if it is announced by registered mail with the reception flag.

The fact that the memorandum was submitted by the opponent constitutes, in any event, a new declaration.

And it is enough to bring the opponent even once before the arbitrator until the judgment has been rendered.

In all of the above, the arbitration shall be settled by arbitration with the judiciary. If the arbitrator renders his judgment on the merits before the expiry of the time limit for the submission of briefs

Without any of the opponents being able to make his defense and statements, he has violated the rights of the defense and his judgment is null and void.

Does the arbitrator have proof of conciliation in a record of his or her freedom to exercise executive power?

If the will of the parties coincides with the arbitrator's judgment. If authorized to settle, the arbitrator shall make public a reconciliation report signed by the parties to the dispute before him.

In both cases, the minutes of the session shall not have the force of the executive bond and shall only be taken into account after they have been filed with the original of the arbitration agreement.

The minutes are of a secondary nature to those of the Court, in accordance with Article 103 of the Code of Procedure.

An initial request may be made to invalidate the agreement in accordance with civil or commercial law rules, as the case may be.

The fourth subject concerns the procedure before the arbitrator

Introduction:

Convention on Procedures - Legal Procedures:

The parties' agreement will improve the penalty of invalidity if the arbitrator violates the procedure on the merits by explicitly accepting the invalidity of the award if the arbitrator does not swear before them before making it.

Or has not published a report to prove everything that happens in the meeting and not to comply with these procedures, the Agreement provides for the invalidity of the arbitrator's judgment

As this amounts to departing from the limits of the document and allowing the initial case to be filed with a motion for annulment,

The arbitrator must observe the basic principles of the dispute, even if he is a conciliator, which is why the arbitrator - like the judge - is obliged to decorate the interests of the litigants with justice, which obliges him to remain neutral but also to respect the appearance of impartiality, which must be............. etc.

And be obliged to: -

1. Principle of respect for the rights of the defense It is sufficient to respect this right for the arbitrator to be able to deduct any claims and excluded defenses before giving his judgment.

And allow the opponent to prove his claims and allow his opponent to exile himself.

Of course, the arbitrator must not interfere with the fundamental defense. A defense that, if true, changes the face of opinion in the case, the opponent may be challenged to prove a substantial defense, or he may deny it by a legal means.

Otherwise, the arbitrator must respond in his judgment to this fundamental defense

If he is to arbitrate reconciliation, the other opponent must be able to respond to this fundamental defense.

2. Equal treatment of opponents cannot be achieved by promoting and taking into account reduction without the other opponent

Allowing a litigant to prove what he or she claims requires in all cases the right to allow the other opponent to deny it.

3. The arbitrator shall allow each objector to examine the documents and materials submitted by the other objector and shall give the parties the time necessary to prepare the defense and respond to the statements and documents.

4 - Conduct investigations in the presence of all lawyers, otherwise the procedure is invalid, one of the arbitrators may not be independent to take evidence measures unless they have all been marked or authorized to do so.

5 - The dispute must be examined in the presence of all the arbitrators otherwise, the procedure would have been invalid with regard to public policy.

6 - The arbitrator must register himself or one of the third parties for what we have submitted or one of the litigants if the other parties accept it

The summary record shall be recorded in the minutes of the arbitration session with respect to the presence or absence of litigants with respect to their claims, defenses or documents

Such a record may confirm the arbitrator's respect for the rights of the defense and the fact that failure to release him may result in a failure to respect the rights of the defense.

The investigation procedures must be documented in a file or, at least, invalid as indicated above.

7 - The arbitrator must reject his mission and leave it for incompetence or response.

Section I

Formation of the arbitral tribunal

How to appoint arbitrators:

The appointment of the arbitrator in person or in his or her capacity or the determination of the method of appointment, an essential element of the arbitration contract.

Nor may it be appointed by the competent court or otherwise by both parties to the dispute,

In addition, the arbitrator's request is considered a satisfaction of the arbitration and, as the judge has the status of judge, confidence in his or her good judgment is equivalent to good judicial judgment.

In addition, confidence in the arbitrator's good judgment in arbitration is equivalent to the judicial guarantees that Parliament has provided to the judiciary,

If the arbitrator does not have the guarantee of his choice from the arbitrators, the arbitration shall be terminated.

It will be agreed that the arbitrator's person will be at the heart of the arbitration contract (condition or involvement) or will be the subject of an independent agreement and will settle this prior agreement independently of the contract or later.

Drafting is necessary for each element of the agreement

If, however, one of the litigants attended an arbitration session and the opponent defined the subject at that meeting, he or she will have accepted the other arbitrator's choice.

It may be prima facie to prove the consent of the opponent to the arbitrator's person by acknowledgement or by decisive oath,

Because all that is required by law is to agree on the arbitration and the arbitrator.

If the arbitration contract provided for three arbitrators, only one of them was chosen and the parties to the hearing attended the arbitration session.

This would be considered as a modification of the arbitration contract and the sufficiency of a single arbitrator if all have demonstrated their defense before him,

But if three arbitrators are chosen, only two are chosen and the parties attend the arbitration session, nullity is required, because when selecting arbitrators,

The implementation of the arbitration contract must be chosen by the third arbitrator and the procedure will then be valid,

If one of the parties to a litigant chooses a person and the other party appears before him and presents his claims and defense before him

This must be considered as an express consent to its arbitration in order to dispense with written confirmation unless the party reserves the right to do so before presenting its defense.

Entities may agree to authorize a particular person on its behalf as an arbitrator or arbitrator

It is also possible to agree to allow the court initially competent for the dispute to appoint the arbitrator(s).

The number of arbitrators:

If the parties have not previously agreed on the number of arbitrators (i.e. one or more arbitrators, provided it is an individual)

Within 15 days from the date of receipt of the notice of arbitration by the claimant, there may only be one arbitrator, The arbitral tribunal shall be composed of three arbitrators.

Appointment of arbitrators:

1. When it comes to the appointment of an arbitrator, either party may propose to the other:

A) The name of a person who will be the sole arbitrator or the names of a group of persons from which an arbitrator may be chosen.

(B) The name of an institution or the names of several institutions or the name of a single person or the names of a group of persons from which the appointing authority may be selected,

If the parties have not agreed to designate an appointing authority.

2. If thirty days have elapsed since the date of receipt of one of the parties, a proposal has been made in accordance with the first paragraph without the parties agreeing to appoint an arbitrator:

He was appointed head of the appointment, which the parties agreed to appoint,

If the parties have not agreed to designate an appointing authority or if the authority they have agreed to appoint has failed within sixty days from the date of receipt of the request submitted to it by one of the parties in this respect,

Either party may request the appointing authority to designate the appointing authority.

3. The Appointing Authority, at the request of one of the parties, shall appoint an arbitrator as soon as possible.

The listing method follows the following procedures

Unless the parties agree to exclude this method,

Or, at its discretion, the Appointing Authority considers that its use is not appropriate in the circumstances of the case and follows the following procedures:

A) The Appointing Authority shall send the parties, at the request of one of them, an identical copy of a list containing at least three names:

(B) Each party shall, within fifteen days from the date of receipt of this list, return it to the appointing authority after the name or names for which it wishes to be deleted.

And number the remaining names on the list in the order they prefer.

(C) After the expiry of the period referred to in the preceding paragraph, the Appointing Authority shall appoint an arbitrator from among the names adopted by the parties on the lists referred to them.

Taking into account the order of preference established by the parties.

D) If, for any reason, an arbitrator cannot be appointed by following these procedures,

The Appointing Authority had the discretion to appoint him.

4. In selecting the arbitrator, the appointing authority shall take into account considerations relevant to the selection of an independent and impartial arbitrator.

And take into account the desirability of the arbitrator being of a non-national nationality with one of the parties to the dispute.

5. When three arbitrators are to be chosen by each party,

The two arbitrators so appointed shall select the third arbitrator who shall preside over the arbitral tribunal.

6. If one of the parties notifies the other of the choice of an arbitrator and the latter does not do so:

Within thirty days from the date of receipt of the notification, notify the first party of the arbitrator's choice.

The independence and impartiality of the arbitrator

Since the arbitrator is the task of the special judicial power,

As we have foreseen, he must enjoy the independence of the opponents and be neutral, and must not judge his goal or desire.

If we have already indicated that the arbitrator must confirm in writing when accepting the task of arbitration by his independence from opponents and by his neutrality,

This recognition is not a condition of the arbitrator's jurisdiction to settle the dispute,

But rather a commitment to his commitment to accept his mission.

The arbitrator's independence and impartiality are part of the conditions that confer on the arbitrator the power to refer the matter to an arbitral tribunal.

Which are required by most arbitration laws and the rules of its organizations.

Case law and case law generally distinguish between the independence and impartiality of the arbitrator. Some argue that the basic rule is that one of the litigants in a case cannot be assigned a judgment, as it is inconceivable that the person should be both litigant and arbitrator.

This rule concerns public policy, as it concerns arbitration procedures and regulations, which is the law of the legislator. Therefore, the arbitrators chosen by a party should not consider themselves to be their representatives or lawyers and, once appointed, they should terminate any association with their choice if there are prior commitments.

The arbitrator appointed by one of the litigants becomes a judge after accepting the task entrusted to him,

Thus, he is neither an agent nor a lawyer of the opponent of his choice,

Rather, it is an elected judge who must have a condition of impartiality and independence from all parties to the dispute, including the opponent he or she has chosen; it is therefore not surprising that the arbitrator appointed by one of the litigants should be prosecuted in the dispute to which he or she is submitted.

Independence means that the arbitrator has no subordinate relationship with one of the parties to the dispute, which is therefore incompatible with the material interests, partnership or financial ties with any of the parties to the dispute in which he or she is dependent, such as employment, family or agency relations.

The arbitrator is not considered independent if he or she performs the personal duties of one of the parties to the arbitration, such as providing advice or technical assistance,

Or if he is an adviser to one of the companies in the group of companies in which the company is involved in arbitration.

If the arbitrator's independence is highlighted by an external aspect,

The arbitrator's impartiality is only an internally difficult state of mind to prove, especially if it is not accompanied by a lack of independence of the arbitrator, this lack of independence leading to non-neutrality.

Neutrality therefore consists in orienting myself and my mind before it becomes external. Therefore, the work was done in international commercial arbitration

The rules of some of its international organizations also require that the arbitrators or at least the arbitral tribunal be non-nationals of the parties to the dispute.

The arbitrators' response:

1 - Whoever appoints an arbitrator shall authorize the person concerned by this nomination in all circumstances likely to give rise to doubts based on his or her neutrality or independence.

When appointing or choosing, the arbitrator shall only declare these circumstances to the parties to the dispute if he has already informed them.

1. The arbitrator may be dismissed if there are circumstances that give rise to justifiable doubts as to his or her impartiality or independence.

2. None of the parties to the dispute may respond to the arbitrator they have chosen, except for reasons that have not been identified until such time as the arbitrator has been appointed.

3. The party intending to dismiss the arbitrator shall send a notice of request for a response within fifteen days from the date of notification of the appointment of the arbitrator or within fifteen days from the date on which it is informed of the circumstances on which the response was based.

4. The request for a reply shall be notified to the opposing party, the arbitrator and the other members of the arbitral tribunal. Such notification must be in writing and must state the reasons for it.

5. When a party requests an arbitral response, the other party may agree to respond.

The arbitrator who has requested a response may also withdraw from the proceedings, as this consent does not constitute an implicit recognition of the validity of the grounds on which the request for a response is based.

In both cases, the appointment of the substitute arbitrator is followed by all previous actions taken in the appointment of the adjudicator.

1. If the other party does not consent to the request for a response and the arbitrator whose request for a response has not been filed, the decision in the request for a response is as follows:

(A) If the appointment of the arbitrator is made by the appointing authority, the latter shall make the decision

(B) If the appointment was not made by the appointing authority, but was designated by that authority, it will be the author of the decision.

(C) In all other cases, the decision shall be taken by the Appointing Authority.

(A) The first party may request the appointing authority, which the parties have already agreed to appoint, to appoint the second arbitrator.

(B) If the parties have not previously agreed to designate an appointing authority,

Or if the appointing authority which has agreed to appoint him or her fails to appoint the arbitrator or does not complete his or her appointment within 30 days of the date of receipt of the request submitted to it by one of the parties in this respect,

The first party may request the Secretary-General of the Permanent Court of Arbitration at The Hague to designate the appointing authority,

He may then request the appointing authority so designated to appoint the second arbitrator,

In both cases, the Appointing Authority exercises its discretion when appointing the arbitrator.

7. If thirty days have elapsed from the date of appointment of the second arbitrator without the two arbitrators having agreed on the choice of the main arbitrator,

The appointing authority chose this arbitrator following the same procedure as the individual arbitrator.

1. When an appointing authority is invited to select an arbitrator in accordance with the provisions of article 6 or article 7,

The party submitting the request must send to the Appointing Authority a copy of the notice of arbitration, a copy of the resulting contract or an attachment, as well as a copy of the arbitration agreement, if it is not included in the contract.

The appointing authority may request each party to provide the information deemed necessary for the performance of its functions.

2. When appointing a person or persons for appointment as arbitrators, their full names, addresses and nationalities shall be indicated, together with their qualifications.

The court's decision to choose the arbitrator is final and without appeal, which guarantees the speed of the arbitral proceedings.

And avoids preventing him from leaving the appeal of the said decision open, in particular, that the opponent of the interest of showing what the defense can mean before the arbitral tribunal, which is ultimately subject to review of the invalidity of the judge.

The arbitrator is required to comply with the law for the same reasons as the judge or for which he or she is deemed unfit to govern.

It should be noted that if the parties to the arbitration are aware of the arbitrator's choice, there is a suspicion of the arbitrator's impartiality and independence and none of them is so categorical.

Or did not respond to the arbitrator within the time limit, it is a waiver of the right to defend impartiality or independence

Because the policy of impartiality and independence are not linked to public order

But also with the interests of the opponents. It is also decided that if one of the parties does not have the arbitrator's answer

Or has not objected, he is no longer entitled, after the arbitral award has been made, to bring an action for a declaration of invalidity based on the arbitrator's non-impartiality or non-independence,

The arbitrator may also be reinstated if he or she has already expressed an opinion on the dispute before him or her or before the request for arbitration is made or if the arbitrator is acting as legal counsel to one of the parties to the arbitration.

Sending a request for a response:

The request for a statement of defense shall be addressed in writing to the Arbitral Tribunal, stating the reasons for the request within fifteen days from the date on which the Respondent requested the Arbitral Tribunal to be constituted or the justified circumstances of the statement of defense.

The adversity of the response between the respondent and the other party is submitted to arbitration,

Therefore, the arbitrator should not be considered as a litigant in the reply action, nor should the arbitration center in which the arbitration takes place in accordance with its rules be considered as an opponent in this case. However, the competent authority shall have the right to decide on the request for a reply. The authority competent to decide on the request for reply:

If the requested arbitrator is not challenged, the arbitral tribunal shall address the request for a response to the court initially competent to hear the dispute.

The defendant may not bring the action for a response directly before the court and the contradictory dispute between the defendant and the opposing party is submitted to arbitration.

Therefore, the arbitrator should not be considered a litigant in the event of a reply. In addition, the arbitration center in which the arbitration is conducted in accordance with its rules shall not be considered an opponent in this case.

However, the arbitrator has the right to intervene in the application if the grounds for the reply are prejudicial to its integrity.

The submission of a request for an answer shall not result in the suspension of the arbitration proceedings:

The submission of a request for an answer shall not result in the suspension of the arbitral proceedings

Consequently, the filing of a request for an answer does not result in the suspension of the arbitration proceedings.

If the arbitration continues until a judgment has been rendered and the arbitrator's decision is subsequently rendered, the arbitration proceedings, including the arbitral award, shall be considered as if they had not been rendered.

This does not mean that the arbitration agreement is terminated, but an alternative arbitrator is chosen, as we will show later,

Unless the parties to the arbitration agree to choose a specific arbitrator appointed in the arbitration agreement,

The judgment of its reply shall entail the termination of the arbitration agreement unless otherwise provided in the agreement.

The parties to the arbitration may agree to terminate the arbitration procedure,

They may, after submitting the request for reply, agree to close the procedure until the request for reply has been settled, In order to avoid any problems that may arise if the arbitral award is made before the judgment of the reply, if the final judgment results in the annulment of all proceedings, including the award,

As mentioned above, it should be noted that the suspension of the arbitration procedure is considered in this case as "an agreement that does not entail the effect of the request for an answer".

Failure to accept the arbitrator's request for a response:

No party to the dispute may reply to the arbitrator who appointed him or participated in his appointment, except for the reasons for which he has been identified

After this appointment has been made and the request for a response is not accepted by those who have already submitted a request for a response from the same arbitrator in the same arbitration.

Effects of the submission and rejection of a request for reply:

The submission of a request for an answer shall not result in the suspension of the arbitration proceedings and if the arbitration continues until the judgment is rendered

In this case, the arbitral award will be reviewed, so that the arbitration procedure, including the arbitral award, will be reviewed if not.

This does not mean the end of the arbitration agreement, but another arbitrator is chosen.

Unless the parties to the arbitration have agreed that an arbitrator be appointed on his or her behalf in the arbitration agreement, the decision of his or her award will not result in the termination of the arbitration agreement.

Effects of the appointment of a replacement arbitrator:

One of the effects of the amendment of the alternative arbitrator is the re-hearing of pleadings in the event of the replacement of the arbitrator.

Or, if necessary, to replace the arbitrator as mentioned above, the pleadings previously submitted must be heard again.

The arbitrator has an expert:

The arbitrator may appoint himself or at the request of one of the arbitrators, one or more experts.

Experts, whether on the list or by others, are granted an absolute right to appear before the court

As well as for the arbitral tribunal, and not in violation of the basic guarantees of opponents and does not affect the basic assets in a dispute.

The arbitrator is not competent to hear the expert's response:

The arbitrator is not competent to hear the expert's response because the adversity in the response exceeds the limits of his authority under the arbitration contract.

And since one of the opponents of this legal action is the expert who is not a party to the arbitration contract and the competent court is the competent court to settle the initial dispute -

Such a case may be closed after the judgment of the Court has been delivered, if the convicted person is not informed of the response until after the judgment has been delivered.

Acceptance of the request for an answer then results in the annulment of the judgment rendered by the arbitrator if it is based on the expert's report.

If the expert's request for an answer is made during the procedure, the expert shall prevent the delay in the assignment of another expert to do the work required.

The judge may hear witnesses after they have been sworn in:

The arbitrator may hear witnesses on his own initiative or at the request of one of the arbitrators. Article 211 of the Code of Civil Procedure provides that "arbitrators must summon witnesses before their testimony is heard by them.

A provision in the form of the obligation to guarantee the validity of the declarations they issue

Especially after the law provided in the statement to make the witness the perpetrator of the offence of perjury provided for in article 252 of the Criminal Code. This required the witness to have been sworn before a body with the power to hear arbitrators are therefore not entitled to dispose of their duty in this regard.

Even if the litigants did not object to this for having violated this procedure during the hearing of witness statements.

The violation results in the invalidity of the arbitral proceedings conducted by the arbitrator and does not prevent the acceptance of the invalidity. The opponent waives his right before the arbitrators' judgment. Since the goal can only be achieved by oath before testifying.

The opponent is entitled to maintain this nullity before the court, even if he did not oppose the arbitrator because of the failure of this procedure,

As stipulated in section 41.2 of the Evidence Act, the oath to be taken by witnesses is in the form of an oath to tell the truth and nothing but the right

The alliance must be in accordance with the religious requirements of each witness if he or she so requests, which means that any other form that does not include the witness's statement in the form of an oath will not be considered fair.

"Discrimination of Dubai Appeal No. 322 of 2004 Commercial - Session 11/4/2005 - S 16 - p. 801"

However, the obituary of the arbitrator's judgment that he had not responded to his request to hear witnesses was an acceptable mourning.

Because the Court does not offer the arbitrators' judgment in an objective manner and their assessment of the evidence presented to them and the extent of its adequacy or otherwise,

It is not valid to challenge the arbitrators' judgment before the court on this ground, which is beyond the arbitrators' control.

"Discrimination of Dubai Appeal No. 225 of 2005 Commercial - Session 10/12/2005 - S 16 - 2008".

The arbitrator may order the following:

The arbitrator may order an investigation on the lines if the person witnessed by the editor refuses his or her signature, seal or fingerprints,

It may identify documents accepted for emulation in accordance with the provisions of the law of evidence and civil procedure or specify them without being bound by these provisions.

The Tribunal may take the oath at the request of one of the arbitrators:

Respect or renounce the conditions of its management and the result of its alliance

Even if the arbitrator is reconciled because the direction of this right is the same - according to the opinion prevailing in the case law and the judiciary, for example, a mandatory reconciliation for opponents and the judge.

- Arbitrators have the right to make judicial and non-judicial decisions:

And the conditions for it to be available to confirm its legal conditions

It is necessary, even as an arbitrator, to accept the court decision because it is considered a decisive argument in this case.

The fifth topic

Arbitration procedures

1. The arbitral tribunal may conduct the arbitration in such manner as it deems appropriate, provided that the parties are treated equally.

And to prepare at each step of the procedure a full opportunity to present his case.

2. At the request of one of the parties at any stage of the proceedings, the arbitral tribunal shall hold hearings to hear the testimony.

Including expert witnesses or to hear oral argument, if neither party has made such a request

The arbitral tribunal shall decide whether it is appropriate to hold such hearings or to proceed on the basis of documents and other documents.

3. Documents or information submitted by one party to the arbitral tribunal shall be communicated simultaneously by that party to the other party.

Place of arbitration:

1. If the parties have not agreed on the place of arbitration, the arbitral tribunal shall determine the place of arbitration taking into account the circumstances of the arbitration.

2. The arbitral tribunal may designate the place of arbitration in the State agreed between the parties.

It shall have witnesses and hold meetings to deliberate among its members at any place it deems appropriate, taking into account the circumstances of the arbitration.

3. The arbitral tribunal may meet at any place it considers appropriate to inspect goods or other funds or to examine documents.

Both parties must be notified sufficiently in advance of the date of such inspections or examinations to be able to appear at the time of their conduct.

4. The award shall be made at the place of arbitration.

Language: English

1. Subject to the agreement of the parties, the arbitral tribunal shall decide, after its formation, to designate the language or languages to be used in the proceedings;

This designation applies to the declaration, the statement of defense and any other written declaration.

This also applies to the language or languages used at oral hearings if such meetings are held.

2. The arbitral tribunal may order that documents submitted in their original language be accompanied by a request or a statement of defense and additional documents or documents -

Which in the course of the proceedings must be translated into the language or languages agreed by the parties or designated by the arbitral tribunal.

Complaint declaration:

1. Unless the notice of arbitration contains the declaration,

During the period specified by the arbitral tribunal, the claimant shall send to the claimant and to each of the arbitrators a written statement in its claim,

A copy of the contract and a copy of the arbitration agreement must be attached to this declaration if this agreement is not included in the contract.

2. The declaration must contain the following information:

A) The name of the defendant and the name of the defendant and the address of each of them;

(B) a statement of the facts in support of the case;

C) Litigation issues.

D) Applications.

The applicant may attach to his declaration all documents deemed relevant to the case.

Or to indicate in the declaration the documents and other evidence to be provided.

Statement of defense:

1. Within the time limit set by the arbitral tribunal, the respondent shall send the claimant and each of the arbitrators a written statement in response to the decision.

2. The declaration must include a response to the action declaration

The defendant may attach to the statement of defense the documents on which he is based for his defense.

Or to indicate in the declaration the documents and other evidence to be provided.

3. The claimant may, in the statement of defense or at a later stage of the arbitral proceedings, if the arbitral tribunal determines that the circumstances so warrant - occasional claims arising from the same contract

Or a right under the same contract to pay compensation.

4. The foregoing provisions apply to interlocutory motions filed by the defendant and to the rights he holds to pay compensation.

Modification of the declaration or defense:

During the arbitral proceedings, each party may modify or supplement its applications or defenses;

If the arbitral tribunal considers it inappropriate to leave the amendment for a period of time at the time of its submission or for any damage caused to the other party or to any other circumstance. However, amendments to an application that would have the effect of deleting such a request may not be made after it has been modified from the scope of the arbitration clause or the separate agreement concluded with the arbitration.

Arbitral jurisdiction:

1. The arbitral tribunal shall have jurisdiction to decide on the defenses to its jurisdiction, as well as those relating to the existence of the arbitration clause or the separate agreement on arbitration or the validity of that clause or agreement.

2. The arbitral tribunal is competent to judge the existence or validity of the contract to which the arbitration clause belongs. The arbitration clause, which forms part of a contract and provides for arbitration, is dealt with. In accordance with this regime, as an agreement independent of the other terms of the contract. Any decision of the arbitral tribunal that the contract is invalid shall not, by law, invalidate the arbitration clause.

3. The payment of the jurisdiction of the arbitral tribunal shall be subject, at the latest, to the submission of the statement of defiance or at a time not exceeding the submission of a response to requests in the case of such requests.

4. In general, the arbitral tribunal decides to rule on its jurisdiction on a preliminary basis. However, the arbitral tribunal may decide to continue the proceedings and decide on the payment of jurisdiction in its final decision.

Other written data:

The arbitral tribunal shall appoint other written statements,

In addition to the statement and defense that the parties must or may submit,

The date of submission of this data must be determined.

Duration:

The time limits set by the arbitral tribunal shall not exceed the submission of written data (Including a court action and a defense) forty-five days. However, the arbitral tribunal may extend the time limit if it considers it justified.

Evidence and pleadings:

1. Each party will have the burden of proving the facts on which it relies to defend or defend its interests.

2. The arbitral tribunal may, if it so wishes, request a party to submit to the other party, within the period specified by the other party, a summary of the documents and other evidence to be submitted in support of the disputed facts as indicated in his defense or defense.

3. The arbitral tribunal may request the parties, at any time during the arbitral proceedings: to submit within the time limit specified by the documents, documents or other evidence.

4. In the event of oral argument, the arbitral tribunal shall inform the parties before the hearing sufficiently in advance of the date, place and place of the hearing.

5. If witnesses are to be heard, each party shall inform the Arbitral Tribunal and the other party at least 15 days before the witness testifies, of the name and address of the witnesses to whom they will testify and the languages to be used for the execution of the certificate.

6. The arbitral tribunal shall make the necessary arrangements for the translation of oral statements made at the hearing and shall take the place of minutes of its meeting. If he considers that the circumstances of the case require the work of the translation or file; or if the parties have informed them at least 15 days before the meeting of their willingness to act.

7. Oral and oral hearings shall be held, unless the parties agree otherwise. The arbitral tribunal may request one or more witnesses to leave the lounge while other witnesses testify. It is free to determine how witnesses are interviewed.

8. The certificate may also be presented in the form of written statements signed by witnesses.

9. The arbitral tribunal decides to accept the evidence presented or a link between the subject or the absence of such a link and the importance of the evidence provided.

Temporary preventive measures:

1. The arbitral tribunal may, at the request of either party, take such provisional measures as it considers necessary with regard to the subject matter of the dispute including procedures for the preservation of the goods in dispute, such as the deposit of the goods with third parties or the sale of perishable goods.

2. Provisional measures may be taken in the form of a provisional award. The arbitral tribunal may require a guarantee to cover the costs of the interim measure.

3. A party's request to a judicial authority to take provisional measures shall not be considered to be contrary to the arbitration agreement or the right to invoke it.

Arbitration sessions and pleadings:

The original is that the pleading is made and the judgment is written in the language of the country, unless the parties agree that the pleading must be conducted in another language, and improve their agreement on the language of advocacy in a multiplicity of languages.

If a foreign language publisher submits the arbitration in the State, the Arabic translation must be a legal translation. Otherwise, the arbitral award shall be null and void if he has accepted these documents as evidence and invoked them in his case.

The Supreme Federal Court ruled that one of the controls to obtain justice was what the legislator had stipulated in article 12 of the Translator's Organization Act No. 8 of 1981, based on the refusal to accept documents that are not translated into Arabic if they are not accompanied by an Arabic translation by a translator.

It is a rule of evidence that the arbitral tribunal cannot violate in two respects, the first being the obligation of the rule of law.

Secondly, in order for the depositary court to exercise its control or power to accept the deposit, it must ensure, under the Civil Procedure Act No. 3 of 1992, that the award is in no way contrary to law or the general rules of justice.

This objective will not be achieved unless the Court realizes that the award is vested. For this reason, the arbitral tribunal should not accept any document not published in Arabic unless it is accompanied by a legal translation of its contents - and that the adoption of a document has no Arabic translation - the body that adopted it under its own knowledge.

This is not allowed for judges and arbitrators. In this context, the President of the Arbitral Tribunal shall correct the translation of a court interpreter under the personal flag.

Unless translation is one of the problems everyone has, because in that case they don't need proof. Since the arbitral tribunal accepted the evidence - some of the documents were published without Arabic language without an accompanying legal translation into Arabic –

The contested judgment may have erred in the application of the law by accepting the filing of the arbitral award despite the violation of the phenomenon by the law, which requires the revocation and annulment of the award.

"Call No. 121 for year 14 - date of the meeting of 27/12/1992 - p. 14 - p. 772"

The Dubai Court of Cassation ruled that it was not a matter of personal knowledge - the use of the arbitrator to know English and listen to observers of the appeal of that language, which is well understood by all present because this science is linked to general questions.

"Call 351 - Advertising of the year 2005 - Session 1/7/2007 AD 17 - p. 1241"

Presence of a session clerk:

The law does not require the presence of a clerk at the arbitrator's office to draft the minutes of meetings and section 212 (5) only requires the court to sign the judgment. However, the arbitrator may use it if he does so or if its existence is required, and opponents may agree that the minutes of the meeting must be written by an author to indicate what is prescribed:

The arbitrators' judgment is not limited to the proceedings of procedural acts other than those relating to the invitation of the litigants, the hearing of their defense and the presentation of their documents. M 11/1.

Arbitration No. 13 of 1990, which was in force in the emirate of Sharjah "and similar to Article 212 / point 5 of the Code of Civil Procedure" as follows:

It is not necessary to file the arbitrator's judgment immediately after its delivery or the presence of a clerk with the arbitrator to write the elements of the arbitration.

"Federal Supreme Court - Appeal No. 176 of the year - the session of 21/11/2005 AD - 16 - 1068".

Public hearings:

Unlike the rule established for the judiciary, the parent should not be held public - but the origin is the non-presence of non-adversaries in these sessions. It goes - that arbitrators do not have the property of judges - with regard to the seizure of the session system with regard to the imposition of sanctions on those who disrupt the regime of opponents or lawyers.

All they have is the publication of a report of what can happen during the session as part of a crime without having the order to arrest those who committed the crime.

Summary of the arbitration procedure

First: Make sure there is an arbitration clause in the contract.

Second: in the absence of an arbitration clause, an arbitration clause must be issued.

Third: if one of the two conditions is met, the following conditions must be met:

(1) The student arbitrator shall write a letter to the arbitrator of his or her choice, informing him or her of his or her appointment as an arbitrator and requesting his or her written approval.

(2) The arbitrator shall receive a letter from the arbitrator appointed by him to accept the arbitration.

(3) The arbitrator shall publish a request for arbitration specifying the name of the project and the dispute, as well as the request to refer the dispute to arbitration in accordance with the arbitration clause of the contract.

This is called an arbitrator and its address gives the defendant an appropriate period of time to choose an arbitrator.

(4) The respondent shall deliver a letter to the arbitrator of his or her choice informing him or her of his or her appointment as an arbitrator and seek his or her consent in writing.

(5) The arbitrator chosen by the defendant against him shall answer to the person against whom he shall notify him of his acceptance of this task.

(6) The arbitrator shall answer against him by accepting the arbitration and shall appoint an arbitrator and his address.

In the event that the arbitrator does not respond to the request for arbitration, the arbitrator first applied to the competent court to examine the dispute in order to appoint an arbitrator in accordance with the arbitration clause of the contract.

7) The two arbitrators shall communicate with each other and publish a file in which the arbitrator shall be appointed.

8) The two arbitrators shall write a letter to the arbitrator to whom he may choose by selecting a potential arbitrator and requesting written consent to accept the arbitration.

9) The arbitrator shall publish a letter to the other arbitrators accepting the arbitration. In the event that the arbitrators chosen by the parties to the dispute do not agree with him, the latter shall apply to the court initially competent to hear the dispute in order to choose the arbitrator in accordance with Law No. 27 of 1994.

10) The arbitrator shall determine the date of the first arbitral proceedings and shall inform the other arbitrators and the parties thereof.

(11) The arbitral tribunal shall meet during the first session of the proceedings to request the arbitrators to prepare an arbitral tribunal or to present a case statement with a timetable for the resolution of the dispute.

12) Hearings continue and opponents are given the right to defend themselves, so that the last interlocutor or depositor is the defendant.

13) Close the door of the argument.

(14) Deliberations shall take place and minutes shall be published without revealing their secrets.

(15) The arbitrator shall be released by the arbitral tribunal and signed by the arbitrators. If one of the arbitrators refuses to sign, the arbitrator's judgment and reasons for the refusal must be proven.

16) The judgment is delivered in open court and each opponent signs the receipt.

(17) The opponent in whose favor the judgment was rendered shall submit it to the court initially competent to hear the dispute and to hear the executive version thereof.

Forms of arbitration documents

Letter of appointment of the arbitrator

Mr. Al-

Peace, mercy and blessings of God

Reference to the contract between us and................ concerning implementation

Project ....

And since a dispute has arisen between us and you regarding this contract, clause n) of the contract provides that:

Any dispute arising from this contract that cannot be settled amicably shall be submitted to arbitration.

The arbitrator shall communicate to the other party his request, the name of the arbitrator and the subject matter of the dispute and shall select an arbitrator within fifteen days of notification of the request for arbitration.

The two arbitrators appointed by the parties shall be appointed within fifteen days of the appointment of the second of them as a possible arbitrator, who shall preside over the arbitral tribunal.

If one of the arbitrators is not selected in time, any interested party may request the Arab Arbitration Centre to appoint him or her.

Arbitration sessions shall be held at the seat of the Centre or at a place to be determined by the Arbitral Tribunal.

Egyptian law is applied to the dispute. The arbitration shall be conducted in Arabic and the arbitrators shall be allowed to reconcile.

On the basis of the above, I advise you to judge me in this dispute. Please confirm and inform me of this book.

Thank you for your cooperation.

Signature and address of the occupant

Free in / / /

Approval of the arbitration by the arbitrator

Mr. Al-

Peace, mercy and blessings of God

With reference to your letter sent to us on.............. Regarding my appointment as arbitrator in the dispute between you and..

I have the honour to inform you that I accept this task and that there is nothing to suggest to me that I am neutral and independent in the face of this conflict.

Sincerely

Signature of the arbitrator appointed by the arbitrator

Free in / / /

Request for arbitration

Mr. Al-

Peace, mercy and blessings of God

Reference to the contract between us and you concerning the project:

....

And as a dispute has arisen between us and you concerning this contract and where clause No........ of the contract states that:

Any dispute arising from this contract that cannot be settled amicably shall be submitted to arbitration.

The arbitrator shall communicate to the other party his request, the name of the arbitrator and the subject matter of the dispute and shall choose a court within fifteen days of notification of the request for arbitration.

The two arbitrators appointed by the parties shall be appointed within fifteen days of the appointment of the second of them as a possible arbitrator, who shall preside over the arbitral tribunal.

If one of the arbitrators is not selected in time, any interested party may request the Arab Arbitration Centre to appoint him or her.

Arbitration sessions shall be held at the seat of the Centre or at a place to be determined by the Arbitral Tribunal.

Egyptian law is applied to the dispute. The arbitration shall be conducted in Arabic and the arbitrators shall be allowed to reconcile.

On the basis of the above, I request arbitration and have been appointed as arbitrator by Mr. Eng.

It is entitled

And his phone number...

Please take the necessary steps to appoint an arbitrator within fifteen days of the date of the appointment. Otherwise, we will have to use the Arab Arbitration Centre to appoint an arbitrator for you.

Thank you and I hope you will be well received

Signature and address of the occupant

Free in / / /

Letter of approval for arbitration

Dear Mr.

Peace, mercy and blessings of God

By referring to the request for arbitration sent to you on: / / I accept the arbitration and I have been appointed as arbitrator by the consulting engineer / ....

And his phone number / ....

Please take note and take the necessary measures.

Sincerely,,,,

The accused against him

Done in / / /

Notify the arbitrator with the consent of the opponent to the arbitration and appoint him arbitrator

Mr. Al-

(The arbitrator appointed against him)

Peace, mercy and blessings of God: -

By referring to the dispute between us and () the implementation of a project:

Please note that the custodian (Company:......................................)

Was appointed arbitrator by Mr. Eng.

His address and telephone number...................................

Please take note and take the necessary steps to select the arbitrator

Sincerely

Signature of the defendant against him

Edit on / / /

M. /

(The arbitrator appointed by the arbitrator)

The dangers of the arbitrator appointed by the court

On behalf of the arbitrator against him

Peace, mercy and blessings of God

Referring to the dispute between us and...

About the project

I have the honour to attach herewith a copy of the letter we received from the defendant against him; please contact the arbitrator appointed to select him.

Sincerely

Custodian's signature

Done in / / /

Minutes of the arbitrators' session

In the arbitration between...

Company

....

About a project..

That on the day / / at 8 p.m., the arbitral tribunal composed of:

Professor / probable arbitrator

The engineer / arbitrator appointed by the company

Professor / arbitrator appointed by the company against which he or she is the subject

His first procedural meeting was decided:

1 - To hold the position of arbitrator professor /... from the seat of the arbitration.

2. Appointment of the professor / lawyer as secretary of the Authority's board of directors and address to the professor's office.

3 - The meeting of.. at 6 p.m." set a date for the first session and the Secretary notified the parties.

The record was closed in its history because it was 8 p.m."

Arbitral Tribunal

The arbitrator appointed by the arbitrator is the arbitrator appointed by the litigant against him............................ ....

Arbitrator ....

The letter from the selected arbitrators to the arbitrator

By appointing him President of the Arbitral Tribunal

Mr. Eng...........

Peace, mercy and blessings of God

With reference to the dispute between.. and.............. ....

Concerning: ....

The two arbitrators appointed by the parties to the dispute have deliberated on the choice of the arbitral tribunal in the above-mentioned case and have agreed to elect you as President of the arbitral tribunal.

Please confirm in writing.

Sincerely

The arbitrator appointed by the arbitrator is the arbitrator appointed by the litigant against him.

Consultant Engineer Consultant Engineer Consultant Engineer

Edit in / / /

Minutes of the first procedural session

Arbitration case filed by

.... (convicted)

Based:

Against:

.... (You are against)

Based:

About:

Project: ....

On the day of the meeting, the arbitral tribunal met:

Engineer / Chairman of the Arbitration Commission.

The arbitrator chosen by the arbitrator

The consulting engineer / .... The arbitrator chosen by the litigant against him

At the invitation of Mr. Eng, Chairman of the Arbitration Commission, where it met at the headquarters of the Arab Centre for Arbitration in Cairo and in the presence of:

M. .... about the center

Engineer / .... about the center

C / D / ....

.... the oppressor against him

The letter of authorization was presented by Mr. Al-Mutairi and Mr. / .... Representatives of the Court together or separately in the presence of arbitration sessions. The arbitrator also submitted a power of attorney to the arbitrator /.....

The Commission decided to postpone the session: .... at 7 p.m. "at the Arab Arbitration Centre in Cairo to prepare the parties to the dispute An arbitration committee closed the case and was signed by the participants.

The conqueror

The accused against him...............

Arbitral Tribunal

In the absence of an arbitration agreement

Any dialogue that may appear in the arbitration agreement shall be corrected at that session.

The session shall determine the language of the arbitration, the applicable law, the duration of the arbitration and the place of arbitration, and the delegation of arbitrators in reconciliation or not minutes of the hearing in the arbitration case.

No. .... for the year 2000

From..

Against..............................

The session held at the Centre's headquarters on / /

Deliver a judgment in the presence of each of the arbitral tribunals

Counsellor Professor. President of the Arbitral Tribunal

Professor of engineering. The arbitrator appointed by the arbitrator

Professor Dr..... ... ... the arbitrator appointed from among the oppressed against him

Session Secretariat: ....

For the controlling party: ....

For the party against whom:

The meeting opened at noon

The arbitral tribunal followed the following sentence:

"For these reasons, the arbitral tribunal decided that:

First: the arbitral tribunal is not competent to rule on claims relating to the contract concluded between the parties to the arbitration on 11/9/1995.

Second: the arbitral tribunal is not competent to rule on claims relating to the contract concluded between the plaintiff against him and the contractor on 11/7/1999.

Third: compel the defendant against him to lead the oppressor unless he pays him the full legal costs.

Unless the fees are paid at the rate of 5% per year from the date of opening of the request on 11/12/2000 until their expiry.

Fourth: oblige the defendant to give him to pay the depositary the legal fees and benefits on this amount at the rate of 5% per annum from the date of the request on 11/12/2000 until the payment is complete.

Fifth: oblige the defendant against him to include the consultant's alternative consultant group and the project on the reference to the insured's task throughout the decade of 10/1/1988 with the same size and clarity.

Sixth: Require the court to present to the accused its drawings and reports prepared pursuant to 10/1/1998.

Seventh: The arbitral tribunal is not competent to rule on the claim for compensation for moral damage resulting from tort liability, depending on the grounds.

Eighth: Rejection in the subject matter other than claims made by both the competitor and the defendant against him.

Ninth: the depositary shall bear twenty per cent of the arbitration fees and costs and the defendant shall bear eighty per cent of the amount of the arbitration fees and its fees and each party shall bear the costs of its counsel.

The meeting was adjourned at 1 p.m. after participants had received a copy of the minutes of the meeting.

Signature of the jury members:

Professor Counsellor / ....

Professor Eng / ....

Prof. Dr. / ....

Date: / / /

Section II Temporary suspension of arbitration proceedings

First: Suspension of the proceedings:

Introduction:

The organization of cases involving the suspension of dispute settlement proceedings is at the heart of procedural issues and in such cases. It is the law applicable to arbitral proceedings that deals with the organization of rules, cases and procedures for the termination and subsequent resumption of the dispute in arbitration.

Suspension of the arbitration proceedings means the absence of proceedings and the refusal to pursue them for reasons that can be assessed by the same parties, the arbitral tribunal or the law applicable to the arbitration proceedings.

So there seem to be three types of stops: -

First: Agreement Suspension:

The arbitration agreement must be agreed and agreed between the parties to the dispute and are bound by the arbitral tribunal, regardless of the status of the proceedings. If the agreement of the parties can thus disrupt the dispute to put an end to its actions, it is strange that the parties are the builders of the arbitration system.

Thus, the power of their will is dominated not only by an agreement on the formation of an arbitration but also in the conduct of the proceedings, as stipulated in article 25 of the Arbitration Law in Egypt to the parties to the arbitration agreement on the procedures followed by the arbitral tribunal.

To the extent that the suspension of the dispute settlement procedure by arbitration is only pure procedure, the opponents may agree on the waivers to which the arbitral tribunal is bound.

The arbitral tribunal is bound by the conditions of the suspension of the agreement, so it is not entitled to follow the procedure in such cases, otherwise its judgment will be null and void.

Whether on the basis of it cannot be in front of one of the parties to the arbitration to present its defense, where it was necessary for the existence of a convincing excuse moratorium prevented the preparation and submission of this defense (53 m / c of the Egyptian Arbitration Law). Either to circumvent the rule of the arbitration agreement of the limits of the parties (53 m / f) or the nullity of the arbitration procedure where it continued to operate the arbitration tribunal in the procedure despite the end-of-series agreement (53 m / g).

On the other hand, it is permissible to agree on the suspension of the arbitration for any period estimated by the parties. In addition, it is necessary for all parties to agree to terminate the dispute settlement procedure, but only one request to the arbitral tribunal and rejects the other.

The arbitral tribunal shall comply with the procedure and shall not give notice thereof unless it is included in the case of suspension by decision.

Third, the moratorium may affect the arbitral tribunal's notice of termination and its decision. If this body is to rule on the dispute in its entirety within 12 months of the opening of the arbitral proceedings (paragraph 45 of the Arbitration Act), it is envisaged that the contractual suspension will result in the end of the time limit for the decision of the judgment.

The Arbitration Act itself expressly recognizes this by stipulating that the arbitral tribunal is required to render its final decision on the dispute within the time period agreed by the parties.

In the absence of agreement, the judgment must be delivered within the legal time limit of twelve months from the date on which the arbitration proceedings are opened.

Moreover, the arbitral tribunal may not expedite the proceedings;

Except after the expiry of the period agreed by the parties, even if one of the parties so requests both parties must be invited to accelerate.

Even if the suspension has expired and the parties have not requested that the procedure be accelerated and the procedure has been followed. They cannot be considered as having left their case until they have agreed otherwise.

However, if the period specified for suspension has expired, the arbitral tribunal shall itself notify that the suspension has expired. So that they can decide to resume the dispute procedure or agree otherwise.

2 - Endowment by the arbitral tribunal decision:

This type of stay is left to the discretion of the arbitral tribunal when it deems it necessary. The waqf begins from the date of its decision and, in most cases; the transfer of the waqf does not fall within the jurisdiction of the arbitral tribunal.

It falls within the competence of a national judicial body, either by its nature or because the parties have not agreed to arbitrate it. In any event, suspension by decision of the arbitral tribunal in general in accordance with the text of article 46 of the Egyptian Arbitration Law requires compliance with several conditions:

The first condition: that there be a preliminary question that goes beyond the mandate of the arbitral tribunal and the main question is any question according to which the judgment in the case depends on the transfer.

The main problem generally arises from this jurisdiction, either because it is not included in the arbitration agreement, because the arbitral tribunal is prohibited from ruling on a matter not covered by the arbitration agreement.

Alternatively, beyond the limits of this agreement, otherwise the arbitral award shall be subject to an action for annulment either the preliminary question arises from the jurisdiction of the arbitral tribunal because of its own nature, where there are issues that cannot be settled by arbitration.

Problems in which non-financial personal matters, criminal matters and public policy matters in general cannot be resolved.

With regard to criminal cases, the text of article 46 that we mentioned cited examples of the challenge of counterfeiting in an official or customary document submitted to the arbitral tribunal.

Alternatively, have initiated criminal proceedings for fraud and criminal proceedings for any other criminal act within the meaning of the General Penal Code. It is sufficient that the waqf has already contested the falsification in the document submitted to the arbitral tribunal or that there is a criminal procedure for falsifying paper or any other criminal act committed.

The second condition is that the separation of the main issue in the preceding sense is necessary for the separation of the subject matter of the dispute. This means that there is a certain degree of correlation between the subject matter of the dispute and the initial question of whether the relationship is established by the element of reason, the element of subject matter or the element of the parties.

The determination of what is a preliminary question and the assessment of its relevance to the subject matter of the dispute is an objective question that is assessed by the arbitral tribunal.

Depending on the circumstances and circumstances of each dispute, and if the arbitral tribunal considers that the settlement of the dispute before it does not depend on the determination of the main issue. It does not stop the conduct of the contradictory procedure and does not continue to examine the dispute.

Otherwise, the Court decided that the proceedings would be suspended until a final judgment was rendered on the matter. It is not enough to make a preliminary or first judgment in this case, as provided for in article 46 of the Arbitration Act in Egypt, it is necessary "until a final judgment has been rendered in this respect", i.e. the provision of an ordinary means of appeal such as an appeal, or the time limit for appeal has expired and has become the subject of the appeal.

Suspension here, particularly with respect to primary criminal issues, this is an application of the rule known in the Code of Criminal Procedure, which criminalizes civil arrests.

In any event, the arbitral tribunal must wait for the competent court, whether civil, criminal or administrative, to give a preliminary final judgment. The suspension of the arbitration proceedings shall terminate the validity of the time limit for making the award. Actions undertaken before the stay remain valid for their effects. What is done during the period of stay is invalid and has no effect.

If the duration of the suspension has expired and the reason for the suspension has expired, the arbitral tribunal shall resume and expedite the arbitration proceedings. The prescribed judgment period must be completed.

Second interruption of the conduct of the dispute:

What is the course of the conflict?

The interruption of the arbitration procedure means that they are not pursued because of the incapacity of the parties or their representatives to defend themselves face to face. The law generally determines the reasons for the interruption of the protection of the rights of the defense.

Article 38 of the Law on Arbitration in Egypt provides that "the dispute shall be suspended before the Arbitral Tribunal in the circumstances and in accordance with the conditions provided for by the Law on Civil and Commercial Procedure".

And in the Code of Civil Procedure, the suspension of the conflict, the loss of the competence of the dispute or the disappearance of the status of the person who initiated the dispute between the parties have the effect of interrupting the progress of the dispute.

On the other hand, the dispute is not interrupted by the death of the agent, the disappearance of his agent or the resignation, where the arbitral tribunal grants an appropriate period of time to the party whose representative has died or whose representative has been dismissed or removed from the mandate of a new representative.

However, the dispute is not interrupted by the arbitrator's death or incapacity. Unless a replacement is appointed in accordance with the procedures followed for the selection of the deceased or incapacitated arbitrator. As the course of the dispute continues to change the representative of the legal person, is interrupted by the absence of this representative.

Type III: final exclusion and termination of the arbitral proceedings

1. Disruption, voluntary dismissal and situations:

(A) Amicable settlement: Arbitration is a system of treaties established by the parties with which it is established and whose agreement expires. The initial agreement on arbitration is authorized for any natural or legal person who has the right to exercise his rights, an agreement that would only cover areas where conciliation was possible.

If the amicable settlement or agreement is reached and the parties agree on its elements and how they are implemented. The arbitration procedure is finally interrupted and the dispute between them ends.

The Egyptian Arbitration Act recognized the possibility of suspension and closure of arbitration proceedings because the parties have agreed to settle their disputes amicably.

Article 41 of the Agreement provided that "if the parties agree to settle the dispute during the arbitration proceedings, they may request to prove the terms of the settlement before the arbitral tribunal. In this case, it must issue a resolution containing the terms of the settlement and terminate the procedure. This decision shall have the force that the arbitrators shall have.

The viewer of these legislative and legislative texts is aware that the parameters of dispute resolution are concluded. The arbitral tribunals that lead to the closure of the arbitration proceedings are as follows:

(A) There is an express agreement between the parties to settle the dispute in a peaceful and friendly manner, either by conciliation or by any other agreement.

That the amicable settlement and the agreement of the parties may be initiated by the parties themselves when they consider that their mutual interests make it necessary not to continue the arbitral proceedings and to negotiate the settlement of an agreement that maintains contact and interaction between them.

Such a settlement may also be concluded at the invitation of the arbitral tribunal itself if it determines that the circumstances of the case and the interests of its parties are not appropriate for a judicial decision.

B. The agreement of the parties for the settlement of the dispute may be reached at any stage of the arbitration procedure. That is, from the opening of the proceedings and the composition of the arbitral tribunal, even before the case has been reserved for the judgment. Leaving the dispute to arbitration: the arbitrator may decide to classify the dispute if the conditions provided for, unless the other party requests the continuation of the proceedings in cases where the opposition based on Article 111 is considered a civil proceeding.

Leaving the dispute is the end of the defendant and all his actions while retaining the right claimed at the origin. If the plaintiff wishes and all his proceedings, while retaining the original of the claimed right, if he wishes to waive his rights before the arbitrator, he has the right to do so, but he does not prevent the other opponent from continuing the proceedings if he does not do so.

II. Disruptions, criminal terminations and causes:

The arbitrator's negligence and negligence: If the arbitrator has the right to leave the dispute proceedings, as we have seen, and thus to terminate his or her free will and the arbitration proceedings. However, he may be forced to terminate this procedure even though he is the plaintiff seeking the protection of the law.

Whenever the arbitral tribunal finds that it has been negligent in initiating or following the proceedings. The termination of the arbitral proceedings is punitive in nature, with the arbitral tribunal making an award against it as a sanction for the arbitrator's negligence.

It is assumed that he is willing to activate these procedures and revitalization and not lazy about them.

Egyptian Arbitration Law, pursuant to the case concerning the resolution of the dispute due to the negligence of the arbitration student.

Article 34/1 provides: "If the claimant does not submit - without valid excuse - a written statement of his claim, the arbitral tribunal shall order the termination of the arbitral proceedings, unless the parties agree otherwise."

The first condition: prove the negligence and failure of the arbitration student and not submit a written statement in the application, whatever the reason for such negligence or negligence, whether after the formation of the arbitral tribunal directly or immediately after the commencement of the proceedings.

The second condition: that there is no acceptable excuse behind the absence or delay of the applicant to submit a declaration of his application and, therefore, that there is no acceptable excuse. The absence of such an acceptable excuse means that the arbitrator has waived his right to continue the arbitral proceedings, thereby ending the arbitral dispute;

However, such a waiver shall not affect the existence of the arbitration agreement, which shall remain valid for the resumption of the arbitral proceedings.

The third condition is that the parties, the occupant and the defendant against him, do not agree to stay the proceedings even though the applicant has not submitted his application.

In the sense that the parties do not agree to prevent the arbitral tribunal from making its award, terminating the proceedings, as a sanction for the failure of the claimant to file its statement.

The latter condition makes it clear that the order to terminate the proceedings in this case is not a duty of the arbitral tribunal. It is optional, but the arbitral tribunal does not have to judge it. Unless there is no agreement between the parties to continue the proceedings even if the arbitrator has not submitted a statement of claim.

If the arbitral tribunal considers for any other reason that the arbitration procedure is unnecessary or impossible. In any event, the arbitral tribunal shall not issue its decision to terminate the proceedings in this case.

Unless there are several conditions:

Condition 1:

Unless factors make the continuation of the arbitral proceedings ineffective or impossible.

The arbitral tribunal will therefore find that the dispute in question concerns matters in which arbitration is not permitted or that the arbitration agreement is similar to what invalidates it, as well as the death of the arbitrator authorized by the conciliation, or ambiguity of the executive future of the judgment to be rendered by the arbitral tribunal.

If the Arbitral Tribunal is satisfied that a judgment is necessary to terminate the arbitration proceedings, it shall refrain, since the making of the award, from taking any such action or accepting any request from the parties.

With the exception of a request for interpretation or correction of the award terminating the dispute settlement procedure.

Closure of the arbitral proceedings

The arbitral tribunal shall apply the rules agreed by the parties to the dispute.

If they agree to apply the law of a particular State, the substantive rules of that State shall be followed without the conflict of laws rules, unless otherwise agreed. If the parties do not agree on the legal rules applicable to the subject matter of the dispute, the arbitral tribunal shall apply the substantive rules of the law.

In deciding the subject matter of the dispute, the arbitral tribunal shall take into account the terms of the contract in question and the standards in force in the type of transaction. The arbitral tribunal may, if the parties to the arbitration expressly agree to authorize the conciliator to decide the subject matter of the dispute in accordance with the rules of justice and equity, without respecting the provisions of the law.

The arbitral tribunal shall apply the law of will chosen by the parties to the dispute voluntarily and if they do not agree on the law applicable to the subject matter of the dispute. The arbitral tribunal had to choose the substantive rules of the law, taking into account its adequacy to the dispute and its adequacy to the case, as indicated above. Unless arbitration with the arbitrators' authorization to reconcile then decides what they consider to be identical to justice and equity. If they are not in compliance with the law, they could, for example, eliminate a right that has passed the limitation period, noting that respect for justice can be achieved through the strict application of the rules of law.

On the other hand, justice and exemption from the application of the rules of law does not mean that arbitrators are free to leave without restrictions. They shall not be judged in the manner requested of them and shall not derogate from the limits of the arbitration agreement.

Nor can they claim the removal of rights that do not refer to the facts that occurred in the case before them or to the judiciary, in violation of public policy and public morals.

The award of an arbitral tribunal composed of several arbitrators shall be made by a majority of the votes cast after deliberation in a manner determined by the arbitral tribunal, unless the parties to the arbitration agree on other measures.

The arbitrators' judgment shall be rendered after deliberation in the manner specified by the arbitral tribunal. The resolution is adopted by a majority of votes. If the majority is not formed in such a way that everyone has a different opinion, he adheres to the smaller team in one of the two teams, otherwise they are considered to be late in settling the case and may be ordered to pay compensation.

If, during the arbitration proceedings, the parties agree on a settlement that ends the dispute, they may request that the terms of the settlement be established before the arbitral tribunal, which must in that case render a decision containing the terms of the settlement. The procedure ends and this decision has the same force as the arbitrator for enforcement.

The arbitral tribunal may make provisional judgments or a part of the claims before the final judgment of the entire dispute is rendered, pursuant to the rule that the property follows the branch.

Arbitration cases:

Either by agreement of the parties to the dispute in accordance with the text of Article 48/1 of Law No. 27 of 1994 on Arbitration in Egypt either the arbitration procedure ends either by agreement of the parties to the dispute, in accordance with article 48/1 of the Arbitration in Egypt Act No. 27 of 1994 or the publication of the final judgment on the entire dispute or an order to close the arbitration proceedings in accordance with Article 45(2) of this Law.

It also ends with a decision by the arbitral tribunal to close the proceedings in the following cases:

A - If the parties agree to terminate the arbitration.

B- If the defendant abandons the arbitral dispute unless the arbitral tribunal decides, at the defendant's request, that it is in the defendant's best interest to continue the proceedings until the dispute is resolved.

C-If the arbitral tribunal considers for any other reason that the arbitration procedure is unnecessary or impossible.

Section IV Arbitral Award

Definition of the arbitral award:

According to the opinion prevailing in the law, the work must be considered as a judgment. The following elements are available:

(A) The judgment shall be rendered by the arbitrators. Decisions of arbitration centres are not provisions.

(B) The judgment is final and decisions regarding evidence do not constitute provisions, decisions concerning the conduct of the dispute (referring to an expert, conducting a review, calling a witness or ending a dispute) are not provisions.

(C) Be binding.

In this respect, the following points arise:

1- Deliberation.

2. The individual arbitrator.

3. Majority judgment

4. The unanimous verdict.

5 - The negotiation process in the access to power.

6. Psychological body.

7 - Is the role of the chosen arbitrator represented by the chosen one?

Types of arbitration:

1- The final decision of the dispute:

An arbitral award ending the dispute is the judgment rendered by the arbitral tribunal. The procedure ends and the dispute expires and the arbitral tribunal has exhausted its jurisdiction.

2. Partial judgment:

However, the arbitral tribunal may make partial judgments and a partial judgment is an objective judgment which is rendered in part in the dispute with the continuation of the arbitral tribunal in considering the other issues before it.

In the case of a partial penalty whose jurisdiction is exhausted when the judgment is revoked, it may not be repeated in its final judgment or in any other partial judgment.

3. Preliminary provision:

The arbitral tribunal may also make preliminary judgments and give an example of this provision before deciding on defenses relating to its jurisdiction, as well as the preliminary provision by appointing one or more experts.

Interpretation of the award:

Either party to the arbitration may request the arbitral tribunal, within 30 days of receipt of the arbitral award, to interpret the ambiguity of its dispositive. The applicant shall declare the other party to the request before transmitting it to the arbitral tribunal, the interpretation of which shall be given in writing within thirty days from the date on which the request for interpretation was submitted to the arbitral tribunal. This body may extend this period by 30 days if it considers it necessary. The interpretation judgment is considered to be complementary to the arbitral award to be interpreted and whose provisions must be interpreted.

1. Either party to the arbitration may request the arbitral tribunal, within 30 days of receipt of the arbitral award, to interpret the ambiguity of the award. The claimant must declare the other party to the request before submitting it to the arbitral tribunal.

2. The interpretation shall be made in writing within thirty days of the date on which the request for interpretation is submitted to the arbitral tribunal. This body may extend this period by 30 days if it considers it necessary.

3. The interpretation judgment shall be deemed to supplement the arbitral award to be interpreted and its provisions shall be interpreted. Of course, interpretation is only required if the text of the ambiguity or ambiguity of the arbitration is difficult to identify about the intention of the intention of the body that rendered the decision.

The correction must be notified in writing to the parties within 30 days of the date of issue. The material errors to be rectified must be contained in the device, as it is the one that affects the opponent's right without the causes. Unless the cause is intrinsically part of or affects the operative part of the operation.

6 - Judgment of the omission of the motions:

Either party to the arbitration may, after the expiry of the arbitration period, request the arbitral tribunal, within 30 days of receipt of the arbitral award, to issue an additional award for the claims submitted in the proceedings and void the arbitral award, this request must be made to the other party before being submitted.

The arbitral tribunal shall render its judgment within sixty days from the date of filing of the request and may extend this period by thirty days if it deems it necessary. It is known that the jurisdiction of the arbitral tribunal ends as soon as the award is made, the arbitral tribunal is therefore required to rule on all the issues raised in the proceedings - nothing more, if she is dismissed in an order that goes beyond the scope of the dispute. Her judgment is null and void, if the question is ignored, it depends on the quality of the question if it is related to the subject matter of the dispute.

The parties to the dispute shall have the right to submit to the Arbitral Tribunal a request for the omission of an additional judgment in claims previously submitted and omitted by the arbitration. But if this issue was raised by one of the litigants and its purpose was to disrupt the separation of the dispute or is outside the jurisdiction of the arbitral tribunal, the arbitral tribunal has the right to make the award inadmissible. The acceptance of the request for omission is subject to three conditions:

1. The request must be submitted to the arbitral tribunal within thirty days from the date of receipt of the award.

2- The arbitral award failed to reject a previously filed application.

3 - The application of the omission to the other opponent before submitting it to the arbitral tribunal.

The arbitral tribunal shall render its judgment on the request for omission within sixty days of the date of its presentation and may extend this period by thirty days from the date of submission and may extend it by thirty days if it considers it necessary.

The judgment in the request for omission is complementary to the previous judgment rendered in the arbitral proceedings subject to the provisions of the arbitral award and found that further judgment was required to satisfy three conditions:

First, the request should emanate from the claims of the substantive opponents

It has been submitted to the Commission in a clear and requested manner, it is not sufficient that the request comes from the defense or formal defenses, such as the payment of non-acceptance, because any omission of the above is considered a rejection.

Second: the Commission's failure to comply with the request is completely ignored and this is not the case, unless it is an omission or error

However, if it is intentional, the judgment may include an explicit or implicit judgment.

The arbitral tribunal is not obliged to follow the claimant in all aspects of his defense and to respond independently to each statement or the argument of its effects as long as the fact that it has abstained and that it contains in its evidence the implicit answer to each argument is contrary.

It is established that the mandate of arbitration is to declare the execution of a declaration against other persons and that the mandate does not benefit from the application of the declaration to other persons and is only a legitimate document of the law or the agreement of persons which, in any case, falls within the scope of what is permitted by law and what is necessary to correct the behavior of third parties' rights of control and correction.

And must be carried out within the legal framework prescribed for it and on its terms and the jurisdiction of the arbitral tribunal in a given dispute is terminated by decision in the present dispute and extends only to the extent permitted by the legal systems and rules, whether to interpret the sentence, correct it or make an additional judgment in the absence of the requirements of the conditions set out in the legal texts and accepted by the parties in this context.

The request for an additional award is made by a party to the arbitral proceedings who submitted requests to the arbitral tribunal during the proceedings and who was ignored by the arbitral award. Therefore, the request for an additional sentence cannot be an excuse to change the sentence, even if it is wrong.

The filing of the said application must not be intended to be the subject of a new debate, since the case has been classified as an application on the merits, regardless of the manner in which those applications are filed. In addition, the request must in no case be intended to refer the dispute or any of its aspects in such a way as to prejudice the foregoing and the judgment.

Consequently, the violation of his pilgrimage and the force of the case ordered as well as it is obvious that the subject of the request implies the request for a judgment on an object or a request that the parties have not agreed to submit to the arbitral tribunal.

Arbitration is a term that requires the signature of a declaration made to third parties. In limiting the execution of the statement of others, the State relies solely on a legitimate document of the law, judgment or agreement of persons.

In any event, it is within the framework of what is permitted by law and what is required for the validity of the conduct with regard to the rights of third parties to proper control and must be carried out within the legal framework prescribed for it and on its terms and the jurisdiction of the arbitral tribunal in a particular dispute is terminated by a decision in that dispute and extends only to the extent permitted by legal systems and rules, whether to interpret the sentence, correct it or make an additional judgment.

Although the requests were not met under the conditions stipulated in the legal texts and agreed by the parties in this context. The request for an additional award must be made by a party to the arbitral proceedings who submitted requests to the arbitral tribunal during the proceedings and who has been overruled by an arbitral award.

Therefore, the request for an additional sentence cannot be an excuse to change the judgment, even if it is wrong.

Such a request shall not be made for the purpose of reviewing the merits of the rejection of the award, regardless of the nature of the rejection of the award, and the request shall not be redirected.

This would prejudice the judgment and thus the violation of the authority and force of the case ordered, it is also clear that the request does not entail the request for a judgment on a subject or request that has not been raised before the arbitral tribunal.

6 - Judgment of reconciliation

If, during the arbitral proceedings, the parties agree to settle the dispute, they may request proof of the settlement before the arbitral tribunal. Who in this case must issue a resolution containing the terms of the settlement and complete the procedure. This decision shall have the power to enforce the arbitrators' decisions. Neither party has the right to withdraw or refrain from implementing it.

The parties to the dispute may agree, during the proceedings and before the adjournment of the case, to settle the dispute between them in a manner that serves their interests. The parties to the dispute shall have the right to request proof of such settlement in the minutes of the hearing, in which case the arbitral tribunal shall render a decision containing the terms of the settlement and the termination of the proceedings.

If the dispute is resolved by reconciliation, no conciliator may renew it, neither by instituting legal proceedings against it, nor by pursuing the legal proceedings instituted by the parties following conciliation and the expiry of the court's jurisdiction to rule on the dispute.

If the contested judgment contravenes this consideration, it violates the law and its application is incorrect. It must be revoked and judged before the end of the dispute, it is necessary for the conciliation to declare that each party must renounce the corresponding part of its request in order to obtain the continuation of the dispute or the dispute between them.

If there are no opposing claims, it is neither a rapprochement nor a dispute between the opponents -The subject's court having the power to understand the reality of the case gets what you see from the opponents' position in this way when it has been shot by a particular distributor in the trial - Agreement on the termination of the proceedings:

If the parties can agree on an amicable settlement of the dispute between them, and the subsequent termination of the arbitration procedure, it is not mixed because of another to end the arbitration of the dispute, agree to terminate existing proceedings, even without an amicable settlement of the dispute between the parties.

Article 48/1 of the Egyptian Arbitration Law provides that the arbitration proceedings shall be closed by a decision of the arbitral tribunal terminating the proceedings in the following cases:

(A) The parties agree to terminate the arbitration proceedings.

It is clear that, until the arbitration proceedings are completed, all parties agree, if one party proposes to terminate the proceedings and rejects the other, the arbitral tribunal must continue the proceedings.

The agreement to terminate the proceedings is expressly stipulated in a written document, however, that the agreement to terminate the proceedings may result from the conduct of the parties, such as not following the proceedings, or to bring them all to state jurisdiction and abandon arbitration proceedings.

3 - Leave the dispute to arbitration:

Ways to leave the dispute in arbitration, to abandon its proceedings by the claimant and to abandon all the consequences, and the return of the parties to the situation in which they found themselves before the start of these proceedings, without making it a waiver of the right filed by the prosecution.

It seems that leaving the arbitration dispute is therefore a voluntary act, one of the parties. However, it remains a unilateral procedural act governed by law and determines the conditions of its effectiveness applicable to arbitral proceedings in general.

I mentioned the abandonment of the dispute settlement procedure by arbitration. Article 48 of the Egyptian Arbitration Law provides that "the arbitration proceedings shall be closed by a decision of the arbitral tribunal terminating the proceedings in the following cases:

If the claimant leaves the dispute in arbitration, unless the arbitral tribunal decides, at the request of the respondent, to take a serious interest in the continuation of the proceedings until the dispute is resolved. Moreover, it is the decision of the arbitral tribunal to leave the arbitration procedure important, as we have seen, in the settlement of the amicable settlement of the dispute, the agreement to terminate the proceedings and, in this case, those who have left the arbitration proceedings may initiate a new arbitration procedure, provided that the law of the case has not been overturned by order or any other reason.

In all cases, the above considerations and controls. This is the consequence of leaving the claimant with his claim, the resolution of the dispute in arbitration with all its procedural and objective effects and procedures. The parties must return to the situation they were in before the arbitral proceedings were opened, while retaining the origin of the applicant's right or legal status, as indicated above.

Decision on the termination of the procedure

Failure and negligence of the demonstrator:

If the arbitrator is entitled to leave the dispute procedure, as we have seen. He thus puts an end to his free will and to the entire arbitration procedure. However, he may be forced to terminate this procedure even though he is the plaintiff seeking the protection of the law. Whenever the arbitral tribunal finds that it has been negligent in initiating or following the proceedings. The termination of the arbitral proceedings must be of a criminal nature, when the arbitral tribunal pronounces an arbitral award terminating the proceedings as a sanction for negligence on the part of the arbitrator.

Under article 34/1, which orders the arbitral tribunal to terminate the arbitration proceedings. Unless otherwise agreed by the parties, it is clear from this provision that several conditions must be met.

Condition 1:

Proof of the negligence and failure of the claimant and not to submit a written statement affirming. Whatever the reason for such negligence or negligence, whether after the formation of the arbitral tribunal directly or immediately after the commencement of the proceedings.

Condition 2:

There is no acceptable excuse for the arbitrator's inability or delay in submitting his statement, so the absence of such an excuse means that the arbitrator has waived his right to initiate arbitration proceedings, and therefore the resolution of the arbitration dispute, however, such a waiver does not affect the existence of the arbitration agreement, which remains valid for the resumption of the arbitration proceedings.

Condition 3:

That the parties, the occupier and the defendant against him, do not agree to stay the proceedings even though the arbitrator did not file his claim in the sense that the parties do not agree to prevent the arbitral tribunal from issuing its judgment closing the proceedings to sanction the claimant's failure to file his claim.

The latter condition makes it clear that the order to terminate the proceedings in this case is not a duty of the arbitral tribunal. However, it is optional for the arbitral tribunal to rule on this question only if the parties have not reached agreement on the suspension of proceedings, even if the arbitrator has not submitted a declaration.

If, however, the arbitral tribunal is satisfied that the award should be made, the arbitration proceedings shall be terminated, it shall refrain from any action in the dispute or from any request by the parties, with the exception of a request for interpretation or correction of the award terminating the dispute settlement procedure.

Correction of material errors by arbitration:

The arbitral tribunal shall rectify any written or arithmetical material errors by decision of its own motion or at the request of one of the litigants. The arbitral tribunal shall make the correction without notice within thirty days of the date of the judgment or file the request for rectification, as the case may be, and extend this period by thirty days if it deems it necessary.

The correction shall be issued in writing by the arbitral tribunal and will be declared to two parties within thirty days from the date of its issuance. If the arbitral tribunal exceeds its power of rectification, the invalidity of this decision may be invoked on the ground of invalidity.

The material errors to be corrected must be contained in the device because it is the one that affects the opponent's right without cause, unless the cause is intrinsically part of the device or allocate the benefit of the latter and the correction of the arbitral award may only be made by the body which rendered the decision contrary to the judicial decisions. If the arbitral tribunal exceeds its power of rectification, the decision may be set aside.

Conditions for the validity of the arbitration

If the parties agree to apply the rules of a particular arbitration institution such as the International Chamber of Commerce of Paris either the London Court of International Arbitration or the American Federation, the form of the judgment is in accordance with the institution's rules.

In a precise description of the arbitrators' judgment, it was stated "that it must be complete in itself and in writing on the subjects in dispute to be decisive as to what is required of the convicted person and not to include an expression of the arbitrators' personal opinions.

This description is accurate: opponents resort to arbitration for a final and binding and enforceable judgment of the dispute. It was, therefore, necessary to establish clear conditions for arbitration.

Arbitration conditions:

The Arab Arbitration Rules in the arbitral award impose conditions in their entirety with the conditions. What are the requirements of comparative law and the rules of international arbitration institutions?

These conditions relate to the form and purpose of the judgment.

Condition 1:

The judgment is rendered after the deliberation, in which all arbitrators must participate, all arbitrators must attend the pre-trial hearing and deliberation is essential.

This is one of the fundamental principles of judicial action involving the omission of public policy. The work of the arbitrators is cancelled if other persons are involved in the deliberation. The purpose of the deliberation is to exchange an opinion between the arbitrators in the case of their multiplicity so that the judgment is rendered as a product of their cooperation.

Whether the law governing the procedure will include a provision on deliberation. This is necessary and agreed in national and international arbitration.

Deliberation must be conducted in a confidential manner to ensure the arbitrator's independence in the opinion expressed and not affected by the opinion of the arbitrator chosen to preserve the secrets of opponents in the arbitration, and if they want to know the arbitrators, they do not want to know the public.

The purpose of confidentiality of the deliberations is not to disclose the exchange of views of the parties to the dispute.

An arbitrator who contravenes this rule is liable to civil liability, but this violation does not invalidate the judgment. Without prejudice to the secrecy of the deliberation, the law provides that a majority may be voted or provides the name of the arbitrator who refrains from signing the judgment and the reasons for his or her abstention.

Arbitration:

The need to deliberate - limited to all members of the arbitral tribunal and to itself. It should be noted that the obligation to deliberate between the members of the arbitral tribunal was binding in two respects.

First: the arbitrators' judgment must be in accordance with the rules of law, even if the arbitrator is authorized to do so, and the deliberations of the members of the arbitral tribunal before their decision is rendered are of public policy.

Second: the secret deliberation between the two arbitrators must take place jointly, without the participation of those who took part and without the defense of its parties. It is also followed by a unanimous or majority vote, the contrary opinion being expressed.

While the arbitral tribunals have accepted their exclusion from the rules of procedure during the examination of the arbitral proceedings in order to accelerate the settlement of the dispute. Another wisdom is that, in many cases, members of the arbitration are not involved in the law

They have neither the know-how nor the experience of procedure, but none of this is done without constraint or restriction.

Since justice requires that arbitral tribunals be bound by all rules of public policy and that the most important of these rules is that the members of the arbitral tribunal deliberate on their decision before making it and that the evidence and proof be fully contained in the documents of the file, the arbitrator cannot decide in the dispute before him. Only after the deliberation, which requires that each arbitrator be informed of the opinion of the other arbitrators, the dialogue and the discussion.

- If there are not many arbitrators, the arbitrator renders his judgment without deliberation, of course. He cannot involve other people with him because his task is purely personal.

The decision is invalidated if it is involved with other people in deliberations and in taking a position. This is the fundamental rule of law for public order. Although the judgment is rendered by a majority, two arbitrators are not sufficient to render a judgment in the absence of the third arbitrator or without deliberation with him, as it is necessary to participate in all deliberations before the judgment is delivered. The Dubai Court of Cassation has ruled that:

Deliberation is the consultation between the arbitrators in the operative part of the judgment and its reasons after the expiry of the pleadings and before they are pronounced and can only be achieved by meeting the arbitrators - who heard the pleading in one place and face to face

In the presence of all, discuss the factual evidence and legal basis after surrounding the case and submitting the claims, defense and documents relating to vision and understanding - The origin of the procedure lies in the fact that they were taken into account by the fact that the judgment and the arbitrator, who is called by one of the parties to the arbitration. Although he is chosen for his self-confidence, he is not an agent, but a judge is chosen from among himself to cooperate with the rest of the arbitrators in order to find a solution to the conflict in accordance with the law and justice. A copy of the arbitral award - the subject of the dispute - indicating that he or she has already participated in the deliberation.

Judgment by a majority of opinions: -

The judgment is made on the basis of a majority of points of view and must be written with the contrary opinion and it is difficult if several points of view of the arbitrators. Everyone had their own opinion, and if that happened in the judicial system, the most recent judges would have to join one of the other opinions.

But do not consider introducing this principle into arbitration because arbitrators do not own a profession, so if the majority of them do not agree - at least if they do not sign the decision on the scheduled date or by agreement, this provision shall be null and void.

This can be avoided in the face of such a situation in an agreement or arbitration clause or clause in order to ensure that the judgment is rendered. The arbitrator or arbitrariness of the arbitrators or their insistence on their position is circumvented by reasonable judgment. In accordance with the provisions of Article 45/2 of the RAK Convention on the Status of Conciliation of "Commercial Arbitration", which provides for a decision against the absence of a majority. This led the President of the Commission to issue alone the final judgment or any decision taken by the Commission during the arbitration procedure inspired by this solution which is compatible with the nature of the arbitration and the methods of constitution of its body, as set out in the text of Article 128 / point 2 of the Code of Civil Procedure which, in the case of court decisions, forced the lower group to join or which includes the most recent judges of one of the two opinions delivered to the largest team after a new position has been taken.

- If the majority of the arbitrators' opinion and without the majority's opinion has been reached, the rule of law and the rule of nullity have been established.

Draft arbitral award:

A draft is not necessary and the arbitral award may be written in any manner whatsoever:

While the legislator, in article 212 of the Code of Civil Procedure, gave the arbitrator the decision to describe the sentence, but it is not really a decision of the Council of the Judiciary.

Paragraph 1 of this article stipulates that the arbitrator shall not be limited to the proceedings in which he renders his judgment, except in the cases provided for in the section relating to arbitration and the procedures set out therein.

This does not include the need to include a draft and does not go beyond what the legislator in the fifth paragraph of the same article requires the arbitrator to write so that the writing is written by the arbitrator.

But includes writing on the launch, whether by hand, in copy or in print without the assignment of a particular type of them. Therefore, the arbitrator's judgment does not apply to the judgment that a project and an original must be received.

It was held that the arbitrators and - in accordance with article 212/1 of the Code of Civil Procedure - were not required to rule on the procedure of the proceedings. Except as provided in the section on arbitration and in the procedures for inviting the parties to plead and hearing their defense and allowing them to submit their documents and the scope of the arbitration referred to in the said Act, is exempted from requiring the arbitrators to issue a draft provision, sufficient to prepare and sign the original copy.

"Discrimination of Dubai Call No. 537 for the year 1999 - 23/4/2000 AD - 11 - p. 342"

And in the same sense Appeal of the Federal Supreme Court No. 22 for the year 22 B.C. - session 3/3/2002 AD - 24 - p. 530 "

Write the sentence and its statements and make it:

The judgment must be one, written, signed and included in its content with the contrary opinion:

The law requires that the arbitrator's decision be in writing in accordance with Article 212 / Section 5, even if the arbitration is valid. In accordance with the above-mentioned article, this provision shall include a copy of the arbitration agreement. A summary of the declarations of the parties and their documents, the reasons for the decision, the date of publication, the place where it was rendered and the signatures of the arbitrators.

If one or more of the arbitrators refused to sign the judgment, this shall be mentioned and shall be given by a majority of the opinions. And will be valid if signed by a majority of the arbitrators.

Writing the Arbitration Award

Written in Arabic, unless otherwise agreed by the parties and accompanied by a translation when filed:

The judgment does not need to be written by the arbitrator, but perhaps in one of the writing methods on the launch, whether by hand or by copying or printing without the assignment of a particular type of them. The judgment must be written in the language of the country in which it was rendered, so that the Registry of the Court and the procedures for its execution can be fully filed.

While the Law on the Judiciary and the Law on the Organization of the Judiciary in the Emirate of Ras Al Khaimah determine that the language of the courts is the Arabic language "Article 15", the provision in force in the United Arab Emirates must be drafted in its original version in Arabic. Unless otherwise agreed by the parties and at the time of filing, an official translation must be attached in accordance with the provisions of Article 212 / Section 6 of the Code of Civil Procedure.

The Federal Supreme Court held that "the Federal Law on Civil Procedure provided that the invalidity of the arbitration should not be specified if the document did not specify where it should take place. It is envisaged that, within the jurisdiction of that court, the consent of the parties to the dispute to settle it outside the State through arbitrators abroad does not constitute a violation of public policy.

In fact, the United Arab Emirates legislature approved article 212, paragraphs 4 to 6, of the Code of Federal Civil Procedure No. 11 of 1992, according to which "the arbitrator's decision must be rendered in the United Arab Emirates.

Otherwise, the rules prescribed for judgments rendered by arbitrators in a foreign country must be followed and the judgment rendered in Arabic, unless the parties agree otherwise.

At that time, an official translation (accompanied by an official translation) must be attached, which means that the original indicates that the arbitrators' judgment must be rendered in the State. Although this does not prevent its issuance outside the country, the rules governing those issued in a foreign country are followed in the latter case. The translation to which the arbitrators refer must be signed if not required by law.

It would be sufficient to include the official translation in the form of the original judgment, which was published in a foreign language and signed by the arbitrators.

If the legislator has authorized arbitration rather than recourse to the competent court and the arbitrator's decision has replaced the court's decision to resolve the dispute between the parties. The law requires that several arbitrators make a single decision to resolve the dispute between the parties.

Consequently, the arbitrator cannot be multiple, even if the parties expressly consent, failing which the arbitration is null and void in relation to public policy, because the multiplicity of arbitral decisions is in contradiction with the guarantee and wisdom of their multiplicity.

And with the guarantee of resolving the dispute under one of their own, and excluding the agreement of opponents to split the government so that each arbitrator of the dispute. In this case, the arbitration is multiple or the parties agree to write several judgments and the arbitral tribunal chooses one of them or establish one, which is signed by a majority of arbitrators, it is the arbitrator who has settled the dispute.

The arbitrators' signature on the judgment:

The judgment must be signed by at least a majority of the arbitrators and the refusal of those who have refrained from signing - Just sign only the last document containing the operator if you contact the reasons. The signature of the judgment is presumed by all arbitrators. However, under Article 212 / point 5 of the Law, the majority can only be signed by the arbitrator with reference to the refusal of the arbitrators' signature at the heart of the decision.

The law does not specify why the abstentionist refused to sign, but it is sufficient to specify that in the judgment.

The judgment in this regard is intended to be the original version, which must be delivered to each party within five days of its publication. At the request of one of the litigants, the court shall examine the procedure for filing the complaint or, in the case of arbitration conducted by the court, the original and the arbitration document, as well as the minutes and documents of the court registry, which is initially competent to hear the dispute within fifteen days of the judgment and must be delivered to each Party within five days of the date of deposit of the property (Article 213 / clauses 1, 3).

He held that "when the appellant, as a contested judge, hates the violation of the law and the inadequacy of the case;

In his defense before the Court of Appeal, he insisted on the invalidity of the arbitral award - the subject of the dispute - which he had not yet brought before the Court of First Instance - namely that the copy of the arbitral award was signed only by the President of the Arbitral Tribunal if it was to be signed by all the arbitrators. His only operation alone in accordance with article 212/5 of the Code of Civil Procedure.

Nor is there any evidence that the arbitrators signed the draft judgment in violation of article 129/1 of the said Act 2. The chairman of the arbitrators alone accepted the documents submitted to him by the applicant during the deliberations, in violation of Article 126 of the said law - the arbitrator - did not participate in the act, as he does not know the Arabic language and the participation of arbitrators chosen by the parties to the debate if they are considered agents.

Since these aspects of disability are related to public order. The Court of Appeal was to examine and respond to them - and I expressed my opposition to this by simply referring to the reasons for the sentence, which, in turn, did not examine these aspects of invalidity.

His contested judgment would have been in violation of the law and would have had a causal defect. As this obituary in its first part is counterproductive - the annulment of the arbitral award in accordance with Article 216 of the Code of Civil Procedure - and of what has been done by this court - is directed towards the judgment of the arbitrators as a legal act. This is a procedural error without a valuation error - and the defects that the claimant for invalidity can invoke have been mentioned in the article cited exclusively to be evaluated - this concerns either the arbitration agreement or the arbitration dispute - and the defects relating to the arbitration agreement consist of an arbitral award other than an arbitration document or on the basis of an invalid document, or beyond the date agreed for the completion of the arbitration - or if the arbitrators remove from the document or the rule violates a rule relating to public policy.

As for those relating to the arbitration dispute and the invalidity of the arbitral award:

The article in question is the publication of a judgment of arbitrators not appointed in accordance with the law or rendered by some of them without being authorized to rule in the absence of other persons - Either failure of the principle of confrontation in the dispute - or violation of the right of defense - or the occurrence of invalidity in the judgment or invalidity of the procedure - effect in the judgment - on the part of the arbitrators in cases other than the previous ones or related to the arbitrators' assessment of the dispute or the inadequacy or inadequacy of the grounds on which their decision is inadmissible - The decision of the arbitrators - and article 212/5 of the Code of Civil Procedure exists only if it is in writing and contains the signatures of the arbitrators or at least most of them - who participated in the proceedings and deliberations - because their signature on its copy is useful to them.

As it stands, the image of the arbitrator's judgment - the subject of the dispute - presented in the appellant's exhibits file bears the signatures attributed to the three arbitrators who participated in the pleading and deliberation.

This is sufficient to say that the publication of this provision is not legally binding on them to multiply their signatures on all pages in particular

The operational document contained a statement - however - and it was useful to associate this device with the previous reasons. However, the same court rendered another judgment in which it was stated:

As stipulated in article 212, paragraph 5, of the Code of Civil Procedure - that among the data. What must be included in the arbitrator's award signature of the arbitrator who reviewed the arbitration.

Considering that, this signature is the only evidence that attests to the existence of the provision in legal terms, and because without it cannot be attributed to the arbitrator and the meaning of the arbitration and its reasons. Therefore, the validity of the arbitrator's judgment is not sufficient, it is sufficient to sign the arbitrator on the document containing the device.

Because the judiciary, as indicated in the operative part, can be listed in the reasons. The purpose of causation is to encourage the arbitrator to make an effort to examine the dispute in order to bring justice to justice. This was not the case, and it is clear from the arbitrator's judgment - the subject of the dispute - that the arbitrator who was appointed - originally, he had not signed any papers containing the reasons and only sign the last document that included the device - it is not enough to be signed on documents containing the reasons.

Since the arbitrator's signature on the grounds and in force of public policy - If the arbitrator contests it and does not sign the reasons for his judgment, the said judgment is null and void - This does not change the fact that the documents that included the reasons at the bottom contain a printed declaration (for verification) because he does not renounce the arbitrator's signature by signing his name or stamping his ring.

If the contested decision contravenes this conclusion and ends with the rejection of the request for ratification of the arbitral award - the subject of the dispute -This has resulted in a valid result in the law and the text of the law is based on unfounded.

Considering that the provision of article 129/1) of the Code of Civil Procedure indicates that the legislator has required that these provisions include the grounds on which they were constructed and the filing of the draft decision containing the grounds signed by the President and the judges when the case was pronounced - Otherwise, the verdict was invalid, and that, although it does not replace this procedure signed by all members of the body that issued the document containing the verdict alone when they separate from the container made the leaves of this article, it reaches this judgment and acquit the judgment of invalidity if reasons released on separate documents. The latter included some of these reasons especially if the whale is useful for its connection to other reasons and its integration with the expression "for these reasons" or "for all of this" or "and then" or other expressions that lead to the operation and reached the reasons that preceded it, which was decided by the Egyptian Court of Cassation for judicial decision.

"The provision of article 175 of the Code of Procedure indicates that the legislator was obliged to file the draft judgment containing the reasons for the minutes signed by all the members of the body that issued them, otherwise the judgment would have been null and void.

This procedure does not diminish the fact that they are all signed on paper containing only the operative sentence if this document is separate from the documents containing its reasons, but if the reasons are written on separate sheets.

These included some of these reasons, mentioned by the arbitrator and signed by all the judges who had rendered them.

The signature on this document is the signature of the operator and the reasons for achieving the purpose of the street, as required by the signature of the judges who rendered the verdict on the project containing the reasons for the decision, is not void.

The Federal Supreme Court also ruled that "the judges who rendered the judgment are not required to sign all the documents on which the draft decision was taken, and it is sufficient to sign them on the last page when they are related to the sentence".

(Call No. 239 - Year 14 - Date of the meeting of 12/6/1994 - Technical Bureau 16)

This rule - which was also decided by the Dubai Court of Cassation published in Appeal No. 537/1991 - could be held on 23 April 2000 - This is consistent with the nature and purpose of arbitration, with the legislator affirming the signature of the operative part and the reasons for the draft rule, which is the rule on public policy.

It must be said that the Dubai Court's judgments do not seek to harmonize the two rules because the first dealt with the signature status of the last paper containing the pattern device, while the second dealt with the signature status on the last paper bearing only the device.

The judgment shall include a copy of the arbitration agreement and a summary of the parties' statements and documents:

Article 212 / Article 5 stipulates that the arbitrator's judgment must include "a copy of the arbitration agreement and a summary of the parties' statements and documents" in order to indicate the factual grounds for the judgment, which is obtained by mentioning the parties' claims and their substantial defense.

The legislator wanted this declaration to be proved by the same provision to verify the arbitrator's judgment within the limits of his powers under the arbitration agreement...

In this sense, it is a fundamental statement necessary for the validity of the judgment, which would lead to its omission.

The inclusion of the arbitral award in the form of the arbitration agreement shall not preclude the presentation of a certificate from the arbitration center stating that the arbitration document has been submitted to it since the beginning of the arbitral proceedings.

Since the provision must be an integral part of the completion of his health conditions so as not to complete the lack of important data by any means whatsoever or by another document separate from it or by reference in the reasons for judgment to the form of the arbitration document without being included. However, the inclusion of an arbitral award in a form of arbitration agreement does not cover the provisions of the Convention.

But sufficient to include its content, including the agreement on arbitration and in order not to derogate from its provisions, the purpose of proving in the judgment is achieved by this declaration because it is sufficient to allow the court responsible for ratifying this provision to review it as soon as the codes are known.

(ADOPTION NO. 328 - 2002 OF DUBAI DISCRIMINATION) S - MEETING DATE 23/11/2002 (S13-819)

The Egyptian Court of Cassation has ruled that:

The legislator, if he does not wish to include the arbitrators' judgment, all the declarations that must be included in the judge's judgment. However, the provisions relating to arbitration contained in the third part of Book 3 of the Code of Procedure must be respected.

Including the provision of Article 507, which requires, inter alia, that the provision include a summary of the parties' statements and documents. Parliament sought to prove that, under the arbitrators, it allowed them to control their work, to verify that the facts of the dispute and the arguments defended were well justified, and to determine the grounds for the award made.

As such, it is necessary and essential data which does not make it possible to achieve the purpose for which the legislator must prove that the decision leads to invalidity. This does not prevent the documents in the file from being filed with the judge in the court register, as the judgment must be an integral part of the completion of the conditions of his state of health, so that he does not accept the completion of the lack of essential data otherwise.

However, the invalidity of the award may be requested in accordance with the last paragraph of article 512 of the Code of Procedure if a judgment or procedure is invalid.

It is clear from the documents that the arbitrators' judgment regarding the dispute did not include a summary of the plaintiffs' statements or the documents on which they relied on the parties' property for the goods, vehicles and equipment indicated in the award, indicating that the arbitral tribunal had heard the plaintiffs' statements and had discussed them orally.

And examined their documents proving the ownership of the candidates to the parties to the dispute without a declaration of the summary of these declarations and documents or the evidence on which they were based and indicating to what extent they are useful to the good and insufficient to achieve the purpose for which the legislator has proved these declarations by arbitrators.

With regard to the contested judgment, it was decided to support the sentence on appeal at the end of the dismissal of the legal action, on the ground that the grounds on which the applicant was not included among the grounds provided for in Article 512 of the Code of Procedure.

The contested judgment was served in support of the appeal on the ground that the grounds invoked by the appellant were not included in the grounds provided for in Article 512 of the Code of Procedure.

It is flawed in the application of the law and in the absence of a causal link, which requires revocation for this reason without the need to discuss the rest of the grounds for appeal.

(Appeal No. 90 - for the year 58 BC - Date of the session of 24/3/1991 x 42 - p. 793)

It was noted that "although article 507 of the Code of Procedure requires that the arbitral award contain a summary of the parties' statements. However, its omission consists in invalidating the judgment only if it is proved that it contained a substantial and effective defense in the outcome of the arbitrators' judgment.

In the sense that if the Arbitration Board had discussed, this result would have been allowed to be modified, as it is considered a deficiency in the reasons for the actual governance leading to disability.

(Appeal No. 573 - for the year 51 BC - Date of the meeting of 3/12/1986 - Q 37 p. 926)

The judgment must include its reasons, the date and place of its publication:

The judgment must be rendered otherwise it is null and void, even if the arbitrator is authorized to reconcile, which is a nullity of public policy, that the arbitrator is not taken by the judiciary with regard to the accuracy determined in the case.

Some participants felt that it is sufficient for the arbitrator to refer to the provisions of the law he or she applied in the context of the dispute, whether in terms of adapting or establishing the rule of law on the facts arising from the dispute. As for the absence of reasonableness or the generality of reason, it does not entail invalidation, as long as this does not include a violation of the law, i.e. what the arbitrator concluded did not violate the law.

The arbitrator's judgment must be explicit and can only contain implicit content, for example, if the arbitrator justifies all the defendant's claims and then declares that he has ruled on all his claims.

The Dubai Court of Cassation ruled that the arbitrator's decision was originally intended to be reasoned but exempt from the obligation to comply with the general form set out in the Code of Civil Procedure.

It is sufficient to include in his judgment a summary of the arguments and documents of the litigants and the reasons for his opinion in the operative part, provided that he has not violated a rule of public policy.

(Appeal No. 269 of 1995 - session on 10/2/1996 - x 7 - p. 107)

The Federal Supreme Court also stated that "the text of the first and second paragraphs of article 212 of the Code of Civil Procedure No. 11 of 1992 stipulates that:

1. Arbitrators shall render their judgments without limiting themselves to the procedures of the proceedings, except in the cases provided for in this section and in the procedures for inviting the parties.

2. The arbitrator's judgment will only be in conformity with the rules of the law if he is authorized to proceed to conciliation "indicates that the legislator intended, on the basis of these two paragraphs, to indicate the formalities of the arbitrator's judgment and the manner in which they were to be rendered.

It is not necessary that all the statements to be included in the judge's judgment be included and that the provisions relating to arbitration be followed.

This includes, in particular, the provision of a copy of the arbitration document and the addendum to the declarations of the parties and their documents, as well as the reasons for the judgment, its scope and date of issue. The place where it was issued and the signatures of the arbitrators indicating that the Court, after ratifying the arbitrator's judgment, has no material and material knowledge of the provisions of the law. Except as regards public policy, but only the procedural aspects mentioned in Articles 212 and 216 of the said Law.

(Appeal No. 449 - for year 21 - Date of the meeting of 04/11/2001 - S 23 - p. 706)

The absence of a declaration of the date of the judgment leads to its invalidity, because the importance of this declaration is essential to determine whether the judgment was rendered within the time limit of the arbitration or whether it exceeded the time limit, which is not related to public policy.

The text of articles 212 and 213 of the Code of Civil Procedure indicates that the law requires that the arbitral award be included in the date of publication.

And set short dates for arbitration, which consists, through the court, in depositing the arbitrator's judgment in the court registry and then determining the hearing for ratification. These are considerations.

The issue date is necessary to calculate these dates as well as to determine whether the arbitrator's decision was rendered within the time limit or beyond its due date in order to allow the Tribunal to verify the arbitral award at the agreed time. Therefore, the date of the arbitrator's judgment will not be invalidated if the court cannot verify that it has not exceeded the specified time for arbitration from the other attachments to the award or the minutes of the arbitration session of a special statement indicating the date on which the arbitrator's judgment was rendered.

This was not the case and the appellant before the Court of Appeal had invalidated the judgment of the arbitrator who had rendered his decision without date.

It is clear from the documents that the arbitrator's judgment is the subject of the case and supports the contested judgment in which the judgment of the main judgment was ratified. The arbitrator did not specify the date of its publication and nothing in the other documents indicates the date of its publication.

(Call No. 400 - for the year 2001) - Date of the meeting of 16/02/2002 -

It should be noted that the decision does not invalidate even if it does not mention the date of publication as long as there is a fixed date that interrupts the arbitrators but their judgment was rendered in time, as if the judgment had been rendered within the time limits of the Court's registry or if one of the arbitrators had died during that period after the judgment was signed.

Judgment:

The arbitrator is required to make the award on the date of the agreement or on the legal date, unless the parties expressly agree otherwise.

Or implicitly to extend the date - the invalidity of the delay is not a matter of public policy.

Article 210 of the Code of Civil Procedure:

1. If the parties to the arbitration agreement do not need a judgment period, the arbitrator shall have jurisdiction within six months of the date of the first arbitration session.

Otherwise, any of the litigants may refuse to bring the dispute before a court or to bring it before it if it has already been filed.

2. The parties have agreed, expressly or implicitly, to extend the time limit set by agreement or by law and may delegate to the arbitrator the extension of a specific time limit.

The Court may, at the request of the arbitrator or one of the litigants, extend the time limit specified in the preceding paragraph by such period as it considers appropriate for the resolution of the dispute.

3. The time limit shall be suspended whenever the dispute ceases or ceases before the arbitrator

It shall resume from the date on which the arbitrator became aware of the suspension or interruption. If the rest of the time is less than one month extended to one month". In accordance with the provisions of articles 203 and 210 of the Code of Civil Procedure, if the parties to the dispute agreed in writing to submit their dispute relating to the performance of a specific contract to arbitration and provided for such a period. The arbitrator had to rule within the agreed time limit, if there was no agreement on a specific time limit to be settled within six months from the date of the first arbitration hearing.

The parties may request the annulment of the arbitrators' award where the court considers its ratification and that this does not prevent the acceptance of the nullity of the opponent's waiver of his right before the arbitrators' judgment under article 216 of the same law and the promoter of those provisions that the law required the arbitral tribunal to take into account the publication of his judgment within the time limit of the agreement or the specified legal form.

The duration may not be extended by itself without the explicit or implicit agreement of the parties to the arbitration, whether in the contract, in the arbitration agreement or in a subsequent agreement, whether in writing or proven in the arbitration report and signed by the court or by a decision.

At the request of the arbitral tribunal, it shall be submitted before the expiry of the term of the agreement or law, provided that such extension is for a certain period if the parties or either of them refuses to extend the dates.

The arbitral tribunal did not render its judgment during the remainder of the initial arbitration period, but rendered it after the overrun. Its judgment could be revoked at the request of one of the parties to the arbitration when one of them requested to ratify or revoke it and to conclude the agreement of the parties to the arbitration to extend the dates fixed for it by agreement or a law or not of the authority of the subject's court when it has established its jurisdiction in this regard on the reasons why the acquisition of a fixed document of immobilization leads to what the decision on this subject is sufficient to cover.

The Federal Supreme Court ruled that "the contested decision does not prevent the request for referral of the case, so that the response to this request does not constitute a right of the opponents to receive a response in all cases".

As long as the documents and evidence are sufficient to form the doctrine of the court and this is not productive because the fact of proving outstanding on the condition is to send written consent to the extension of the arbitration period, which has not been done".

(Appeal No. 640 of the 22nd session - Date of the meeting of 19/11/2002 - S 24, p. 2146)

The Dubai Court of Cassation also ruled that:

The judgment shows that the applicants have had recourse to the arbitrator for more than two years from the date of the first session, thereby expressing their implicit consent to the extension of the six-month time limit imposed by the civil proceedings under Article 210, so that the arbitrator may render his judgment.

If the parties do not agree on the extent to which the date is extended, the satisfaction of extending the duration of the judgment is considered as an expeditious arbitration agreement.

The time limit is six months and until one of the litigants declares that he does not want to approve the renewal or to go to court to rule at the end of the previous period.

(Appeal No. 178 of 1996 - Date of the meeting of 25/1/1997 - p. 58)

And this:

Among the assets established in the optional arbitration agreement of the parties to the dispute contained in the arbitration agreement at a specified date for the end of the arbitrators' work

It shall not prevent the extension of the agreed period for a period or any other period, nor shall it prevent the arbitral tribunal from deciding on such extension.

Such an agreement may be implied by the presence of the parties to the dispute during the examination of the arbitration and the discussion of the matter after the time limit has expired.

(Appeal No. 13 of 1991 - 9/6/1991 - p. 2 p. 418)

And judged that:

"The provisions of Article 210 of the Code of Civil Procedure - The agreement of the parties to the arbitration on a given date on the arbitrator shall not prevent their agreement - then explicitly or implicitly - to extend that period for any period of time or to authorize the arbitrator to fix that date.

The Court may also extend this time limit for such period as it considers appropriate for the determination of the dispute at the request of either party or the arbitrator, in order for there to be an extension of the duration of the arbitration - as such - the duration of the arbitration - either by agreement of the parties, or by the arbitrator's award, or by a court decision - must be linked to the previous period and not separate from it. If there is a time interval between the two periods, there is no additional time - and if the renewal of the terms and conditions of the parties' agreement to a new arbitration period - The duration of the arbitration is bound and therefore extended by the presence of the parties to the arbitration before the arbitrator and the failure of either expressly to the presence of the parties to the arbitration before the arbitrator and not adhering to any or explicitly to the fall of the arbitration document has exceeded the first date.

According to the text of article 216 of the same law - the fall of the arbitration document exceeded the time limit set for the arbitrator to give his judgment - unrelated to public policy - The court cannot judge by itself but it must be in the interest of the parties to the arbitration to adhere to it explicitly and clearly - either before the arbitrator when considering the dispute, or before the court when considering the request for ratification of the arbitral award or by requesting its nullity".

(Call No. 9 of 1996 AD - Date of the meeting of 13 July 1996 - S 7 - p. 396)

And the date on which the arbitrator must rule on the case is suspended each time the dispute ceases or ceases and the date of his appointment resumes from the date on which the arbitrator became aware of the disappearance of the ground, although the remaining period is less than one month, which may be up to one month (see the commentary on article 209 of the civil procedure) when is the decision considered valid and is it allowed to invoke the decision leading to it?

The judgment shall be deemed to have been rendered from the date of its signature after its entry, the judgment may be authoritative from the same date:

The importance of determining the timing of the judgment to verify the validity of the proceedings appears and take into account the time limit indicated in the text of the law or by mutual agreement between the parties to render its judgment Article 210 / Point 1.

This is also important if a person dies or makes one of the reasons for the response or if one of the litigants dies or loses his or her eligibility.

If one of the litigants dies before the judgment is delivered, the judiciary must put an end to the dispute.

Decisions taken during the interruption are not valid and Article 212 / point 7 provides that the judgment is deemed to have been rendered on the date of the arbitrator's signature after his writing.

Therefore, the effects of the judgment at that time may be authoritative, even if it may be challenged or the order has not been made. The parties may not bring the dispute before the courts.

Otherwise, it is permissible to maintain the inadmissibility of the case before it is decided. Arbitrators may not examine the judgment they have rendered in order to exclude the dispute from their jurisdiction.

They may not modify any of the terms of the judgment, and if they can correct the material errors it contains, either purely in writing or by arithmetic or an interpretation of its functioning, if it is ambiguous or if the rejection of a claim on the merits has been neglected.

Provided that this is done before the filing of the arbitrator's judgment by the court registry or, as the case may be, in accordance with article 213 of the Code of Civil Procedure

The Egyptian Court of Cassation has ruled that:

"If it is established that the parties to the dispute have reached arbitration insofar as they have engaged in numerous disputes concerning the culture of their own palaces.

The arbitrators' judgment was finally settled in these disputes and one of them was granted the right to receive certain sects, including agriculture.

This culture was already in place at the time of the arbitrators' judgment, as they were the right of the convicted person against others.

And the latter's claim for his right to this agriculture is refunded under this provision of the power of the order, this does not mean that he is the sower of this agriculture, nor does it change the fact that the judgment cannot be enforced by receipt. Non-application of the provisions shall not affect their undeniable authority for any reason that has legally expired.

(Call No. 93 of year 23 S - Date of the meeting of 14/3/1957 - p. 229)

The Federal Supreme Court ruled that:

"Arbitration is intended to be one of the means organized by law as an exceptional means of settling deductions and to make it a judicial body to which adversaries may appeal and to render the judgment rendered by it the authoritative command ordered once it has been rendered.

This provision remains valid as long as it remains in force and has not been revoked by the competent court.

Even if its decision is subject to appeal, even if it does not receive the execution order.

(Call No. 317 for year 19 S - Date of the meeting of 29/11/1998 - S - 20 p. 1257)

The Dubai Court of Cassation has ruled that:

"It is decided - and what has been done by this court - that the judgment rendered by the arbitrators shall have the authority of the order rendered once it has been rendered.

The parties to the dispute may not resort to justice or to the resumption of the dispute in which, in the case of the unification of the subject matter and the case, in any subsequent proceedings before the courts, even with legal or factual evidence that has not been raised in the arbitration dispute. Until the court has ruled that it has been invalidated or refused to ratify it. He shall refrain from presenting the dispute in an objective manner and to the extent that it complies with the law.

It is not empowered to refer arbitrators to arbitration for consideration of arbitration cases, except when considering the request for ratification when such a request is made, in accordance with articles 213 and 214 of the Code of Civil Procedure.

(Appeal No. 126 of 2001 - Date of the meeting of 27/5/2001 - 12 p. 487)

The Federal Supreme Court also stated that:

"According to article 215 of the Code of Civil Procedure, two judgments may only be executed if they are ratified by the court that filed its pen.

After reviewing the decision and the arbitration and confirmation document, there is nothing to prevent its implementation.

This court is competent to correct material errors in the arbitrators' judgment, at the request of the parties concerned.

It is also determined that the invalidity of a party's decision to deviate from the limits of the arbitration document invalidates the arbitrator's judgment unless the annulled party does not affect the other party and is not indivisible. "

(Call No. 9 - for the year 20 s - Date of the meeting of 13/2/2000 - Q 22 p. 196)

It also decided that:

"If the arbitrator's judgment as soon as it is rendered has validity among the opponents, but that authority is maintained when challenged by invalidity and the fate of the decision depends on what is required in this appeal"

(Appeal No. 21 - 2003 - Q 14 - p. 448)

Article 214 stipulates:

That "when considering the request for ratification of the arbitral award, the court may refer it back to the arbitral award for consideration of the arbitral tribunal's decision or clarify the judgment if it is not specified to the extent that it can be enforced and the arbitrators in these cases make their decision within three months of the date of notification of the decision unless the court decides otherwise.

The decision may only be challenged with the final judgment rendered by the ratification or annulment of the decision".

Arbitration:

The law does not require that the sentence be pronounced in public - and it is not necessary to pronounce it in accordance with the original, unless otherwise agreed between the opponents.

The law does not require that the judgment be pronounced in public or in the presence of the parties, unless they have accepted it, and even in such a case, there is no invalidation, even if the sentence was pronounced without their presence.

Since the judgment is rendered from the date of the arbitrators' signature after writing it, speaking in open court does not constitute a guarantee for the parties.

This is not a fundamental or fundamental measure, and therefore the arbitrators cannot make a decision at all.

Invalidity of the contract, including the arbitration clause - the nullity of the arbitration contract - and the invalidity of the dispute in arbitration and the invalidity of the judgment rendered therein:

The invalidity of the arbitration contract is an objective invalidation of the arbitration contract, for example, the annulment of the loss or absence of one of the litigants, and operates under the rules of civil transaction law, if it is null and void any opponent in the case to enforce this nullity, and the court decides for itself, but if the contract can be revoked, the person who adheres to it is only bound by the invalidity to his advantage in accordance with the general rules, the nullity of the arbitration contract leads to the nullity of the dispute in the arbitration and the annulment of the decisions rendered and judged as if they were not.

The invalidity of a dispute in arbitration, for example the lack of eligibility of one of the parties.

The invalidity of the judgment rendered by a person who is incapacitated is a procedural invalidity which follows the proceedings and acts in accordance with the rules of the Code of Civil Procedure.

Ultimately, all types of cancellations are called:

The invalidity of the original contract, including the arbitration clause, shall invalidate the condition unless she herself has an independent entity.

2. The invalidity of the arbitration contract inevitably leads to the invalidity of the dispute and the arbitral award.

However, the invalidity of the arbitration dispute shall in no way imply the invalidity of the arbitration contract and the invalidity of the arbitral award shall in no case imply the invalidity of the arbitration dispute.

3. The nullity of the relative arbitration contract does not mean that the dispute in arbitration is null and void in relation to public policy, the first invalidity being the nullity of the contradictory arbitration procedure for the nullity of public policy.

4. The invalidity of the dispute in the arbitration relating to public policy shall not invalidate the arbitrator's award contrary to public policy.

The Federal Supreme Court ruled that:

The invalidity of the initial contract shall entail the annulment of the arbitration clause accordingly

The court of nullity of the contract remains subject to the jurisdiction of the general court to rule on the dispute.

It is legally and legally determined that the contract must be returned to a place subject to its judgment and be a valid, valid and valid purpose and description, and not accompanied by a condition that corrupts it, so that if its corner, place or purpose is violated. This has no effect and no leave is returned. Any interested person may maintain his disability and the judge may judge him by himself.

The contested judgment having established its jurisdiction on the fact that the contract is the subject of the case is the contract of an agency, as mentioned in the contested judgment, indicated in the text of clause 2/3 of the competitor against whom the customer orders the bank to buy or sell the currency and the bank executes the orders.

However, this description does not make this contract legitimate, but the contract remains void because the power of attorney is prohibited and is contrary to Islamic law.

The examination of the texts of the contract governing the relationship between the parties and the supporting documents for foreign exchange transactions provides that the applicant or one of the applicant banks is subject to low and high exchange rates in order to benefit from the price differences of these currencies on foreign exchanges Client to the bank

For the latter to contact the London and Tokyo stock exchanges and enter, on behalf of the client, transactions purchased by saying $1 million at the rate in effect at a given time on the stock exchange. Then he sells by saying an additional hour on the same or a later day at the rate in effect at that time and date without being delivered for purchase or sale for sale.

But the customer benefits from the high price recorded on his account with the bank amount resulting from this increase or records a loss in case of low prices as the text of rule 4.9 of the contract governing the relationship between the parties involved shows. However, there is no delivery of the foreign currency with which the customer deals.

In addition to clause 2.3, the client must order the bank to buy or sell one or more currencies to the client at the price or exchange rates applied by the bank for the client. And execute orders provided that the investment account has a cash balance of at least $5,000.

At least 5% of the value of the proposed investment situation and the total amount of the client contract must not exceed fifty million dollars and that all the client's obligations to the bank do not exceed ten million dollars and it is clear from the verification of the bank's transaction cheques for the defendant, with the exception of two transactions, that each transaction represented not less than $1 million or £1 million.

While the amount deposited by the plaintiff against him did not exceed $177,173, that is, the delivery and receipt of the contract, and the figures that the agreed transactions.

Which was carried out by the applicant on behalf of competitors does not bet on the rise in currency prices and the fall in prices.

And record the resulting differences in loss or profit and the content of the transaction vouchers concluded showing that the agency's position represents a bet on exchange rate differentials, some of them before the US dollar against the Japanese yen and the British pound sterling and that the intention of the parties does not tend to enter into actual foreign exchange contracts in which the pound sterling or Japanese yen is purchased in US dollars or vice versa, and recognizes the allocation - the prize - and receives the physical sales receipt and the receipt. As it is the condition of place in Islamic law, but it was agreed to conclude future contracts in which the buyer does not have the price. But the exchange rate is visible on the agreed maturity date and the seller pays the price difference. If the price of the currency sold increases. The buyer pays the difference if the price drops and the price is unknown at the time the contract is concluded.

It cannot be determined at that time, but it is determined by circumstances unknown to both sides. They have no income in terms of supply and demand and price fluctuations.

The contractors of these futures contracts also operate in the currency of the contract before the non-existent arrest.

They exchange positions in the contract and the liquidation period becomes a seller and the seller is a buyer without delivery.

What are the essential characteristics that form the core of futures trading on the stock exchange?

And would lead to a defect in the contract of sale and misplacement, which is characterized by arrogance and play because its real objective is to speculate on the upward price, which leads to its nullity and the absence of any impact on it in accordance with the text of Article 1021 of the Civil Transactions Act and Articles 3 and 4 of the Federal Criminal Code No. 3 of 1987. "

(Call No. 209 for year 15 S - Date of the meeting of 22/1/1995 - XVI - 63)

The Dubai Court of Cassation also ruled that:

"If the lease agreement between the parties is based on all the elements of the moral and material commercial enterprise, the commercial license was only one of its components, and it was not the intended destination. Rather, the contract is conceived as a combination of the material and moral elements that make up this institution, including a permit from the licensee to the other party to exploit them - whatever the face of the opinion in this declaration or nullity - do not organize the nullity of the contract or the arbitration clause, which guaranteed ".

(Appeal No. 399 of 1994 S - Date of the meeting of 7/5/1995 - S 6 p. 396)

It also held that: "The nullity of the initial contract containing the arbitration clause must be annulled or terminated.

It shall not preclude the effectiveness of the arbitration clause with regard to the consequences of the annulment, termination or termination of the original contract, unless the invalidity extends to the same arbitration clause.

In such a case, this would have no effect since the arbitration clause had its own subject matter - this excludes the dispute for which arbitration is required from the jurisdiction of the courts. And assign the arbitration mandate to the "arbitral tribunal.

(Appeal No. 167 - for the year 2002 - p. 13 p. 486)

It also decided that the invalidity of part of the arbitrator's judgment concerning his departure in a dispute in which he had departed from the limits of the arbitration document would inevitably require the invalidity of the other party's dispute. Which are linked to the old inextricably linked. It is provided that the link with non-fragmentation is a question of fact that is left to the discretion of the competent court.

(Appeal No 10 of 1995 S - Date of the meeting of 8/10/1995 AD - S 6 p. 568)

In arbitration before the court: -

The arbitrator must file the arbitral award, the original of the arbitration document, the minutes, the acts and a copy of the judgment, which must be registered within fifteen days of the delivery of the judgment.

In extrajudicial arbitration:

The arbitrator shall provide a copy of the award to each of the parties within five days of the award - and to the parties to the dispute or one of them may request certification or the heroes of the judgment through the usual channels of filing the application. The arbitral tribunal may require the delivery of the photo by paying the costs. Insofar as it provides for the list of centers on which the arbitration took place.

Article (213) of the Code of Civil Procedure

1. In the arbitration conducted by the court, the arbitrators shall file the judgment with the original of the arbitration document, the minutes and the documents. The court registry, which initially had jurisdiction to hear the case within fifteen days of the judgment. They shall also file a copy of the judgment with the Registry of the Court, which shall be delivered to each party within five days of the filing of the original.

The clerk of the court shall make a declaration of such filing and the judge or the President of the Chamber shall, where appropriate, determine a hearing within 15 days of ratification of the judgment and shall so declare to the parties.

2. If the arbitration is the subject of an appeal, the filing is filed with the registry of the court that originally has jurisdiction to hear the appeal.

3. In arbitration between opponents out of court.

The arbitrators shall provide a copy of the award to each party within five days of the award

At the request of one of the litigants, the court examines the ratification or the merits of the decision according to the usual procedure for filing the case.

The third paragraph of Article 213 of the Code of Civil Procedure provides that arbitrators must be arbitrators. Between litigants outside the court to deliver a copy of the award to each party within five days of the award. If the invalidity does not result in the delivery of a copy of the judgment on that date.

The failure to communicate this image does not constitute - and what has been done by this court - one of the grounds for invalidating the arbitrator's judgment, because its subsequent procedure does not allow for its self-determination.

The Federal Supreme Court ruled that:

"The appellant's defense being based on the nullity of the arbitration on the basis of Article 213/3 of the Code of Federal Civil Procedure. It did not overturn the arbitral tribunal's refusal to provide the parties with a copy of its judgment within five days.

Or any other period within which it is stipulated that in arbitration between parties not parties to the tribunal, the arbitrators shall deliver a copy of the award to each party within five days of the award. The court will consider ratification or revocation of the decision at the request of one of the litigants in the normal procedure.

(Call No. 279 - Year 18 s - Date of the meeting of 14/12/1997 - Q 19, p. 816)

It also decided that:

"Collect an understanding of the facts of the case, evaluate evidence and documents and interpret the forms of contracts, agreements and correspondence. On the part of the authority of the subject's court when the subject has established its jurisdiction to obtain sufficient grounds for its judges to be conducted.

The list of conciliation and commercial arbitration procedures at the Abu Dhabi Commercial Arbitration Centre, which governs the relationship between the parties to the arbitration and that center. Its commercial conciliation and arbitration procedures are in accordance with the principles and provisions set out therein. This shall be interpreted and supplemented by the requirements of the parties and their agreements regarding the resolution of their disputes through conciliation and arbitration with the Centre, unless such provisions or agreements contain a provision contrary to the principles and provisions of the Rules pursuant to paragraphs 1 and 3/3 thereof.

Article 10/36 of these Rules provides that "the Centre's management shall grant the parties a copy of the arbitral award after payment of all costs, expenses and fees provided for in the case, if the party wishes to receive a copy of the judgment, it will reimburse the fees, expenses or fees due to its opponent.

The Centre's management grants the said party a certificate attesting to the payment of the amounts indicated as a deduction, which means that the payment of the prescribed fees, expenses and honoraria is a condition for the parties to obtain a certified copy of the arbitral award. The Arbitral Tribunal and the Centre shall not be entitled to hear the arbitral proceedings and make the award without filing the parties or any of the parties for the prescribed fees governed by Rule 5.15 of the Rules. The deposit center waived its right under the article mentioned in the collection of fees and charges.

Consequently, the Applicant invoked the agreement reached with the Arbitral Tribunal and the Centre not to commit to pay more than his share of fees before the arbitration and the Centre not to commit more than his share of fees before the arbitration and the verdict.

The provision of the preceding article shall not be interpreted in such a way as to be binding if it is in a hurry to pay the fees, expenses or fees due by its opponent to obtain the form of the arbitral award and shall not be in contradiction with the provisions of article 3/213 of the Code of Civil Procedure.

Nor with the provisions of article 1-46 of the Civil Transactions Act, since the obligation to submit a copy of the arbitral award does not prevent the right of the administration of the arbitration center to meet the fees, expenses or fees.

As a condition for the award of the arbitral judgment in accordance with the above-mentioned rules to which arbitration proceedings have been conducted in accordance with their provisions".

(Appeal No. 546 for year 22 - The date of the meeting of 12/11/2002 - XX 24 - p. 2055)

The arbitrator may be sued if he fails to fulfil his duty to file or arbitrate. The Dubai Court of Cassation has ruled that:

"The case is the right to have recourse to the courts to protect and enforce this right to lift those who are entitled to such protection and against those who must protest against it, the first paragraph of article 213 of the Code of Civil Procedure promulgated by Federal Law No. 11 of 1992.

I have bound the appointed arbitrator by filing his judgment with the original of the arbitration document and the files and documents of the registry of the court initially competent to hear the case within fifteen days of the pronouncement of the award, and a copy of the judgment to be given to each party within five days of filing the original;

It also required the clerk of the court to draw up a report of this filing, which must be submitted to the judge or head of department, as the case may be, in order to schedule a hearing within fifteen days for the ratification of the verdict and be announced by both parties.

Nothing in the Act provides that the arbitrator shall fail to comply with the provisions of the aforementioned article, which prevents the parties concerned from seizing the competent court to hear the dispute in order to implement the provisions of that article with the usual procedures for filing the case.

Thus, the action to compel the arbitrator - appointed by the court competent to hear the dispute, to file his judgment with the original of the arbitration document and the minutes and documents of the registry of the court initially competent to hear the case - to

He must be submitted to the arbitrator, since he is the defendant in the dispute which is bound by the obligations imposed on him under the first paragraph of Article 213 above, and the request for formal notice addressed to him to attach the documents in his possession and no other in the arbitration dispute relating to these obligations incumbent on the arbitrator.

(Appeal No. 31 of 2001 - Date of the meeting of 11/3/2001 - Q 12 p. 214)

Arbitration costs and expenses:

The arbitrators may estimate their fees and arbitration costs and bind the losing party under the supervision of the competent court. Article 218 of the Code of Civil Procedure It is up to the arbitrators to estimate their fees and arbitration costs, which may judge all or part of them on the losing party.

Article 218 of the Code of Civil Procedure allowed arbitrators to assess their fees and arbitration costs and allowed them to be judged by the losing party or to judge some of them.

However, at the request of one of the litigants, the legislator placed this estimate under the control of the Court. Depending on the efforts made, the nature of the dispute and its value, etc., the amount of time required to resolve the dispute will be determined.

The Federal Supreme Court stated that "the arbitrator is entitled to be convicted under Article 218 of the Civil Procedure Act. As long as the arbitral award has been rendered in time without exceeding the legal time limit and the court of first instance has accepted the filing of the arbitral award and ratification.

(Appeal No. 365 for year 17 BC - session on 9/3/1997 - Q19 p. 189)

The Dubai Court of Cassation also ruled that "the text of the sixth apartment is counterproductive because nothing in the law prevents arbitrators from deciding on the determination of their fees and the costs of the arbitration after their publication.

Considering that their jurisdiction to arbitrate still exists with respect to the determination of such fees and expenses, as their jurisdiction in this regard is not related to the subject matter of the dispute after the decision is rendered.

In this regard, it was sufficient for their judges to make a declaration for each amount spent on arbitration costs and arbitration costs.

In the case of the contested judgment, the appeal is dismissed and the appellant's defense is dismissed because it invalidates the arbitrators' second arbitral award concerning the determination of the arbitrator's fees and arbitration costs.

(Appeal No. 537 of 1999 - Session 24/3/2000 - Q 11 p. 342)

Arbitration and arbitration procedures in the light of the status of the Ras Al Khaimah Conciliation and Commercial Arbitration Centre:

Preface:

Law No. 5 of 2007 was promulgated to regulate the Chamber of Commerce and Industry of Ras Al Khaimah. Following the publication of the Chamber's Executive Regulations in 2008.

On 7/9/2008, the Chamber's Board of Directors initiated the approval of the status of the Ras Al Khaimah Conciliation and Commercial Arbitration Centre, in response to the aspirations of the legal and economic community. In order to serve it in the field of the fight against commercial disputes through arbitration - as indicated in the introduction to the Statute itself -

The system consists of seven chapters, the first of which deals with the general provisions that define the terms contained in its texts.

Its scope and the supposed formulations of those who wish to settle their disputes in accordance with these Rules for the conciliation and arbitration clauses and for both points. The second chapter dealt with the declaration of the establishment of the Conciliation and Arbitration Committee at the Centre.

The number of its members, the duration of their membership and the method of electing its president, seat and the way it holds its meetings and the quorum, and the contraindications of the participation of its members in its work and skills.

Chapter III deals with the mandate of the Centre's secretariat.

And their duties and responsibilities.

Chapter IV deals with the composition of the conciliation commission and the arbitral tribunal

The method of selection of arbitrators, the conditions to be met by them, the place of the meeting and the conduct of the proceedings

Chapter V also deals with conciliation procedures.

Chapter VI deals with arbitration procedures. Chapter VII deals with the costs of conciliation and arbitration.

A list of the fees of the Centre's arbitrators, adopted on 12 March 2009, is attached to the Statute and entered into force on the same date.

It included ten articles, including the determination of the annual membership fees for conciliation and arbitration tables and the expert table and translation by penalty for non-payment.

The percentage of their costs and the specific costs for submitting requests for conciliation, arbitration, experience and translation;

It included a table indicating the Commission's minimum and maximum fees in proportion to the value of the amount in dispute.

1. Proposal for the wording of the arbitration clause and the conciliation and arbitration clauses:

The Act provided a comprehensive formula for including contracts for the settlement of disputes relating to the contract, its performance, interpretation, annulment, annulment or invalidity, Or what it consecrates or concerns in any way whatsoever to arbitration or conciliation and arbitration in accordance with the provisions of the Statute of the Centre.

It is a complete formula that is sufficient to refer to arbitration and coverage in its procedural status by reference to what is contained in the Statute, which makes arbitration. It has been incorporated into the wording of the arbitration clause and the procedures, and the provisions of this clause are in accordance with the text of article 203 / clause (1) of the Code of Civil Procedure.

This allowed contractors to require the base contract or a subsequent agreement to offer their tendency to "perform" a particular contract to one or more arbitrators. This is stipulated in the proposed wording - the rest of this wording concerns the inability of this provision according to which "an arbitration in a given dispute may be agreed upon under specific conditions".

However, the proposed wording may be arbitrated "in any dispute relating to the contract", as the arbitration clause itself - if included in the disputed contract - It will only be effective if it determines the validity of this meeting and then the validity of the contract and the execution of the arbitration clause. However, it is true that this provision is included in an arbitration clause.

2. The parties may agree not to submit to the Centre's statutory procedures

Determination of arbitration procedures and elimination of deficiencies in statutory procedures:

Article 4 allows the parties to agree in writing on the arbitration by applying different provisions to manage the arbitration process. Including the selection of arbitrators, the appellability of the arbitral award and the limitation of the role of the RAK Chamber of Commerce and Industry to the mere organization and sponsorship of the arbitration;

Provide the services made available to it at the request of the arbitrators or arbitrators

This helps to define the Centre's ability to provide services to assist the arbitration process.

The Centre's ability and experience to lead the entire arbitration process.

Arbitration procedures not provided for in the Statute may also be agreed.

In the event of disagreement, the arbitral tribunal shall act in accordance with the provisions of article 6 of the Statute.

3 - Report on the independence of the arbitration clause from the initial contract: -

Article 5 / clause (1) establishes the rule that the arbitration agreement is considered to be independent of the original contract that is the subject of the dispute it contains. Initially, I promised to do so, unless the parties expressly agreed otherwise.

This is difficult to comply with - and this rule was intended to maintain the arbitration clause valid and enforceable even with the invalidation of the original contract. Indeed, the recognition of the status of this rule as a general asset remains to be seen.

Because the revocation of the original contract - in many cases - necessarily entails the revocation of the arbitration clause for several reasons, for example, their commitment and indivisible association or the nullity of the contract because of the forfeiture of the contractor or be subject to arbitration (and contract) contrary to public policy, morality or Islamic law.

4. Jurisdiction of the competent arbitral tribunal and related defenses.

Article 5 / clause (2) establishes the rule known in the field of arbitration as the principle of "jurisdiction" or an arbitration whose judgment inevitably implies the competence of its author, The arbitral tribunal shall have jurisdiction to determine whether it has jurisdiction to hear the dispute before it. The provision of this rule is in line with this rule established in the field of arbitration and has been reinforced by the provision on the argument of lack of jurisdiction. Whether or not to cover the subject matter of the dispute and all matters relating to jurisdiction. It does not go beyond its scope and its explicit provision enshrines the established principle. The provision clarifies the questions asked of arbitrators, particularly those who do not have legal expertise.

5. Confidentiality of information provided by the claimant for conciliation and arbitration purposes:

Article 7 defines the rule of confidentiality of information accessible by reason of their work and their disclosure is prohibited except with the joint consent of both parties or at the request of a competent judicial authority.

6. Notify the Parties by registered mail with knowledge of arrival or by any acceptable means of communication.

Article 9 provides that parties may be notified by registered mail or by any acceptable means of communication, for example by fax and e-mail.

Article as well as its ambiguity in determining what is meant by acceptable means. Do not allow, for example, reports on fixed or mobile phones, as they may be considered unacceptable means - in some cases for some - of reporting.

The text should have been drafted in such a way that notification is possible by all means, provided that finality and certainty can be verified. This makes it possible to use all the means of modern technology.

The legislator's purpose is to ensure that the notification is made in accordance with the provisions of the Code of Civil Procedure relating to arbitration.

7. Right of the data subject to veto the non-application of the provisions of the Staff Regulations:

The article of the rule decided that the right to oppose or refrain from the application of the provisions or rules of the Statute of the Centre lapsed, unless there was a timely objection.

The text, based on a vague and vague standard of objection, is a "bad time". In particular, it is agreed in the report on cases of compliance with appointment procedures that they must be resolved conclusively or defined by a standard that would lead to their final determination.

8. Establishment of the Conciliation and Arbitration Committee and definition of its terms of reference and procedures:

Articles 10 to 15 concerned the formation of a conciliation and arbitration committee from among its members.

They have done well by adding "other" specialists to meet needs that can be assigned by disciplines or provide the expertise they may need. It also defined its competence in the selection of the conciliator or arbitrator, determine the place of arbitration in the event of disagreement between the parties and decide on requests for review of the appointment of arbitrators.

Determine their fees and the costs of conciliation and arbitration in general and the deposit, establish the criteria by which arbitrators and experts are included in the Centre's lists;

Propose the rules of procedure necessary for the application of the Statute, as well as the necessary amendments to it and the corresponding regulations, it also decided on the method of convening the meeting at the invitation of its President or the Chairman of the Chamber's Board of Directors. The voting system is determined by a majority of the votes of the members present.

In the case of equality or the Secretary of the Centre in his absence, and also made his meetings confidential.

It has prohibited a member from attending or participating in its work or discussing what is offered to it if it is a party or has a direct interest or relative of one of the parties or an affiliation up to the fourth degree or an agent of its own company or a legal representative or guardian or agent, it also required those who have such an obstacle to disclose it.

We can think that a certain degree of independence of this committee from the Board of Governors of the Chamber of Commerce and Industry should be ensured

Given the important and influential skills

He practices with respect to arbitration, which is a judgment in dispute. He must ensure that he has the greatest guarantees of intervention or influence the choice of arbitrators or the president of the arbitral tribunal in deciding on requests for reconsideration of their appointment, it is appropriate to limit the invitation to the Committee's meeting to its Chairperson or former members in his/her absence, and to chair the meetings alone without the intervention of the President of the Board of Directors or the Secretary of the Centre.

9. Form the Centre's secretariat and define its competences:

Article 16 made the Centre's secretariat the administrative arm of the arbitral tribunal

It receives the requests for arbitration, the response and all documents, informs the parties of the requests for arbitration and prepares a summary of the dispute to be submitted to the Conciliation and Arbitration Commission and to announce the dates and place of the sessions, if the arbitral tribunal so requests.

In addition to maintaining the registration of claims submitted to the committee and preserving the assets of judgments and lists of arbitrators and experience and record the minutes of the sessions of the committee and the arbitration and conciliation bodies - This administrative organization will undoubtedly contribute to facilitating the arbitral tribunal's task. It is dedicated to the study of litigation and settlement, which makes it possible to make judgments quickly and resolve disputes, which is the primary objective of the arbitration system itself.

10. Selection of arbitrators:

Article 18 of the parties to the dispute chooses arbitrators from among the members of the Conciliation and Arbitration Committee and the Secretary-General or from the list of arbitrators approved by the Chamber. If they agree not to submit to the Centre's status and may appoint an individual arbitrator, chosen by the Committee in the event of disagreement at the request of one of the parties;

If it is agreed to select a panel of several arbitrators, each party may choose to appoint one arbitrator. Otherwise, the committee shall, at the request of one of the parties, appoint the arbitrator on its behalf: The parties may also choose the chairman of the arbitral tribunal or assign him to the arbitrators. The members of the committee or the lists of arbitrators before or outside the chamber have a final decision.

- Article 19 specifies obstacles to the arbitrator's task, such as being a minor or being prohibited.

It echoes the provisions of the Code of Civil Procedure.

- Article 20 also specified the place of the arbitral tribunal and the need for the presence of all members of the arbitral tribunal to examine the disputes before it. It allowed procedural decisions to be taken and required unanimity in this case, as authorized by its President in this regard, it decided that its sessions would be confidential and that it would not be present, except for those authorized by the arbitral tribunal.

To what extent is arbitration preferable to the use of alternative means of conflict resolution (conciliation, mediation, etc.)? This is very different from the choice between state courts and arbitration.

The arbitration clause precludes the intervention of the State courts in the subject matter of the dispute. Conciliation or mediation shall not exclude the use of arbitration nor does arbitration exclude the use of conciliation or mediation.

Authority of arbitrators by issuing temporary and provisional orders.

Interim and provisional orders are those issued by the judiciary at the request of the person concerned during the dispute or before the commencement of the hearing in order to temporarily preserve his or her rights until the dispute is resolved or face circumstances in which it is feared that it is too late to lose or ignore the right.

This rule is complemented by another principle, namely the right of the person against whom an interim order has been made to bring an action before the courts to bring an action and request its revocation.

Sometimes, the law provides that a substantive claim must be filed in accordance with the law within a specified period of time, starting from the day on which the safeguard order is executed, until the court considers supporting or rescinding it as in the case of preventive fixing of the furniture.

The jurisdiction of the judiciary to make such interim orders is based on the fact that they are governed by minutes and the use of force, where applicable.

On the other hand, these are actions that affect the interests of citizens and their money, although they do not affect the origin of these rights.

It must be through orders on petitions submitted by stakeholders and examined by the judiciary to be under its control.

Some of these orders are refused when the judge finds that there is no document that seems to corroborate the plaintiff's position.

The Egyptian Court of Cassation has defined temporary measures as a specific qualitative competence, namely the publication of a provisional verdict in which aggressiveness is obvious at first sight from one party to the other or stop the resistance from one to the other, by demonstrating it as illegal or by taking urgent measures to protect the object of the right or evidence of that right)

The use of justice in the context of an urgent request for an interim or provisional measure shall not constitute an infringement of the right of arbitrators to refer the matter they have accepted to the arbitral tribunal or assign its full jurisdiction to decide it, even if this is in contradiction with the conclusion of urgent justice or if its justice is not based on it later.

An appeal to urgent justice before the formation of the arbitral tribunal is an urgent requirement if the parties to the arbitration always find a full-time judge to decide their urgent claims.

It shall order such provisional and protective measures as it deems appropriate. It is a sufficient guarantee to limit the arbitrary nature of a party to the arbitration in a judicial or other test, so as to extend the procedure to complete the composition of the arbitral tribunal.

The subsequent loss of benchmarks or evidence that should have been proven at that time would have rendered his claim unnecessary after the formation of the Commission after its characteristics had been changed or its effects had been removed.

The competence of the interim relief judge to order provisional or protective measures is a specific question of public policy.

Therefore, no other party has jurisdiction to request any of these measures except this judge, unless they are related to a substantive application before another court.

There is no doubt that the use of urgent justice has the following advantages:

1. The judiciary has an assistance function that helps the plaintiff prepare the evidence he or she may need in a substantive case on which he or she may rely in the future.

2 - This is a case of precaution or precaution, which is why the case submitted to it is abstract and independent of the substantive case of the admission conditions.

3 - It is a time spent with the impact of the judgment on the merits. On the other hand, the emergency judicial power, in accordance with article 45 of the Egyptian Code of Procedure, is only competent to process the urgent request without the temporary request, which does not have emergency status.

Consequently, the Court of Cassation ruled that the urgent matters falling within the competence of the substitute judge are those limited to summary proceedings or an urgent precaution without prejudice to the purpose of the law and which must be differentiated between the two hypotheses.

The first concerns the jurisdiction to make temporary and interim orders before the formation of the arbitral tribunal.

The second concerns this jurisdiction after its formation.

For these two hypotheses, we present the following details:

First: The authority competent to issue interim orders before the formation of the arbitral tribunal:

That an agreement on arbitration would not prevent the use of justice in an urgent request for interim or provisional action, as long as the arbitral tribunal has not yet been constituted, it has already justified the following:

1. The agreement on arbitration and the allocation of jurisdiction to settle the question to be referred to the arbitrators, excluding the courts of the States, shall not affect the right of either party to appeal to the court of first instance to fill the void by taking provisional or protective measures before the formation of the arbitral tribunal. This would not prejudge the origin of the law submitted to arbitration.

Therefore, the urgent tribunal must not follow an agreement on arbitration until the trial judge has examined the merits of the dispute in order to conduct the appropriate inquiry as evidence in a particular case. Establish or maintain realistic evidence so that it can be used when considering a substantive dispute.

This does not mean that the parties to the arbitration have waived arbitration, which remains the means to be decided in the dispute.

This is clear from the foregoing and from what is stated in the second paragraph of Article IX of the Arbitration Act that (the court which is competent in accordance with the preceding paragraph - exclusively - has jurisdiction until the end of any arbitration proceedings).

It is also clear that the court with jurisdiction to hear the dispute has become the one with qualitative jurisdiction to deal with all matters to which the arbitration procedure is submitted.

To the extent that the Arbitration Act grants it jurisdiction to take provisional and protective measures, it exceeds the qualitative competence of the judge on urgent matters, either before the commencement of the arbitration procedure or during its conduct, unless the parties to the arbitration agree that the arbitral tribunal should order such measures.

It also extended the same urgent requests of the Court of First Instance or the order for interim and provisional measures on the merits.

It is not valid to state that it is possible to appeal to the judge for urgent cases before the beginning of the arbitration procedure or during the course of the procedure for that:

"Position of the legislation and comparative rules of international arbitration centers and bodies in determining the competent authority to issue interim or provisional orders before the formation of the arbitral tribunal."

Extrapolation of the laws governing arbitration in most countries of the world, as well as arbitration rules, shows that arbitration centers and courts are almost unanimously or explicitly. Either party to the arbitration before the formation of the arbitral tribunal to use the courts of the State to obtain an order for interim measures or an interim measure deemed necessary in the subject matter of the dispute that is the subject of arbitration proceedings or that may constitute grounds for invoking it, except that such laws. These measures differ from each other as regards judicial authority.

The New York Convention on the Enforcement of Foreign Judgments has created a tendency for many States that have signed it not to have jurisdiction to judge interim or provisional measures.

The Convention on the Settlement of Investment Disputes between States and Nationals of Other States, in the light of its article 47, has been followed by judgments accordingly.

UNCITRAL Model Law on International Commercial Arbitration

Article IX authorizes one of the parties to the arbitration to bring an action before the State courts to take provisional preventive measures before or during the arbitration proceedings

This is stipulated in Article 8/5 of the ICC Rules and Article III of the Rules of the American Arbitration Association as well as the Rules of the London Court of Arbitration in Article 14.

Second: The authority competent to make interim and provisional orders after the formation of the arbitral tribunal.

According to the case law, once the arbitral tribunal has been formed, it is competent to consider the application for temporary and interim orders and to support its opinion for the following reasons:

(A) That, by the formation of the arbitral tribunal, the reason why the judicial power of the State has been vested with the power to assist the arbitral tribunal in its task nullifies the necessity of the necessity of such a tribunal.

(B) The assessment of the relevance or rejection of an interim or provisional order shall be made by the arbitral tribunal competent to rule on the subject matter of the dispute.

Being more capable than the state's judiciary, which may be difficult to issue an interim or precautionary order, does not affect the origin of the right before that body.

C) It is when the parties choose the path of arbitration. They accepted it as an alternative to the state's judiciary.

(D) Where the parties to the dispute have agreed that the arbitrators may rule on a dispute between them, they shall not refrain from implementing the provisional or protective measures ordered by them. According to another view, physical and legal barriers who can cope with orders made by arbitrators for such measures that would justify the maintenance of the State's jurisdiction, namely:

Order the implementation of interim and provisional measures

The provisional or protective measures taken by the competent court to hear the dispute are urgent.

At the request of one of the parties to the arbitration, either before the commencement of the proceedings or during his or her conduct, it is enforceable without bail, unless the court decides to submit it.

However, the question is different if it is issued by the arbitral tribunal after the agreement of the parties to the arbitration to award it and the issuer's failure to apply it.

This body has also been allowed to authorize the issuer to take the necessary measures to implement it, specifying that it must not affect its right to ask the President of the Court referred to in Article 9 above to order enforcement by annex to the enforcement form.

Enforcement of the arbitral award

The arbitral dispute ends when the arbitral tribunal has terminated the award ending the dispute. The mandate of the arbitrators ends only in cases of interpretation of a judgment, correction of material errors or additional judgment, as indicated above. The sentence then begins after the judgment is pronounced.

The arbitral award, if it is not enforced by the convicted person on an application for a declaration of invalidity, is also optional. The sentenced person may, in his or her favor, request the judiciary to issue an execution order. That is, after the judgment is rendered, the judicial review stage after the judgment is rendered begins. First of all, we note that the arbitral award itself is not an executive act.

If the convicted person does not accept the execution of the judgment voluntarily or before its partial execution and the other parts of the judgment are rejected, the convicted person:

If he wishes to enforce the judgment in its entirety, he will have recourse to the courts of the State where he intends to enforce the arbitral award.

As the arbitral tribunal is a special judicial power, it does not have the power to make reparation, but must call upon the State's justice system to give it the status of an executive act.

However, the arbitral award shall not be considered an executive act until the execution order has been issued.

It allows the convicted person in his or her favor to sign a provisional seizure of his or her property,without the permission of a judge to detain or make a claim for the validity of the seizure, if such seizure can be signed under the arbitral award as an inapplicable provision.

The decision of the judicial authority to enforce a refusal to enforce an order shall not preclude the imposition of preventive detention under the arbitral award.

Explanation of the new Arbitration Act

In the United Arab Emirates

Published by Federal Law No. 6 of 2018

Preface:

Law No. 3 of 1970 on Civil Court Procedures in force in the Emirate of Abu Dhabi - for the first time a legal organization of arbitration

Chapter IX, Arbitration System - Articles 82 to 96

The provisions of this Act are applicable to federal courts. Its provisions have been applied to the disputes before it (with the exception of some of the provisions of Resolution No. 13 of 1990 of the Sovereign of Sharjah on the arbitration of disputes within the Emirate).

Federal Law No. 11 of 1992 was subsequently promulgated by promulgating the Code of Civil Procedure

The third section included articles 203:2018, which organized arbitration .Its provisions remained in force until the adoption of the last Federal Law No. 6 of 2018 on arbitration

His texts are set in the following context:

The first chapter

Definitions and scope of application

Article (1) Definitions

In applying the provisions of this Act, the following words and expressions have the meaning assigned to them, unless the context otherwise requires.

Country: United Arab Emirates

Arbitration:

A means governed by law by which a dispute between two or more parties must be settled by a binding award of the arbitral tribunal with the agreement of the parties.

Arbitration agreement:

The parties agree to refer to arbitration, whether this agreement was reached before or after the dispute.

Arbitral Tribunal

The body formed by an arbitrator or more than one person to settle the dispute shall be submitted to arbitration. Court:

The federal or local court of appeal approved by the parties or within the jurisdiction of the arbitration.

Arbitration institution:

An entity or centre established to regulate arbitration proceedings.

Authorized organization:

Any natural or legal person, the parties agree to grant any of the powers prescribed pursuant to this Act.

The party concerned:

The authority authorized by the arbitration or court.

Parties:

The arbitrator and the arbitrator against him, no matter how many.

The referee:

The party initiating the request to open arbitration proceedings.

The plaintiff against him:

The party against whom the arbitrator has initiated the arbitration proceedings.

Article 1 provides, as is customary in modern legislation, definitions of certain terms related to law. These include the definition of arbitration, its agreement, its body and its parties.

Although these definitions have not deviated from the consensus of most case law and have been settled by judicial decisions, they fall in many cases - a good way to determine the concept of a particular word or expression in the context of a procedure.

The implementation of the provisions of the same law to create the confusion that may arise, but it was free for the legislator. This approach should no longer be confusing by defining the term "arbitrator".

It defines it as the body empowered to arbitrate and another one before the competent court.

The Code of Civil Procedure - the pre-arbitration organization - did not include such definitions.

Egyptian Law No. 27 of 1994 on Arbitration in Civil and Commercial Matters, contained in Article IV

Definition of arbitration and what the court says and the terms of the arbitral tribunal - the parties to the arbitration saying:

Article: (4)

1. The term "arbitration" in the provisions of this Law shall be subject to arbitration agreed voluntarily by the parties to the dispute.

If the arbitrator under the agreement of the parties is an organization or permanent arbitration status or not.

2. The term "arbitral tribunal" shall be transferred to the tribunal composed of one or more arbitrators to decide the dispute submitted to arbitration.

The term "court" refers to the court of the State's judicial system.

3. The term "parties to the arbitration" in this Law shall be transferred to the parties to the arbitration, even if there are many of them.

What is meant by arbitration in court decisions:

- The will of the contracting parties creates arbitration and determines its scope according to the matters dealt with and the applicable law

Formation of the arbitral tribunal, its powers, arbitration procedures, etc.

- Decision of the court's jurisdiction that arbitration is an exceptional means of resolving postponements based on a deviation from normal litigation methods

The competence of the arbitral tribunal to decide the dispute is essentially based on the rule of law authorizing the withdrawal of the jurisdiction of the judiciary.

However, the legal organization of arbitration is based on the consent and acceptance of the parties as a means of resolving all or part of the disputes that have arisen.

Or may arise between them in the course of a certain contractual or non-contractual relationship is the will of the entrepreneurs who create the arbitration

It specifies its scope in terms of matters covered and the law to be suspended

Formation of the arbitral tribunal, its powers, arbitration procedures, etc.

(Appeal of the Egyptian Court of Civil Cassation No. 145 for the year 68 B.C. - session 28/5/2007)

The arbitration shall be subject to the will of the parties as expressed in the arbitration clause signed by them.

The usual judicial procedures are not applicable to it and are not subject to the supervision of a court.

Except within the limits of the principles of fair trial in matters of confrontation, the right of defence and public order requirements.

(Federal Supreme Court - Appeal No. 51 of 2016 - Hearing of February 28, 2017)

Arbitration is based on the willingness of the parties and their agreement to choose this path to resolve the resulting dispute

Or may result from the interpretation or execution of the terms of the contract between them,

Such an agreement provides the legal basis for the arbitration process and determines its scope and scope.

The dispute does not fall within the jurisdiction of the ordinary judiciary and the general jurisdiction to settle disputes.

(Federal Supreme Court - Appeal No. 224 of 2014 - Hearing of 16/11/2014)

Considering that the General Shariah on the arbitration of civil and commercial articles in the UAE

In accordance with the provisions of Title III of Book II of the Code of Civil Procedure, arbitration in matters of conciliation is permitted in the agreement

This agreement was the legal basis on which it was based and determined its scope and scope.

The dispute does not fall within the jurisdiction of the ordinary judiciary and the general jurisdiction to settle all disputes

The arbitrator thus obtains the power to decide the subject matter of the dispute in the same way as the arbitration is internal or external.

Whether a prior or subsequent agreement is concluded in the form of an arbitration clause contained in a contract or in the form of a separate agreement,

Anyone who agrees to award him an arbitration, considering that the provisions of the Code of Civil Procedure are decisive in indicating the consensual nature of the arbitration resulting from the will and resulting from it,

The imposition of arbitration in disputes arising from a particular relationship is therefore contrary to the nature of arbitration in its origin and structure,

This implies a breach of dispute by denying access to justice to the persons concerned

In addition necessarily introverted for an assault on the jurisdiction of the judiciary, as it was,

Decision of the President of the Securities and Commodities Authority No. 1 of 2001 on the arbitration system in disputes arising from securities and commodities trading

Published under the Securities and Commodities Authority and Market Act No. 4 of 2000,

It is clear from the text of Article IV that the legislator's objective is to authorize the Commission to set up an arbitration system

Given the nature of transactions on financial markets with its special rules and mechanisms

This requires the prompt resolution of disputes arising from such transactions.

In such a way that litigants refrain from going to court to save time, effort and time, with the aim of providing traders with an easy way to facilitate the settlement of disputes arising from the circulation of securities and goods.

The law does not intend to authorize this body to establish a system that would impose arbitration on persons who do not request it or refuse to enter it contrary to the nature of the Arbitration Convention and result in the loss of the right to a trial

Article 2 of the decision of the said authority stipulates that disputes arising from the application of the provisions of this law shall be settled. among securities and commodity traders exclusively by arbitration.

Negotiating in the marketplace is an acknowledgement of the acceptance of arbitration and an obligation to enforce the court's judgment and a waiver of appeal methods, except as prescribed in these rules.

This provision establishes a jus cogens rule that cannot be violated by imposing arbitration on investment dealers, which goes beyond the scope of allowing them to violate the text and requirements of the law, as well as the rules of legal fundamentalism.

The jurisdiction of the arbitration depends in each case on the agreement of the parties and makes it possible to settle the dispute between them (Federal Court - Appeal No. 42 of 2009 - hearing of 26 May 2009).

The starting point of the text of Article (1) is the use of the words - the arbitral tribunal - and the words - the parties - the arbitrator - the arbitrator against him and excessive in the statement.

1. Most Arab laws governing arbitration, including the laws of the United Arab Emirates and Egypt, have always used the term "arbitral tribunal" instead of "arbitral tribunal".

Although the model law prepared by the United Nations Commission on International Trade Law, known as UNCTAD -

The United Nations General Assembly has recommended that the States that benefit from them should not be modified at all in order to unify the arbitration system.

The term "arbitral tribunal" is used to avoid any confusion between the national courts established by the Constitution and national legislation.

It is dominated by the judiciary and the ambiguity of the arbitral tribunal's expression "the right reserved exclusively for the State to establish courts

Or to be understood as giving individuals the right to create courts which, as some may see, may infringe upon the sovereignty of the State.

And then the Egyptian legislator and then the Emirates text on the expression "arbitral tribunal"

Appoints the body formed by one or more arbitrators to rule on the dispute submitted to arbitration;

While retaining the designation of its verdicts "with the judgment in custody of the term" court "of the federal or local court of appeal accepted by the parties or within the limits of its jurisdiction.

2. Describe the UAE legislator by defining the parties as the arbitrator and arbitrator

He then identified the arbitrator and the arbitrator against him as the party initiating the request for commencement of the arbitration proceedings, which he called the arbitrator and the party to whom the arbitrator had initiated the arbitration proceedings against him and called the arbitrator against him.

While it was sufficient to define one of the three words of the parties to the case, the first part being the plaintiffs no matter how many and the second part are the accused whatever the many who have made this definition suspicious and excessive in the declaration that avoids legislations and laws.

Article 2: Scope of the law

The provisions of this Act shall apply to:

Any arbitration conducted in the State, unless it is agreed to be subject to the provisions of another law on arbitration, provided that it does not conflict with the public policy and morals of the State.

2. Any international commercial arbitration conducted abroad and the parties agree to submit it to the provisions of this Law.

(3) Any arbitration arising from a dispute concerning a contractual or non-contractual legal relationship governed by the law in force in the State;

Except what is excluded by a special text.

The Law on Civil Procedure and Pre-Arbitration Procedure did not contain a similar provision. The text of Article II was intended to broaden the scope of the law, making it applicable to home arbitration, regardless of its commercial or non-commercial nature, whether the dispute results from a contractual or non-contractual legal relationship.

However, it linked its applicability to arbitration conducted abroad as international commercial arbitration. It can be assumed that the legislator intended commercial relations in the strict sense of what he was spending on purely commercial materials. This is limited by commercial law, which limits the validity of the law in international arbitration.

The UNCITRAL Model Law cites many examples, including the provision of goods or services commercial agencies, construction contracts, engineering and technical expertise and industrial and tourist licenses, technology transfer, development contracts, transport, exploration and extraction of natural resources and the supply of energy and the construction of gas and gas pipelines and the construction of roads, agricultural land reclamation, environmental protection and nuclear reactors. Most are considered, by traditional business standards, as civil engineering works.

International commercial arbitration must therefore be understood in the sense that it is intended to have a broader specific definition and meaning under the Arbitration Act.

In order to keep pace with the rapid development of international trade, which has led to the emergence of modern activities that did not previously exist

It is linked to international investment and achieves the adoption of the international model that the world has come to know in the field of international trade.

It should be noted that Egyptian Law No. 27 of 1994 on Arbitration took up this criterion but was cited - to show that the meaning intended to describe arbitration as commercial is the meaning to which UNCITRAL

These examples are cited in article 2, including all cases in the model law

International arbitration in judicial judgments:

Text contained in article II, paragraph 1, of this Convention (New York Convention on the Enforcement of Foreign Arbitrators)

Each Contracting State shall recognize the written agreement by which the parties are required to arbitrate all or part of the disputes that have arisen or arising between them on a subject of contractual or non-contractual legal relationships relating to a matter that can be settled by arbitration. In the second paragraph of its first article, the arbitrators' decisions are not only intended for decisions rendered by specific arbitrators for the purpose of a decision in specific cases.

But also the verdicts of the permanent arbitral tribunals invoked by the parties "together demonstrate that an international arbitration agreement is valid in return for its legal effects.

Including exclusion from the jurisdiction of the national judiciary, even if its arbitrators have not chosen or appointed arbitrators where there is in this Agreement what expressly refers to or imply that the will of the parties to the referral to a permanent arbitral tribunal has been deviated arbitrators shall be chosen in the event of a dispute in accordance with its rules. This is not what the Convention requires from a certain method of expression.

(Al-Muayyadah Court of Appeal No. 2660 of 59 BC - Hearing of 27/3/1996 of 47 p1 p. 558)

International arbitration

Article 3:

Arbitration is international in nature if it is conducted within the State in one of the following cases:

1. If the parties have several business centers, the lesson is the one that best suits the purpose of the arbitration agreement.

If one of the parties to the arbitration does not have a business center, the course will be held at his or her usual place of residence.

2. The place of performance of a substantial part of the obligations arising out of the commercial relations between the parties or the place, which is closely related to the subject matter of the dispute.

3. If the subject matter of the dispute that is the subject of the arbitration agreement involves more than one State

4. If the parties expressly agree that the subject matter of the arbitration agreement concerns more than one State.

The Code of Civil Procedure - the organization that precedes arbitration - did not contain a similar provision

Although Egyptian Law No. 27 of 1994 on the Arbitration of Civil and Commercial Goods contains a similar provision stipulating that:

"Arbitration is international within the provisions of this Law if its subject matter is a dispute relating to international trade in the following cases:

First: if the principal place of business of each party to the arbitration is located in two different States at the time the arbitration agreement is concluded,

If one of the parties has several business centers, the course is the most relevant for the subject matter of the arbitration agreement.

If one of the parties to the arbitration does not have a business center, the course will be held at his or her usual place of residence.

Second: If the parties to the arbitration agree to resort to a permanent arbitration organization or a seat inside or outside the Arab Republic of Egypt.

Third: If the subject matter of the dispute covered by the arbitration agreement is related to more than one State.

Fourth: If the main focus of the work of both parties to the arbitration

It is located in the same State at the time the arbitration agreement is concluded and one of the following places is located outside that State.

(A) The place of arbitration specified in the arbitration agreement or by indicating its mode of appointment;

(B) The place of performance of a substantial part of the obligations arising from the commercial relations between the parties;

C) The place most closely related to the subject matter of the dispute.

Article 3 of the United Arab Emirates Law, defining the meaning of international arbitration, defines the cases in which arbitration is international.

In accordance with its provisions, it has taken the advice of the Model Law on International Commercial Arbitration in this regard.

As if the law - having broadened the meaning of the term trade in terms of provisions relating to international arbitration, it has returned and expanded further in the sense of "international arbitration".

Agreement on the arbitration abroad of judicial judgments:

- The Egyptian legislator approved the agreement on arbitration abroad by acceding to the Convention on the Decisions of Foreign Arbitrators and his execution took place in New York in 1958 (Appeal No. 2660 of 59 BC - meeting 27/3/1996 S 47 C 1 p 558)

Chapter II Arbitration Agreement

Eligibility to accept arbitration

Article 4:

1. The arbitration agreement shall be concluded only by the natural person having the capacity to dispose of the rights or the representative of the legal person authorized to enter into the arbitration agreement, otherwise the agreement will be null and void.

2. Arbitration cannot be agreed in cases where reconciliation is not permitted.

3. In cases where this law requires the parties to agree on the procedure to be followed for the determination of a particular issue each of them may authorize other persons to choose or

decide on this procedure. Any natural person or arbitration institution within or outside the State shall be considered a third party in this regard.

4. The arbitration agreement shall not terminate with the death or expiry of a party. It may be implemented by or against the legal successor of that party, unless otherwise agreed by the parties.

Article 203(3) of the Code of Civil Procedure - Pre-Arbitration Rules provides:

(ii) arbitration may not be conducted in cases where reconciliation is not permitted.

The arbitration agreement can only be valid for those who have the right to dispose of the disputed right. Article 11 of the Egyptian Arbitration Law provides that arbitration can only be accepted by the natural or legal person who has his or her rights. Arbitration is not permitted in cases where reconciliation is not permitted. This is provided for in paragraphs 1 and 2 of Article IV.

It is simply a repetition of the general rules that impose it without the need to provide for it (whether it is the ability to dispose of the rights of the individual) or the representative of the legal person authorized to conclude the arbitration agreement or, in the absence of arbitration, in cases where composition is not permitted, this chapter of the book entitled "What cannot be arbitration is entitled").

Eligibility - in court decisions:

- The arbitration must have the right to dispose of the disputed right (Federal Court, Session 24/5/2000, Technical Office Q22-p. 871)

- Although it is not permitted to arbitrate to determine the liability of the offender for a criminal offence. Otherwise, it is considered null and void for violation of public policy, but if the agreement provides for arbitration by the judiciary in disputes where it is not permitted, like all other contracts, it is valid for what can be arbitrated. Invalidity is limited to the false part only, unless the person making the request proves that the invalid or voidable part is inseparable from the total contract.

(Appeal No. 1479 of the year 53 BC - hearing of 19/11/1987)

- In accordance with the fourth paragraph of Article (501) of the Code of Procedure.

Article (551) of the Civil Code stipulates that no arbitration may be made to determine the liability of the offender for a criminal offence.

Otherwise, it is considered null and void for violation of public policy and if the case is the subject of arbitration so it was a reason for engagement in Sindh, but about the crime itself.

It aims to determine who is responsible and who is in charge and who is in charge of public order, peace cannot be restored and, therefore, it is not valid to be arbitrated. This implies that the obligation established in the bond will be null and void for the illegality of his case.

(Appeal No. 562 for year 47 BC - Session 2/12/1980 AD 31 p. 1989)

- Arbitration is provided for in articles 502 and 503 of the Code of Procedure, which are shared between the parties; any agreement on mutual obligations to dispose of the arbitrators' judgments. The invalidity of the incompetence provisions stems from Articles (131 and 132) of the Civil Code, a relative invalidity of the decision to challenge, which are not admissible.

(Appeal No. 73 for the year 17 BC - hearing from 18/11 to 1948)

Article 4, paragraph 3, did not contain a similar provision in the Code of Civil Procedure - Pre-Arbitration Organization.

- While Egyptian law No. 27 of 1994 on arbitration in civil and commercial articles included the text of article 5, which was as follows:

"In cases where this law does not allow the parties to arbitrate to choose the procedure to be followed in a given case, this includes their right to authorize other persons to choose that procedure. Any arbitration organization or center established inside or outside the Arab Republic of Egypt shall be considered a third party in this regard.

Selection of third party procedures and licenses in judicial decisions.

Arbitration through an arbitral institution or arbitration center within or outside the State.

The parties to the dispute shall sign the arbitration contract, which shall enable them to satisfy and accept the procedures and arrangements governing the operation of the Centre.

Failure of the Centre to stop its work and initiate the process entrusted to it as a result of actions taken by one of the parties to the proceedings to prevent the completion of the arbitration task or to delay the recognition of the rights of the other party.

An example of a defective ground for the invalidity of the arbitral award is that it is not accompanied by an arbitrator's willingness to rely on the arbitrator's person. Notwithstanding the arbitration procedures governed by Legislative Decree No. 6 of 2004 of the Emirate of Ajman regulating the work of the Emirate Arbitration Centre.

(Appeal No. 213 of the Federal Supreme Court for the year 2014 - hearing 26/11/2014)

(Federal Court Appeal No. 627 for the year 2013 - hearing on 29/04/2014)

1. Article 25 of Act No. 27 of 1994 promulgates a law on the arbitration of civil and commercial articles indicates that the legislator has granted the parties to the arbitration the freedom to agree on one of the procedures.

What the arbitral tribunal must follow, whether it is in force in an organization or arbitration center in Egypt or abroad. In the absence of agreement on the introduction of any of these rules of procedure, the arbitral tribunal shall be free to choose the procedures it considers appropriate.

(Egyptian Court of Cassation Appeal No. 414 of 71 - Hearing of 8/2/2009)

2- The decision of this court that the consent of both parties to submit the arbitration to the rules of the International Chamber of Commerce in Paris would obscure the provisions of Egyptian Arbitration Law No. 27 of 1994, except as regards public policy.

(Appeals No. 1041, 1154 for the year 74 BC - sitting 13/4/2010)

Decision of the court of this court that the legal organization of the arbitration

It is based on the will of the entrepreneurs who create arbitration

Its scope is defined according to the matters covered and the applicable law

The composition and powers of the arbitral tribunal and the arbitral procedure;

The documents stated that the arbitration clause included the agreement of the parties to submit any dispute arising from the contract to arbitration before the Rotation Support Fund in Alexandria. Thus, the willingness of both parties to apply the rules and provisions of this body in the selection of arbitrators was rejected. Considering that the text of Article 7 of the Arbitration Rules of this Fund has made it possible to specify the rules relating to the composition of the arbitral tribunal.

Although it is established in the documents that these rules have been respected in the composition of the arbitral tribunal, the arguments put forward by the applicant in this respect are unfounded.

(Appeal of the Egyptian Court of Cassation No. 261 of 68 BC / 97 of 73 BC - hearing 8/2/2011)

Article 5: Copies of the arbitration agreement

1. The arbitration agreement may be prior to the establishment of the dispute, whether it is independent of itself or contained in a specific contract concerning all or part of the disputes that may arise between the parties.

2. Arbitration may be agreed after the dispute has arisen, even if a legal action has been brought before a court, in which case the agreement specifies the issues covered by the arbitration.

3. Arbitration may be agreed by reference in a contract Or any other document containing the arbitration clause if this assignment is clear when you consider this clause to be part of the contract.

Article 203 (1) of the Code of Civil Procedure - Pre-Arbitration Organization - stipulates that:

1. As a general rule, contractors may require, in the basic contract or in a subsequent agreement, that any dispute that may arise between them in the performance of a particular contract may be submitted to an arbitrator or more may also be agreed to arbitrate a particular dispute under particular conditions.

(Refer to the body of this book under point 3: Arbitration clause and participation)

Egyptian law No. 27 of 1994 on arbitration of civil and commercial articles included the text of article 10, which reads as follows:

1. The arbitration agreement is the agreement of the parties to use arbitration to settle all or part of the disputes that have arisen. They may also arise between them in the course of a particular legal relationship, whether contractual or not.

2. The arbitration agreement may be prior to the establishment of the dispute, whether it is independent or indicated in a specific contract concerning all or part of the disputes that may arise between the parties. In this case, the subject matter of the dispute shall be specified in the statement referred to in the first paragraph of Article 30 of this Law.

The arbitration agreement may also be concluded after the dispute has arisen, even if legal proceedings have been brought before a judicial authority. In this case, the agreement shall specify the matters covered by the arbitration, failing which the agreement shall be null and void.

3. Any assignment contained in the contract to a document containing the arbitration clause shall be considered as an arbitration agreement. If the assignment is clear, you must consider this condition in the contract.

Arbitration agreement: arbitration clause and participation in court decisions:

Considering that these terms have ensured that the elements necessary for the establishment of a compromise by the first applicant according to the Arbitration Act - in a way that prevents courts from dismissing with regard to any dispute that may arise between the two parties on this subject, when one of them has referred it to it.

If the other does not succeed in the arbitration procedure from the appointment of an arbitrator, it shall represent. In the written statement to be sent to the opponent and the members of the arbitral tribunal upon agreement, the contested judgment shall be this was taken into account and terminated in support of the contested judgment in its decision not to accept the case because of the existence of the arbitration agreement, it would be in accordance with the law. The Court of Cassation may establish new legal grounds that complement these grounds without revoking it.

The validity of its judicial system did not prevent it from not dealing with the subject matter of the dispute after it had resulted in the non-acceptance of the case for the reason of the declaration as a formality when it accepted it, refrained from considering the issue and then sacrificed the reasons for the appeal as a whole on an unfounded basis.

(Appeal of the Egyptian Court of Cassation No. 574 of 65 BC - Session 9/4/2002)

The inclusion of the arbitration clause in the charter in a general and unclear wording is not sufficient to say that this clause is available.

- If it is decided to look at the origin of the lease during the dispute, it is accompanied by the documents of the appeal, which are generally mentioned in the bill of lading, as indicated in the letter.

Clause 11 of the twentieth clause shall be replaced by the words that general losses, if any, shall be held in London in accordance with the Antwerp Rules 1974, as set out in clause 11, including what is stipulated.

This means that the eleventh part of clause No. 31 is replaced by "arbitration in London" and is mentioned in clause 8 of the special conditions activity: arbitration in London.

The wording of these articles was in general wording

The lack of clarity that does not reflect the tendency of the parties involved in the chartering of the vessel to regulate arbitration procedures and the method of appointing arbitrators and their number, specifying the dispute or disputes to which their agreement belongs.

It was not enough to say that the arbitration clause was available to affirm that the arbitration in London, with reference to the amended terms not included in this undertaking, is such that the execution of this clause is not fulfilled.

If the contested judgment had ruled in favor of the contested judgment, which concluded that the case had not been accepted because of the existence of the arbitration clause based on an incorrect interpretation of these provisions, it would have infringed the law and departed from its duration.

He broke the law and deviated from his words.

(Egyptian Court of Cassation Appeal No. 607 of 63 B.C. - Hearing 27/3/2007)

The reference in the contract to a document containing the arbitration clause:

- The decision of our court that arbitration is a means of settling discounts by the usual methods of dispute, including guarantees, with the bill of lading originally constituting the shipper's or consignee's evidence before the carrier. The parties to the contract of carriage shall use arbitration to settle any dispute which may need to be expressly stipulated in this bond, including the selection of arbitrators or referral to a permanent arbitral tribunal. The contested judgment undertook to examine in depth its disadvantage is that it is mentioned in its blogs that the contested person's call to conduct arbitration after the filing of the complaint has its effect.

(Appeal No. 4837 of 65 BC - hearing of 26/11/2001)

- An agreement - for the parties to the letter of guarantee - to use arbitration to settle their disputes either by specifying it or by referring to a document containing it that is severed in the terms of this letter.

(Appeal of the Egyptian Court of Cassation No. 495 of 72 before JC - session 13/1/2004)

An agreement on arbitration is not presumed.

Article 150/1 of the Civil Code stipulates that, in accordance with the Court's jurisdiction, the law is required to take the clear words of the contractors as they stand and may not, under the guise of interpretation, deviate from their apparent meaning for any other meaning. Arbitration is an exceptional way to resolve disputes through the usual methods, and the opponent should seek justice to commit to refer the dispute to an arbitrator. Or the more the case is about arbitration, the more the case is about. Arbitration is not supposed to clearly express the departure of the opponent's willingness to follow this path by specifically including the dispute or disputes in which he or she is involved. According to the knowledge of the origin of the lease contracts involved in the dispute, attached to the appeal documents, they do not contain any particular requirement, but this is mentioned in paragraph 26:

Under English law, any arbitration will take place in London

- Where applicable, the arbitration takes place in London, in accordance with English law, which means that, in the case of an arbitration agreement, it will take place in London and in accordance with English law, and if the contested judgment decides not to accept the applicant's case because of the existence of the arbitration clause based on his interpretation of the said clause. According to the agreement of the parties to resort to arbitration in any dispute arising from the contract of carriage between them, this would have violated the law by departing from the clear clause of the reversal clause.

(Appeal of the Egyptian Court of Cassation No. 1115 of 52 BC - session 16/11/1987)

Article 203 of the Code of Civil Procedure also aims to indicate the legislator's tendency to consider that the arbitration agreement between the parties to the contract is independent of the basic contract and that it may be subsequent to the contract and, of course, that it is envisaged or considered as a condition of the contract. Don't deny his self and his independence.

(Federal Supreme Court - Appeal No. 166 of 2008 - Hearing 1/2/2010)

- Evidence - according to the award codes - that both parties have filed a complaint with the other and that they have filed arbitration sessions and approved the arbitration agreement and signed it before the Commission. The objection that the arbitral award is not available in the form of an arbitration agreement is unacceptable.

(Federal Supreme Court - Appeal No. 524 of 28 - Session of 22/12/2009)

- Article 203/1, 2 of the Code of Civil Procedure stipulates that the same agreement between the parties or a subsequent agreement must contain a clause providing for referral to arbitration, so that, in contracts and in accordance with the principle of proportionality, the arbitration clause of the main contract concluded between the contractor does not apply. The employer of the subcontract must, unless the subcontract and, in particular, aim at the application of the above-mentioned arbitration clause.

(Federal Supreme Court - Appeal No. 25 of year 21 - hearing of 9/1/2001 23 p. 10)

Article 6: Independence of the arbitration agreement

1. The arbitration agreement is independent of the other terms of the contract.

(2) The payment of the nullity, cancellation or termination of the contract, which includes the arbitration agreement, shall not result in the suspension of the arbitration proceedings.

The Code of Civil Procedure (pre-arbitration organization) did not contain a similar provision)

Egyptian Law No. 27 of 1994 on arbitration in civil and commercial articles contained a similar provision. Article 23 stipulates that:

"The arbitration clause shall be considered as an agreement independent of the other clauses of the contract and the invalidity, cancellation or termination of the contract shall not affect the arbitration clause contained therein if that clause is true in itself."

- The principle of the independence of the arbitration clause is confirmed by the text of article 21 of the United Nations Commission's rules, which is technically well known and preceded by article 2 of the New York Convention, although exceptional circumstances may justify a derogation from this principle, as if it were the illegality of the original contract. The International Chamber of Commerce in Paris issued two arbitrary judgments, the first of which implicitly rejected the application of the principle of independence.

The arbitration agreement was pointless and not competent, while the second explicitly took the principle of independence on the grounds that the illegality of the original contract did not go into the arbitration agreement, which remains valid because of its effect on the arbitration contract.

Principle of the independence of the arbitration clause in court decisions

Where the appellant is vitiated by an erroneous judgment in the application of the law and in a statement before the arbitral tribunal that there was no arbitration clause because of the termination of the contract, it having been terminated by the express termination clause, The Commission rejected this defense on the ground that the arbitration clause was independent of the rest of the contract and that the contested verdict was confirmed and confirmed by the judiciary, whereas the arbitration clause itself was neither immune to judicial review nor to the unconstitutionality of the text of Article 23 of the Arbitration Act No. 27 of 1994. The arbitration clause is considered as an independent agreement Other terms of the contract,

The nullity, termination or termination of the contract shall not affect the arbitration clause contained therein if it is true), which indicates that it is one of the fundamental rules considered as one of the pillars of arbitration, namely the independence of the arbitration clause forming part of a contract from the other clauses of this contract. Nothing shall affect the contract resulting from the cancellation or the grounds for cancellation or termination. Thus, the dissolution of the initial contract, its cancellation or termination does not prevent the production of the arbitration clause for its effects as long as it is true. Under the terms of the original contract, he enjoys legal independence allowing him to be free from any initial anaphylactic dissolution agreement or the consequent annulment may lead to is the arbitration decision pro governing the contested decision is committed on this subject and has refused to pay the dispute and that the arbitration clause guaranteed by a contractual dispute is true in itself, the notice of death in this respect are unfounded.

As for the argument invoked by the applicant as to the unconstitutionality of article 23 of the Arbitration Act invoked, it is unacceptable, since the court of that court considered that this payment was not linked to public policy and could not be invoked before the Court of Cassation to exercise its power of appeal. Do not accept it.

(Appeal No. 824,933 of the Egyptian Court of Cassation for the year 71 BC - Session 24/5/2007)

- The purpose of the arbitration clause is to exclude the arbitral dispute from the jurisdiction of the courts and to transfer it to the arbitral tribunal, an agreement on two different subjects, one concerning the same law and the other concerning the determination of the agent in the settlement of the dispute requiring arbitration, arbitration being an exceptional means of carrying out arbitrations. And the consequence that the removal of the arbitration clause is subject to its invalidity.

The invalidity, annulment or termination of the base contract containing the arbitration clause shall not prevent the arbitration clause from remaining in force and from producing its effects for the dispute requiring arbitration with regard to the rights and obligations of the parties to the base contract resulting from its invalidity, termination or termination. Its judiciary confirmed the decision of the first instance to refer the dispute to arbitration, invoking the inclusion of the arbitration clause itself in the 21st clause of the basic contract concluded between the two parties. Respect for the appellant does not invalidate the arbitration clause, because his independence does not follow the presence or nothing.

(Appeal of the Federal Supreme Court No. 166 for the 2008 hearing session of 1/2/2010)

Article 7: Drafting of the arbitration agreement

1. The arbitration agreement shall be in writing, otherwise it shall be null and void.

2. The arbitration agreement shall be deemed to satisfy the writing rule in the following cases:

(A) If it appears in a publisher signed by the parties or received by exchange of letters or by other means of communication in writing or by electronic message in accordance with the rules in force in the State concerning electronic transactions.

(B) If reference is made to a fixed contract by writing the provisions of a standard contract, international agreement or other document containing an arbitration clause and if the assignment is clear, considering that clause as part of the contract.

(C) If the arbitration is agreed at the hearing of the dispute by the competent court, the latter shall render its decision confirming the arbitration agreement.

(D) If written memoranda exchanged between the parties during the arbitration proceedings or recognized before the courts, in which one party requests that the dispute be submitted to arbitration, do not oppose the other party to the defense.

- The Civil Procedure (Pre-Arbitration Organization) Act contained a similar provision which stipulated that Article 203 / Clause 2 reads as follows: "2 The arbitration agreement shall only be in writing".

Egyptian law No. 27 of 1994 on arbitration in civil and commercial articles contained a similar provision: article 12 stipulated that an arbitration agreement must be in writing or otherwise void. This agreement had to be in writing if it contained a publisher signed Telegrams or other written means of communication.

The arbitration agreement is written, otherwise it is null and void in court decisions:

- The stipulation of the arbitration must be proven in writing and include the subject matter of the dispute, with a copy of the arbitrator's judgment, failing which the arbitrator's decision shall be null and void. Articles 203/2, 3, 212/5, 216 Civil procedure. On sufficient and justified grounds for the campaign} Federal Supreme Court - Appeal No. 101 of 19 - Session of 17/5/1998 Technical Office Q 20-52 {

- It was decided that it was sufficient for the arbitration of some of the related disputes to contribute to preventing the courts from considering it when one of the parties has it, which was done in writing, specifying the place of arbitration in Egypt or abroad.

(Egyptian Court of Cassation - Appeal No. 654 of 79 B.C. - Hearing of 25/5/2010)

Article 8: Settlement of the dispute involving an arbitration agreement

1. The court seized of a dispute before an arbitral tribunal shall decide on the inadmissibility of the case if the defendant submits it before making a claim or payment relating to the

subject matter of the dispute, unless it finds it invalid or impossible to perform the arbitration contract.

2. The filing of the complaint referred to in the preceding clause shall not prevent the opening or continuation of the arbitral proceedings or the issuance of the arbitral award.

The Civil Code (regulations under the Act on Prior Arbitration) contains a similar provision: article 203 stipulates that: (5) If the parties agree to arbitrate a dispute, it cannot be referred to the courts. At the first hearing, the case may be heard and the arbitration clause is considered null and void.

Egyptian Law No. 27 of 1994 on arbitration in civil and commercial articles contained a similar provision that deleted article 13 as follows:

Article 13:

1. The court seized of a dispute before an arbitral tribunal shall decide on the inadmissibility of the case if the defendant submits it before any claim or defense in court.

2. The filing of the complaint referred to in the preceding paragraph shall not prevent the opening or continuation of the arbitral procedure or award.

Claim the existence of the arbitration clause and the impact of the action on the arbitral proceedings:

1. The argument that the arbitration clause was not admissible because of the arbitration clause - and what was done in the jurisdiction of that jurisdiction - was a non-public defence, even if the name of the admissibility was taken, because the lesson to be learned is payment and its purpose, and not by the name given to it and that the participant must do Before deciding on the merits of the action and removing its right, the appellant's right to pay this payment will be lost if it has not appeared before the court of first instance and indicated it on the action sheet.

2 - to draw an implicit link with the formal defenses of the Court of Matters as long as such extraction was based on justified grounds.

3 - If it is established that the applicant did not appear before the Court of First Instance and that he adhered to the appeal log, the first of the grounds for appealing the existence of the arbitration clause in the contract is placed Arbitration The contested judgment, considering that what the applicant had stated in its appeal sheet concerning the arbitration clause constituted a defense and not an explicit and unequivocal payment, which caused it to lose its right to pay the non-acceptance contained in its above-mentioned defence brief. Corruption can be spoiled by deductions and errors in law enforcement.

4. If the contested verdict is overruled by its refusal to accept the non-admissibility of the case because of the existence of the arbitration clause and its acceptance, it also annuls the judgment rendered pursuant to Article 271/1 of the Code of Procedure.

(Egyptian Court of Cassation - Appeal No. 2372 of 75 BC - hearing of 19/12/2006)

Arbitration is an exceptional means of settling disputes based on ordinary litigation; the arbitration clause does not concern public policy, the court cannot impose its execution on its own initiative, but it must be maintained before it and its waiver may be explicit or implicit. It is established in the documents that the applicant, at the hearing of 10/12/1991, accidentally requested to proceed with the judicial set-off between what was due to him on the amounts pending against the first applicant.

And what can be judged in the initial case and that the prosecutor against them filed a defense brief at the hearing of 31/12/1991 in which he did not claim not to accept this request because of the arbitration clause. They were questioned at a hearing held on 25/2/1992 at certain points in the case.

At the hearing on 20/10/1992, the appellant's attorney was present and asked that the case be maintained without any reference to this argument.

Thus, their right to enforce the arbitration clause would have been removed, as it would be deferred until after they had spoken on the matter. If the contested decision contradicts this consideration and decides in the sub-litigation not to accept this condition and does not fall, it would have violated the law and errors in its application, and this error prevented it from examining the subject of the sub-litigation, in addition to the above is vitiated by invalidated deficiencies and must be annulled for this reason Without having to discuss the rest of the grounds for the appeal.

(Hearing of the Egyptian Court of Cassation No. 1466 of 70, 30/1/2001)

- While Act No. 27 of 1994 on arbitration of civil and commercial articles allowed the appeal to invalidate the arbitrators' verdict, but limited the invalidity to the applicant to the arbitrators' judgment based on the obituary does not justify the invalidity. The argument that the arbitration agreement does not cover the issues raised by the other party during the examination of the dispute (amendment of claims) is withdrawn immediately before the arbitral tribunal, failing which its right is forfeited in accordance with article 22/2 of the same law.

(Appeal of the Egyptian Court of Cassation No. 291 of 70 BC - session 17/6/2001)

Payment term:

- The arbitral tribunal shall decide on the defenses based on the absence of an arbitration agreement, its fall, its invalidity or its non-inclusion in the subject matter of the dispute. Arbitration in civil and commercial matters.

(Appeal of the Egyptian Court of Cassation No. 291 of 70 BC - session 17/6/2001)

- that the party who accedes to the arbitration adopt a positive attitude to oppose at the first session the use of its opponent in the judiciary to assert the right to claim, despite the agreement on arbitration, if there is no objection at this hearing

The arbitration clause becomes null and void and the first hearing is deemed to be the session at which the accused or his lawyer is present for the first time in court.

(Federal Supreme Court Appeal No. 19 of 2015 - hearing on 11/3/2015) Example.

- Appeal No. 357 for 2009 - hearing of July 18, 2009 - example)

- The first hearing is the session during which the defendant represented himself or his agent. The agent's request for a period of time does not change the question of whether the arbitration clause must be respected during the first session, except when the opponent offers to consider the matter or not.

- The presence of an agent of the disputed person against this preliminary hearing and the request for a time limit to respond to the trial without complying with the arbitration obligation, which will be considered null and void because it will not be retained because the arbitration clause was not retained at the initial hearing. In his request, he refrains from taking into account the subject matter of the trial.

(Federal Supreme Court - Appeal No. 556 of year 29 - hearing 15/4/2008)

- Article 203 / section 5 of the Code of Civil Procedure - a provision relating to arbitration proceedings which cannot rely on the provisions relating to defenses contained in Chapter I of Chapter VI of the Code of Civil Procedure and the text of which is clear and explicit and cannot be withdrawn Interpret and search the street intentionally.

(The main body of the book criticizes Article 7, Article 203/5 of the Code of Civil Procedure.)

Chapter III The Arbitral Tribunal

Article 9: Composition of the Arbitral Tribunal

1. The arbitral tribunal shall be formed by agreement of one or more arbitrators between the parties. If this is not the case, the number of arbitrators shall be set at three, unless the body concerned decides otherwise.

2. If there are many arbitrators, their number must be chained, otherwise the arbitration will be invalid.

Article 10: Conditions to be fulfilled by the arbitrator

In addition to the conditions agreed by the parties, the arbitrator must be a natural person who is not a minor, prohibited or deprived of his or her civil rights as a result of bankruptcy, unless he or she is rehabilitated or convicted of a crime or offence violating honour or honesty. For him the spirit.

2. The arbitrator shall not be a member of the board of directors or administrative body of the arbitral institution competent to organize arbitral proceedings in the State.

3. The arbitrator shall not be of a specific gender or nationality, unless the parties or the law agree otherwise.

4. Any person notified of his candidature for arbitration shall declare anything that may raise doubts as to his impartiality or independence. Unless he has previously informed them of this circumstance.

Article 11: Selection of the Arbitral Tribunal

1. The parties may agree on the procedures to be followed for the appointment of the arbitrator(s), as well as on the time and manner of their appointment.

2. If the Arbitral Tribunal consists of an arbitrator and the parties cannot agree on the arbitrator within fifteen (15) days from the date on which one of the parties has requested in writing to inform the other party to do so, the designated party shall appoint him/her at the request of one of the parties. The parties shall not accept an appeal of this decision in any way whatsoever, without prejudice to the provisions of Article 14 of this Law.

3. If the Arbitral Tribunal is composed of three arbitrators, each party shall select one arbitrator on its own side and the two arbitrators appointed shall agree on the choice of the third arbitrator. if one party does not select an arbitrator within fifteen (15) days of receipt of the request by the other party The arbitrators shall appoint the third arbitrator within fifteen (15) days of the date of the last appointment, at the request of the party concerned, at the request of one of the parties, without appeal, without prejudice to the provisions of Article 14.) Of the law.

4. The party concerned shall take into account the conditions required by this Law and those agreed by the parties for the appointment of an independent and impartial arbitrator.

In cases where the authorized party does not appoint the arbitrator in accordance with the procedures specified in the agreement of the parties or in accordance with the provisions of this Law, in the absence of an agreement, either party may request the court to take the necessary measures to complete the training and appointment of the members of the arbitral tribunal. In this respect, there is no possibility of appeal.

6. If a request for the appointment of an arbitrator is made to the party concerned, the claimant shall simultaneously send copies to all other parties and to any arbitrator previously appointed in the same dispute. And all measures taken to appoint any remaining members of the arbitral tribunal.

7. The arbitral tribunal shall be appointed by the third arbitrator appointed in accordance with the provisions of this article, which shall apply in the event that the arbitral tribunal consists of more than three arbitrators.

8. The Court may, at the request of either party, request any arbitration institution of the State to provide it with a list of its specialists.

The Code of Civil Procedure (Pre-Arbitration Legal Regulations) contained provisions that included certain provisions similar to these sections in sections 207.205.20.204.

Egyptian Law No. 27 of 1994 on the arbitration of civil and commercial articles contained similar provisions in articles 15-16-17.

The arbitrator is not a party to the arbitration dispute but a person who enjoys the confidence of the litigants

And their willingness to give him the power to separate the trees from each other by allowing the verdict to be passed once it exists and then do not imagine that the opponent and one disposition at a time.

Due to the complexity and diversity of the dispute, a large number of arbitrators are required in some disputes for which arbitration is necessary, while others are unlikely due to their size and limitations. Cost reduction requires only one arbitrator. They decide what is good for them and determine the number of arbitrators required by the dispute, provided that their number is multiple, which is in accordance with the provisions of article V of the rules of the United Nations Commission, which increases the number of arbitrators to one or three.

3. Unique conditions, eligibility, nationality, independence of the arbitrator, acceptance of his mission and drafting in court decisions:

Although the arbitration is judicial in nature, the arbitral tribunal must respect the basic principles of the dispute

The impartiality and independence of the arbitrator are considered as the fundamental guarantees of the dispute, but the arbitrator has as its origin the fact that he is neutral and independent as long as he has accepted his mission. The appellant did not submit to the trial court evidence of his claim that the arbitrator was invalid in relation to the holding company, which the appellant sued against it for not disclosing this status, and did not receive his response within the time prescribed by law. He cannot adhere to this ground in the field of his application for invalidation of the arbitral award and that the contested judgment is committed in this respect, the obituary in this respect is based on a foundation.

- Although the arbitration is considered to be of a judicial nature, the arbitral tribunal will observe the basic principles of the dispute, whether it is a normal arbitration or an arbitration with a delegation of conciliation, and that the impartiality and independence of the arbitrator are essential qualities of the dispute, but its origin is that it is neutral and independent as long as it has accepted its mission and anyone who claims that the arbitrator is neither neutral nor non-independent must comply with it and prove it as long as he or she became aware of the defect before the arbitral award was made and not after. Consider and set up a judge Dismissing the appellant's defense appeal in light of the obituary notice on the pillar of his conclusion, she was aware of the facts on which she relied on the arbitrators' denial of impartiality before the arbitral award was issued and therefore did not prevent them from relying on them to seek nullity.

- The arbitral award in respect of which the order was sought was in violation of the International Chamber of Commerce in Paris, which requires the arbitrator's independence and impartiality. The administrative body in charge of the arbitration department approved the candidate of the National Committee without informing the parties to the arbitration and, during the arbitration, discovered that the President The arbitral tribunal cannot be objective and impartial, so he asked to be heard, but the administrative body in charge of supervising the arbitration rejected him, considering that the steps of the arbitration had progressed well and that the decisions of the organs of the International Chamber of Commerce in Paris were not beyond the control of justice. The challenge in his blogs does not include a response to the appellant's defense (and to the second) that the arbitrator refrained from participating in the arbitration and Egyptian arbitration law required that the arbitral award include a statement of the reasons why one of the arbitrators refused to participate in the delivery and signing of the arbitral award. Arbitration without disclosing the reasons for the refusal of one of the arbitrators to sign the final verdict, which means that the decision of two persons to voluntarily authorize incompetent persons to pass between them or to settle the dispute by arbitrator or conciliator accepts the conditions.

3. Selection of the arbitral tribunal in judicial decisions

Under articles 204/203 of the Code of Civil Procedure, if the parties to the dispute accept arbitration and have not agreed on the arbitrators' persons, or if one of them abstains from working, withdraws or is dismissed, or if his dismissal is prevented, or if he is prevented from doing so, a dispute will arise between the parties. Concerned The court initially competent to hear the dispute relating to the arbitration and at the request of one of the litigants, the necessary arbitrators may not be the subject of any appeal against the judgment rendered.

(Federal Court of Appeal hearing No. 206 of 27 of 27/12/2015, Technical Office p. 2938)

- As is clear from the contested verdict, he concluded the appointment of an arbitrator to resolve the dispute between the parties as to what the candidate needs in exchange for the creation of drawings by order of the appellant's inheritance. Under the tenth clause of the contract concluded between the parties and the fact that the court is under the general jurisdiction of the arbitral tribunal and that it has been established that the parties have not agreed on the person of the arbitrator, the court's intervention to appoint him does not constitute a violation of the law, but a coherent and effective article of article 204 / of the Civil Procedure Code.

(Appeal of the Federal Supreme Court No. 91 of 27 - hearing 6/3/2006)

- Actors of the provisions of articles 9/17 of the Arbitration Act No. 27 of 1994 - Modification of the fact that the parties to the dispute agree on the choice of arbitrators and on the choice of arbitrators, if they are not and that the arbitral tribunal is composed of three arbitrators, The court referred to in Article IX of the Arbitration Act shall choose an arbitrator within 30 days at the request of one of the parties to the dispute, the arbitrator chosen by the arbitrators appointed or chosen by the arbitrator being chosen by the arbitrator appointed by the other party. The arbitral tribunal shall take into account the arbitrator chosen under the conditions required by law and those agreed by the parties and shall render its decision to choose the arbitrator as a matter of urgency. Cairo, published on 29 April 2003, appointing the potential arbitrator, established in its judicial system that the parties to the arbitration, after having chosen each of the courts, had not appointed a particular arbitrator, which was the cornerstone of the arbitral award rendered on 1 July 2004 before its court and confirmed the contested judgment. To build it on the pleasant grounds of origin Considerable in the newspapers enough for his judicial power to be assured, he would have reached a legally correct conclusion.

(Appeal of the Egyptian Court of Cassation No. 3969 of 75 BC - Session 22/3/2011)

(The date and time of the selection of arbitrators by agreement and the selection of arbitrators by the court:

- Article 9-17 of the Arbitration Act No. 27 of 1994 on civil and commercial articles leading the parties to the dispute to agree on the choice of arbitrators, as well as on the method and time of their selection, the arbitral tribunal being composed of three arbitrators. If one of the parties does not appoint a tribunal within thirty days of receipt of a request from the other party, the arbitrators appointed shall not agree on the choice of the third arbitrator within thirty days of the other party's request, or the arbitrators appointed shall not agree on the choice of the third arbitrator. The tribunal referred to in article IX of the Arbitration Act shall be chosen by the tribunal at the request of one of the parties to the dispute.

The arbitrator chosen by the arbitrators appointed or chosen by the Court shall preside over the arbitral tribunal.

The court must, in the arbitrator of its choice, respect the conditions required by law and those agreed by the parties.

If the parties were asked if they had any objections as to its composition, they replied, denying that this was a new agreement on the selection of arbitrators and not an erroneous order, but the applicant did not submit her new application subject to obituary, except to the referring court after the decision of the Court of Cassation on appeal No. 941 For the year 71 BC in its memorandum of 7 June 2003, after the dispute had continued before the arbitral tribunal and then before the court of invalidity

And willing to spend it by dismissing and rejecting the appeal and it was for good reasons to have its origin fixed in the papers and to achieve a result which eventually sufficed to bring the termination of the contested judgment to that correct result - and that the means

This court can do it the same way as before without breaking it and the obituary becomes unproductive.

(Appeal of the Egyptian Court of Cassation No. 145, 221 for the 74th session of 22/3/2011)

The law is governed by the arbitration agreement and by the fact that arbitrators do not choose their arbitrators:

- Article 17 of the Arbitration of Civil and Commercial Articles Act No. 27 of 1994 stipulates that the parties to the arbitration shall agree on the selection of arbitrators.

If they do not agree, follow the following instructions:

If the arbitral tribunal is composed of an arbitrator, the tribunal referred to in article 9 of this Law shall be chosen by the arbitral tribunal at the request of one of the parties. If the arbitral tribunal is composed of three arbitrators, each of the parties shall choose one arbitrator. If the arbitrators appointed do not agree on the choice of the third arbitrator within 30 days of the date of the last appointment, the court referred to in Article 9 of this Law shall choose him at the request of one of the parties. These judgments apply in the case of the formation of the arbitral tribunal of more than three arbitrators, indicating that the legislator has asked the arbitrators to choose those who decide, otherwise the tribunal has imposed them on the basis of the aforementioned article. Law 27 for the year 1994 in force from 21/5/1994 in the first article of the publication of which imposes its provisions on each arbitration existing at the time of entry into force or after it, even if it is based on an arbitration agreement concluded before its entry into force Against it was put in place under the work of this closely The law of the contested judgment violated this question, and started from the arbitration agreement invoked by saying that without persons identifying the arbitrators, he may have committed an error in the application of the law.

(Appeal of the Egyptian Court of Cassation No. 4791 of 71 BC - session 24/11/2002)

Refrain from participating in the selection of the arbitrator:

- If the opponent's refusal to participate in the selection of the arbitrator or his choice of court is considered as a failure to perform the arbitration contract, the result of his invalidity is absolutely null and void because his case was without purpose. Appeal to the courts having general jurisdiction in all disputes.

- (Call No. 4122 for year 62 BC - Session 27/6/2005)

- (The main body of the book reviews the entitled items that cannot be appointed arbitrators and the appointment of arbitrators in the case of arbitrators or some of them, abstaining from work or retiring, or the dismissal or rejection of arbitration or the bringing together of arbitrators and the identification of arbitrators).

Article 12: Issuance of decisions concerning arbitral proceedings

Any decision in the arbitral proceedings involving more than one arbitrator shall be taken by a majority of the members of the arbitral tribunal, unless the parties agree otherwise.

However, the presiding arbitrator may make decisions on procedural matters if the parties or other members of the arbitral tribunal so permit.

Article 13: Breach of the selection procedures of the arbitral tribunal

If one of the parties does not comply with the procedures for the selection of arbitrators, which have been agreed or have not been agreed, or if the arbitrators appointed do not agree on a necessary matter to be agreed or if others, including the authorized party, do not perform the tasks entrusted to them in this respect, one of the parties shall take the necessary measures, unless the agreement provides for another means of carrying out this procedure and appeals against this decision are not accepted by any means.

The Code of Civil Procedure (Pre-Arbitration Legal Regulations) did not contain a similar provision and Egyptian Law No. 27 of 1994 on the Arbitration of Civil and Commercial Goods contained a similar provision.

Including the right to subject these procedures to the rules in force in any arbitration organization or center inside or outside the Arab Republic of Egypt.

Memorandum on Arbitration Procedure of the Egyptian Law on Arbitration Procedures dealt with in Chapter IV (Articles 25 to 38). The provisional regulatory rules established by the legislator to counter the imposition by which the parties agreed on the procedural rules and noted in those rules left the arbitral tribunal considerable scope to choose the most appropriate procedural rules.

Agreement on the procedures followed by the arbitral tribunal in judicial decisions:

- Article 25 of Act No. 27 of 1994 promulgating a law on arbitration in civil and commercial matters states that the legislature has granted the parties to the arbitration the freedom to agree on one of the procedures to be followed by the arbitral tribunal, whether it is in force in an organization or in an arbitration center. In Egypt or abroad, in the absence of an agreement on the application of any of these rules of procedure, the arbitral tribunal is free to choose the procedures it considers appropriate.

This Court has decided that one of the statements to be included in the judgment on the rules of procedure.

(Appeal No. 414 of 71 BC - hearing on 8/1/2009)

Rules of procedure that Egyptian law does not allow to derogate from the agreement of the parties on the referral of the arbitration and its proceedings to the arbitration rules of the Cairo Arbitration Centre.

Article 1 of the Arbitration Rules of the Cairo Regional Arbitration Centre read as follows:

1- If two parties agree in writing to submit disputes relating to this contract to arbitration in accordance with the arbitration system of the Regional Centre for International Commercial Arbitration in Cairo, such disputes shall be settled in accordance with these Rules, taking into account any amendments agreed in writing between the parties.

2. These Rules shall govern the arbitration, unless it is incompatible with a rule in which a provision of the law applicable to the arbitration cannot be infringed by the parties. Article 22 of the Civil Code stipulates that the rules of jurisdiction and all procedural matters provided for in the law of the country where the proceedings are instituted or prosecuted shall apply, the rules of procedure which Egyptian law does not allow to derogate shall prevail over the agreement of the parties concerning the referral of the arbitration and the proceedings. Arbitration procedure and rules of arbitration of an arbitration organization or centers, including the Cairo Regional Arbitration Center.

(There were 648 appeals filed by the Egyptian Court of Cassation in the year 73 BC, 5745, 6467, 6787 in the year 75 BC - hearing 13/12/2005)

The Code of Civil Procedure included a pre-arbitral legal regulation similar to some of the provisions of this article of article 207

The Egyptian law No. 27 of 1994 concerning arbitration in civil and commercial articles contained similar provisions in articles 18-19-20-21 years.

Article 18:

1. The arbitrator may only be dismissed if circumstances raise serious doubts as to his impartiality and independence

2. No party to the arbitration may dismiss the arbitrator appointed or who participated in his or her appointment, except for a reason determined after that appointment.

Article 19:

1. The request for restitution shall be submitted in writing to the Arbitral Tribunal, stating the reasons for the reply, within ten days of the date on which the claimant became aware of the formation of the Tribunal or the circumstances on which the reply was based.

2. A person who has already submitted a request for restitution from the same arbitrator in the same arbitration will not be admitted.

3. The appellant may appeal against the judgment by dismissing his application within 30 days from the date of its announcement to the court referred to in Article 9 of this Law, without being able to appeal against his judgment.

4. The filing of a request for restitution or an appeal against an arbitral award rendered by refusing to suspend the arbitral proceedings shall not entail the suspension of the arbitral proceedings, and if the arbitrator is dismissed, either by the arbitral tribunal.

Or from the court at the hearing of the appeal, the consequences of the arbitration proceedings, including the arbitral award, are considered as if they were not.

Article 20:

If the arbitrator is unable to perform his or her duties or fails to perform his or her duties or interrupts the performance in such a way as to cause undue delay in the arbitration proceedings and does not withdraw and the parties have not agreed to dismiss him or her, the court referred to in Article 9 of this Law may order the termination of his or her duties at the request of the parties.

Article 21:

If the arbitrator's term of office ends by dismissal, removal, revocation or for any other reason, a replacement shall be appointed in accordance with the procedures followed in the selection of the arbitrator whose term of office has ended.

Egypt's arbitration law was discussed in response to the Minister of Justice to explain the legal philosophy that led to the idea of submitting a request for a response to the same body, said Dr. Edward Ghali Golden, a member of the board, said it would be difficult to prevent this and that a request for a response would not be feasible. Arbitration As I said earlier, in order to reduce delays and procedure, the request for restitution is addressed directly to the Court of Appeal.

Mr. Minister of Justice:

Of course, the idea of shortening the time limits and procedures for bringing cases directly to the Court of Appeal is an opposite thought to another thought and remember from the Code of Procedure that we said that when you want to answer the judge, the judge considers that this answer has pushed defenses and then annexed to the subject. The case was then referred to the Court of Appeal, which prompted the judge to react in order to speed up the processing of the case.

Therefore, the speed of the decision in these cases requires that the court or body that is being pushed to decide on this request be a trend and a philosophy of the philosophies on which the examination of the law of oral argument is based if this draft has adopted this view. He requested a response, continued the case and then referred the entire case to the Court of Appeal and thus upheld what had been concluded.

Response of the arbitral tribunal or one of its members to court decisions:

- The submission of a request for restitution shall not result in the suspension of the arbitration proceedings. The litigants are in their neutrality in order to be on an equal footing with the judicial system applicable to courts of all types and degrees, so that if the litigant considered that he or she would not have the right to do so because of his or her suspicions to the arbitrator, it was justified to submit a written request within a specified period to the arbitral tribunal. If the arbitrator does not withdraw If the appeal is submitted free of charge to the competent court in accordance with Article 9) of the same law, without prejudice to the right of the Authority to complete the arbitration proceedings, the claimant shall reply.

If his request to complete the proceedings of this application before the above-mentioned court is granted, in accordance with Articles 148 to 165 of the Code of Procedure, as common law in this area for contentious proceedings

Considering the absence of the articles of Law No. 27 of 1994 in the declaration to what was so it was determined on the basis of the judgment codes issued at the hearing of 21/2/2007 that the company against which the chairman /........... of the jury asked to reply on the grounds that his brother, the adviser /... works for the bank, raises doubts as to whether the arbitrator should refer the case to the competent court and continue to hear the request for arbitration, in accordance with the above-mentioned law, the arbitrator must submit a request for referral by the chairman of the Authority, in accordance with his justification, in this case he must refer the request to the competent court. However, as the Commission did not forward the request for an answer, he only specified that the brother of the President of the Arbitral Tribunal was not an employee of the Bank, but a foreign legal adviser who had consulted on certain issues, including the subject of the dispute, as well as on his withdrawal from the legal profession after having been appointed Chairman of the Dispute Resolution Committees. In this respect, the Authority itself lifted the assignment and chose the applicant to bring an appeal alone before the competent court, by submitting his application, even if he decided to reject his application on the basis of the justifications mentioned, contrary to the text of Article 19 above. Law No. 8 of 2000.

Considering that the contested judgment contradicted that examination, it was concluded that the arbitral tribunal was not required to refer the arbitrator's request for referral to the court referred to in Article IX on its own initiative until the applicant applied to that court as an interested party who had submitted the request for a reply. It is inconceivable that the claimant for the execution of the claim should be referred to the competent court, but the arbitral tribunal is entrusted with the transfer of this claim and completes the remaining proceedings in accordance with the previous declaration. Other grounds for appeal.

(Appeal of the Egyptian Court of Cassation No. 9568 for the year 79 BC - hearing 14/3/2011)

Article 16/3 of Act No. 27 of 1994 promulgating a law on arbitration in civil and commercial law provides that "the acceptance of the mission by the arbitrator shall be in writing and shall disclose, upon acceptance, any circumstances that might cast doubt on his independence or impartiality"; Article 18 stipulates that "the arbitrator may be dismissed only if there are circumstances that raise serious doubts as to his impartiality or independence. No party to the arbitration may remove the arbitrator who appointed him or her or participated in his or her appointment, except for the reasons for his or her determination after that appointment." "The request for restitution shall be addressed in writing to the Arbitral Tribunal, stating the reasons for the reply within fifteen days from the date of receipt. If the arbitrator whose request is not accepted is not granted within fifteen days from the date of submission of the request, he shall be referred without charge to the court referred to in Article 9 of this Law for a decision by a non-reviewable judgment. However, in the event of circumstances that cast doubt on the arbitrator's independence or impartiality, the arbitrator shall disclose them as soon as he accepts his mission.

However, if he does not disclose it after having established that it does not raise doubts as to his independence or impartiality, the arbitral party must be informed of these circumstances after his appointment and considers that they give rise to them. The arbitrator may not be referred to the court provided for in article 9 of the same law within fifteen days from the date of filing of the request and may not be the subject of a judgment that is not subject to appeal, so that the arbitration proceedings continue without opposition. An arbitral award cannot be complied with simply because the arbitrator has not disclosed the circumstances that may give rise to doubts. If a party objects to the arbitrator, the arbitrator may withdraw from the arbitration, but the arbitrator may continue to act despite this objection. Neither party replied and obtained a verdict in this response. Considering that the contested verdict correctly indicated in his reports that the applicant did not take the necessary steps to dismiss the arbitrator appointed by him within the time limits prescribed by law and presented his defense in this respect, which he raises with regard to the failure to disclose this arbitrator when accepting the arbitration of the circumstance mentioned The obituary will be lost until it has made the restitution provided for by law.

(Appeal of the Egyptian Court of Cassation No. 240 of 74 BC - Session 9/2/2010)

Note: As there are no judicial decisions rendered by the Federal Supreme Court in the United Arab Emirates pursuant to the provisions of this article, we cite for domestication some of the judgments rendered under arbitration provisions in the Code of Civil Procedure (the legal regulation before arbitration)

- The legal obstacles that make the judge unfit to hear the case are the same as those that prevent the judgment from being exercised.

- Whereas the parties are free to choose the arbitrator if their appointment is not provided for, as long as the agreed arbitrator is not a party to one of the parties or a person who has already made his opinion known in this dispute, he loses his independence and impartiality

And the necessary integrity in the arbitral tribunal, which constitutes an alternative to the judiciary with inherent jurisdiction to consider all disputes, except what is excluded by a special provision.

(Federal Supreme Court - Appeal 3.3 for the year 2012 - hearing of 13/11/2012)

Respond to his condition every time he has a reason for disability.

- Example of a defective court favorable to the applicant's decision not to accept the arbitrator's request for referral, even though he has already submitted a report on the dispute, which loses the necessary impartiality, independence and impartiality of the arbitral tribunal.

(Federal Supreme Court - Appeal No. 379 of 2013 - Hearing of 21/01/2014)

(The body of this book will be reviewed under the headings Appointment, Revocation and Invalidity).

Death or dismissal of an arbitrator in court decisions

- The arbitration clause is a consensual contract if its elements are positive and acceptable, and it is possible to arbitrate.

(Egyptian Court of Cassation Appeal No. 6529, 6530 for the year 62 BC - hearing on 12/1/2000)

- If it is clear from the documents that the arbitration consultation took place with the right of acceptance and acceptance issued by both parties and that two arbitrators were revoked with the consent of the parties to the dispute and signed by the names of the individual arbitrators, there is no effect on the validity of the participation as long as the will of the parties was chosen If the contested judgment violated this consideration, the arbitration provision was invalidated on the ground that the dismissal of two of them constituted a cancellation of the arbitration provision.

As indicated by the judgment on the grounds that the appointment of the person of the arbitrator of the basic pillars of the arbitration board and the rejection of this arbitration are collapsing, the violation of the law is vitiated.

(Egyptian Court of Cassation Appeal No. 6529, 6530 for the year 62 BC - hearing on 12/1/2000)

- If the arbitration clause is the subject of the proceedings, which must be null and void, it is a consensual contract whose elements are valid and acceptable between the two parties, the subject matter of the dispute being subject to arbitration having been signed by two arbitrators. The motion to set aside a judgment is unfounded. This opinion does not alter the first appellant's argument against the death of the arbitrator, who cannot be appointed by the court because he was an arbitrator authorized by the conciliation.

Because this is due to the fact that the arbitrator died after the participation became valid, this death is only an obstacle to the implementation of the participation is not a reason for his invalidity, because - and what has been done by the judiciary of this court - when the arbitrator authorized reconciliation can only be appointed with the agreement of the parties, and the result If, after the arbitration procedure, there is a reason preventing the arbitrator from ruling, the arbitration contract shall be performed only by a new agreement between the parties in dispute against another arbitrator, in accordance with article 824 of the previous Code of Procedure applicable to the case, whose judgment shall be considered as a public policy.

All this shall be without prejudice to the conditions of detention of the subject matter of the dispute that were available prior to the arbitrator's death.

(Appeal of the Egyptian Court of Cassation No. 489 out of 37, hearing in British Columbia, 24/2/1973)

Article 18: Jurisdiction in arbitration matters

1. The courts shall be convened to deal with arbitration matters referred by this Law to the competent court in accordance with the procedural law in force in the State and shall be the exclusive jurisdiction until the end of any arbitral proceedings.

2. The President of the Court may order, at the request of either party or the arbitral tribunal, to take such interim measures as he may deem necessary for the purposes of an existing or potential arbitral procedure, either before or during it.

3. The taking of the measures referred to in the preceding paragraph of this article shall not result in the suspension of the arbitral proceedings or a waiver of the arbitration agreement.

4. If the President of the Court makes an order in accordance with paragraph 2 of this Article, the effect of this order shall be terminated only in whole or in part, except by decision of the President of the Court.

Article 19: Jurisdiction of the arbitral tribunal to decide on its jurisdiction

(1) The arbitral tribunal shall decide on any payment relating to its lack of jurisdiction, including on the basis of the absence of an arbitration agreement, its nullity or the non-inclusion of the subject matter of the dispute.

2. If the arbitral tribunal determines, in a preliminary decision, that it has jurisdiction, any party within fifteen days from the date of its announcement may request the tribunal to rule. The arbitral proceedings shall be suspended pending the decision on such request, unless the arbitral tribunal decides to continue them at the request of one of the parties.

3. The party requesting the continuation of the arbitration proceedings shall bear the costs of the arbitration.

If the court has decided that the arbitral tribunal does not have jurisdiction.

Article 20:

Time limit for maintaining payment of the non-jurisdiction of the arbitral tribunal

1. The argument that the arbitral tribunal has jurisdiction for a period not exceeding the time limit for the presentation of the defense of the arbitrator referred to in article 30 of this Law shall be followed. The arbitral tribunal may in any event accept the delay in payment if it considers that the delay is due to reasonable cause.

2. The appointment or participation in the appointment of an arbitrator by either party shall not entail the loss of the right to exercise the defenses referred to in point (1) of this Article.

The Code of Civil Procedure - the pre-arbitral legal organization - did not contain a similar provision.

Egyptian Law No. 27 of 1994 on the arbitration of civil and commercial articles contained provisions similar to article 22, which stipulated that:

Article 22

1. The arbitral tribunal shall decide on the defenses based on its lack of jurisdiction, including those based on the absence, fall, invalidity or nullity of the arbitration agreement.

2. These defenses shall be maintained within a period not exceeding the time limit for the defense of the defendant referred to in Article 30(2) of this Law so that the appointment of an arbitrator or participation in his appointment does not deprive him of his right to present any of these defenses. The argument that the arbitration agreement does not cover the issues raised by the other party in the course of the dispute must be raised immediately, failing which the right will be forfeited.

3. The arbitral tribunal shall decide on the defences referred to in paragraph 1 of this article before deciding the case or adding it to the subject-matter to decide them together; if it decides to reject the payment, it may only be invoked by filing an action for annulment of the arbitral award terminating the dispute in accordance with article 53 of that law

It is established that the rule of granting the arbitral tribunal the power to rule on defences based on its lack of jurisdiction, which is known in arbitration case law - jurisdiction - is a rule that constitutes a fundamental pillar of the arbitration system.

Jurisdiction is the power to legislate in a dispute and lack of jurisdiction is the loss of that power.

The French Court of Cassation has retained the right of the arbitral tribunal to determine its jurisdiction and to continue to hear the dispute despite the nullity of the original contract. Allegations concerning the basis and scope of its jurisdiction, a problem known as (jurisdiction) and confirmed by the new legislative text, the principle of the independence of the arbitration contract from the initial contract in the fields of purely national relations (Professor / Samia Rashid in International Relations of the special edition in 1984, p. 86).

Determination of the arbitral tribunal in the defenses related to its lack of jurisdiction before court decisions

- Under article 21/1 of the UNCITRAL Rules on the Application by the Parties of the Arbitral Tribunal of the Application of Defenses Based on Inconsistency, including the Existence of the Arbitration Clause or the Separation or Validity of the Arbitration Clause.

(Call No. 196 for the year 74 BC - Session 23/2/2010)

- When the contested verdict has established its judgment, rejecting the payment made by the claimants to invalidate the arbitral award for non-compliance with that payment, the arbitral tribunal being competent to rule on the defenses to the invalidity of the arbitration agreement. The court may not deal with the relationship of litigants with their agents unless the person concerned refuses to represent his or her agent. The provisions of the decision are in conformity with the law, especially since invalidity is a decision in favor of the dispute, the obituary is unfounded.

(Call No. 196 for the year 74 BC - Session 23/2/2010)

The decision - within the jurisdiction of that court - that arbitration is an exceptional means of settling discounts is based on a departure from standard dispute resolution methods and on the cost of guarantees. It is based on the consent and acceptance of the parties as a means of resolving all or part of disputes that have arisen or may arise between them in a contractual or non-contractual relationship. And other arbitration procedures,

Article 21/4 of the 1976 UNCITRAL Arbitration Rules (UNCITRAL) stipulated that the arbitral tribunal in general should decide on such payment in its final judgment.

Considering that it has been established from the documents that the 1993 contractual agreement containing the arbitration clause concluded between the applicant company - the business establishment Al Manara in the emirate of Abu Dhabi in the United Arab Emirates - and the contested company - the Moawad Company for Jewellery and Watches in the Kingdom of Saudi Arabia - was included in Article X. The parties agree to settle any dispute between them amicably by arbitration with the Regional Centre for International Commercial Arbitration in Cairo.

The arbitral award rendered by majority vote shall be final and binding on both parties, who shall have the broadest powers to apply the laws, commercial customs and principles of justice between the parties.

This means that the parties to the arbitration have determined the law applicable to the arbitration between them if they are willing to allow the arbitral tribunal to apply the law and the customs and principles of commercial justice between the parties, which has led the body to apply the law of civil transactions of the United Arab Emirates, the law of the State of the company concerned. As the law of the State in which the contract was concluded and began to apply it, the parties have also defined the issues that the arbitral tribunal is entitled to decide, namely all disputes and disputes that arise between them in the performance of the contract.

Thus, the arbitral tribunal may decide on the lack of jurisdiction after having concluded that the contract of the agreement in question is a contract distinct from the contract of 4/4/1980 for the difference between its parties, and the settlement of the case after both parties have expressed their defence and submitted Their compensation, as a dispute between the parties resulting from the implementation of the agreement concluded between them, will be judged in accordance with the will of the parties and will therefore not have exceeded the limits of its mandate and will not be imposed. The arbitration clause was a means of settling disputes based on ordinary litigation; the arbitration clause does not concern public policy and can be lifted explicitly or implicitly. The applicant company has not yet invoked before the Court of Appeal the annulment of the arbitration for the purpose of its execution. The arbitration contained in the agreement, the act of the case, despite the waiver of the contested company against it, does not agree to raise it for the first time before the Court of Cassation and, consequently, the conclusion of the contested company's verdict has been duly approved by law and sacrifices this text on the merits.

(Appeal of the Egyptian Court of Cassation No. 145 of 68 BC - hearing 28/5/2007)

Article 21: Provisional or protective measures

1. Subject to the provisions of Article 18 of this Law, unless the parties agree otherwise, the arbitral tribunal may, at the request of one of the parties or on its own initiative, order one of them to take such provisional or protective measures as may be required by the nature of the dispute, in particular.

(A) order the preservation of evidence that may be essential to the resolution of the dispute;

(B) takes the necessary measures to preserve the products in dispute, for example, by ordering that they be deposited with a third party or that you sell perishable products;

(C) the maintenance of assets and funds through which a subsequent decision can be implemented;

(D) Maintain or restore the status quo until the dispute is resolved.

(E) order an action to prevent the occurrence of imminent damage or prejudice to the arbitral process or order a failure to act that could cause damage or prejudice to the arbitration.

2. The arbitral tribunal may require the applicant for interim or provisional measures to provide sufficient security to cover the expenses incurred by such measures and may also incur all damages resulting from the enforcement of such orders if the arbitral tribunal subsequently decides not to have the power to make them.

3. The arbitral tribunal may modify, suspend or cancel an interim measure ordered at the request of one of the parties or on its own initiative in exceptional cases and with prior notification to the parties.

4. A party whose interim order has been made in its favor after having obtained the written authorization of the Arbitral Tribunal may apply to the Tribunal for an order to enforce the order made by the Arbitral Tribunal or any party to it within fifteen (15) days from the date of receipt of the request. Application for authorization or enforcement under this Article to all other parties at the same time.

The Civil Procedure (Pre-Arbitration Judicial Organization) Act did not contain a similar provision.

Egyptian Law No. 27 of 1994 on Arbitration of Civil and Commercial Goods contained approximately the same text. The content of article 24 was as follows:

1. The arbitral tribunal may decide that the arbitral tribunal may, at the request of any of them, order any of them to take such interim or provisional measures as the nature of the dispute requires and request that sufficient security be provided to cover the cost of the measure it has ordered.

2. If the person to whom the order is made fails to comply with it, the arbitral tribunal may, at the request of the other party, authorize that party to take the necessary measures to comply with it.

Without prejudice to the right of that party to request the President of the Court, referred to in Article 9 of this Law, to order its execution.

- Article 21 of the Arbitration Act of the United Arab Emirates lists the provisional and interim measures taken by the arbitral tribunal, which are mentioned, but are not limited to, and specifies the guarantees for the issuance of such decisions and the modalities of appeal before the court competent for their implementation. The new arbitration procedure takes such interim or protective measures from the jurisdiction of the courts to the jurisdiction of the arbitral tribunal - only the role of the competent court is to enforce them, which was contrary to the practice prior to this legislation if the Federal Supreme Court decided that the courts had jurisdiction to order remuneration. If the contracting parties do not agree in the basic contract or in the arbitration clause on the competence of the arbitrator or arbitrators to take provisional or urgent measures, their agreement to arbitrate the dispute concerning the interpretation of the execution order. The contract concluded between the parties does not give the arbitral tribunal the right to have the authority or competence to decide such proceedings or cases and does not prevent individuals from having recourse to the courts to order or judge them to own the general and inherent jurisdiction, thus benefiting from asylum. In this case, the courts may waive adherence to the arbitration clause, the scope of which is limited to the merits of the dispute.

(Federal Supreme Court - Appeal No. 225 of 24 - hearing 16/11/2002 Technical Office Q 24-2198)

Fourth item

Arbitration procedure

Article 22: Introduction or intervention of new parties to the arbitration

The arbitral tribunal may authorize the inclusion or occupation of a third party among its parties by arbitration, at the request of one of the parties or the intervener, provided that it is a party to the arbitration agreement and after having given all parties, including the third party, the opportunity to hear their statements.

Article 23: Determination of the procedures to be followed

1. Subject to Article 10.2 of this Law, the parties may agree on the procedures to be followed by the arbitral tribunal in carrying out the arbitration, in particular by subjecting them to the rules in force in any arbitration body inside or outside the State.

2. In the absence of agreement on the observance of certain procedures, the arbitral tribunal may determine the procedures it considers appropriate, in accordance with the provisions of this Law and without prejudice to the fundamental principles of the dispute and the international conventions to which the State is a party.

Article 24: Declarations

(1) The provisions of this Article shall apply unless the parties agree otherwise:

(A) Any written communication shall be deemed to have been received: if delivered to the addressee in person, or to his place of work or habitual residence or to the postal address known to the parties, specified in the arbitration agreement or in the instrument governing the relationship covered by the arbitration; The addressee shall be deemed to have received such addresses if they were sent to the addressee's last known place of business, his habitual residence or postal address by registered mail or by courier or by any other means providing written proof of attempted delivery. Any fax or then e-mail address already Parties to use it in their relations with each other or already a statement of the parties by the other party in a message.

B. The message is deemed to have been received by the addressee on the day it is delivered, in accordance with this Act. In all cases, the receipt will be deemed to have been received if it was received or sent before 6 p.m. in the country in which the correspondence was received.

2) To calculate the time limits under this law: The time limit from the day after the day on which the message was received or any other correspondence. Public holidays or working holidays during this period are included in the calculation of this period.

3. The provisions of this article shall not apply to correspondence made in judicial proceedings.

Article 25: Waiver of the right of objection

If one of the parties continues the arbitration proceedings with knowledge of a violation of the arbitration agreement or a provision of this Law that may agree to violate it, no objection to such violation shall have been filed within the agreed time limit or within seven (7) days from the date on which the flag was made in the absence of an agreement. This was considered a violation of his right to object.

Article 26: Equality between the parties to the arbitration

The parties to the arbitration shall be treated equally and shall have every opportunity to present and defend their claims.

Article 27: Opening of arbitration proceedings

1. The arbitral proceedings shall commence on the day following the completion of the composition of the arbitral tribunal, unless the parties agree otherwise.

2. A declaration of arbitration is considered as an action for the signature of the pre-trial detention.

Article 28: Place of arbitration

1. The parties may agree on the place of arbitration, failing which the arbitral tribunal shall determine the place of arbitration.

This takes into account the circumstances of the case and the relevance of the venue of the meeting to its parties.

2. The arbitral tribunal, unless the parties agree otherwise:

(A) To hold arbitral hearings at any place it considers appropriate for any arbitration proceedings, the parties having been announced well in advance of the date of the hearing.

(B) Arbitration sessions shall be held with the parties or shall be the subject of deliberations using modern means of communication and electronic technology; the Arbitral Tribunal shall deliver or transmit the minutes of the hearing to the parties.

Article 29: Language of the arbitration

1. The arbitration procedure shall be conducted in Arabic, unless the parties agree otherwise.

2. The agreed or specified language shall apply to the arbitral proceedings and to any written memorandum submitted by the parties as well as to any oral argument and to any arbitral award, decision or other statement made by the arbitral tribunal, unless otherwise agreed.

3. Subject to the provisions of Federal Law No. (6) of 2012 on the organization of the profession of translator, the Arbitral Tribunal may decide to attach all or part of the written documents submitted during the proceedings in the language or languages used in the arbitration;

In the case of several languages, translation may be limited.

Article 30: Brief and defense

1. Unless the parties otherwise agree or the Arbitral Tribunal decides otherwise, the arbitrator shall, within fourteen (14) days of the composition of the Arbitral Tribunal, send to the arbitrator against him and to each of the arbitrators a written statement containing his name, address, address and explanation;

A determination of the issues, its claims and any other matters to be agreed between the parties is indicated.

2. Unless the parties agree or the Arbitral Tribunal decides otherwise, the arbitrator shall, within fourteen (14) days from the day following the receipt of the statement sent by the arbitrator referred to in the preceding paragraph of this article, be delivered to each of the arbitrators. The Tribunal may include any incidental or compensatory claim related to the subject matter of the dispute or claim a resulting right to pay compensation, even at a later stage of the proceedings, if the Arbitral Tribunal considers that the circumstances so warrant.

3. Unless otherwise agreed by the parties, each party may amend or supplement its claims or defenses or file a counterclaim during the arbitral proceedings, unless the arbitral tribunal decides not to accept it in order to avoid delays in the settlement of the dispute or because it is beyond its jurisdiction, the arbitral tribunal in its decision shall determine the principles of the trial and the rights of the defense.

Article 31: Documents in support of the declaration and in response to the defense

Each party may attach a statement of the case or a defense brief, as the case may be, to copies of the documents on which it is based or may indicate all or part of the documents and evidence to be presented, while respecting the right of the other party to have access to them. The claim has the right to request the presentation of the original documents or documents on which the parties are based, as well as the right of the parties to examine them.

Article 32: Failure to fulfil the obligations of the parties

1. Subject to the provisions of Article 30 of this Law, unless the parties agree otherwise, the following points shall be observed:

If the arbitrator fails to submit, without valid excuse, the statement of the arbitral proceedings in accordance with the provisions of this Law and the parties have agreed to follow the proceedings, the arbitral tribunal may decide to terminate the proceedings if it is satisfied that there is an undue and unjustified delay by the arbitrator in pursuing his claim. Fair or unfair against the defendant against him.

2. If the arbitrator fails to file a defense, the arbitral tribunal shall continue the arbitration proceedings without the arbitrator acknowledging his claim against the arbitrator, but the same decision shall apply if the arbitrator fails to present his defense in response to a counterclaim.

3. If a party fails to attend the hearing or submit the requested documents or take action without valid excuse, the arbitral tribunal may continue the arbitral proceedings and conclude what it considers appropriate in the light of the actions and violations of that party, justified by the circumstances of the arbitral proceedings. Judgment of the dispute based on the evidence at their disposal.

Article 33: Sessions and evidence

1. Arbitral hearings are confidential, unless the parties agree otherwise.

2. Unless the parties agree otherwise, the arbitral tribunal may decide to hold pleadings to present evidence or pleadings, or to continue the proceedings on the basis of the presentation of documents and other material evidence. Appropriate procedures at the request of a party.

3. The sessions can be conducted through modern means of communication that do not require the presence of the parties.

4. The arbitral tribunal shall notify the parties of the dates of the meetings to be held well in advance of the date specified by the arbitral tribunal.

5. The parties may, at their own expense, engage legal experts, attorneys and other persons to represent them before the arbitral tribunal.

6. The summary of the proceedings of each session of the arbitral tribunal shall be recorded in minutes and a copy shall be provided to each of the parties.

7. Unless otherwise agreed by the parties, witnesses, including experts, shall be heard in accordance with the law in force in the State.

8. The arbitral tribunal has the discretion to determine the rules of evidence to be followed and the extent to which the evidence presented by one of the parties concerning the fact or opinion of the experience is admissible, correlated or assessed.

It may also specify the time, manner and form in which such evidence is exchanged and the manner in which it is submitted to the Commission.

Article 34: Use of experts

1. Unless otherwise agreed by the parties, the arbitral tribunal may decide to appoint one or more experts to present its report, determine its mandate and duration, and send a copy of its decision to the parties.

2. Each Party shall provide the expert with information relating to the dispute and shall allow the expert to examine and examine such documents, property, immovable property or movable or immovable property in connection with the dispute,

The arbitral tribunal shall decide any dispute between the expert and a party in this respect.

3. Before accepting his appointment, the expert shall submit to the arbitral tribunal and the parties a statement of his qualifications, as well as his impartiality and independence.

The arbitral tribunal shall decide on any objection to the appointment of such expert and its decision shall be final.

4. No Party may object to the qualifications, impartiality or independence of the expert unless the objection is based on grounds known to that Party after its appointment.

5. The arbitral tribunal shall transmit to each of the Parties a copy of the expert's report as soon as it is filed and shall give them the opportunity to submit its observations on the report within the specified time limits.

6. After submitting the expert's report, the arbitral tribunal may decide on its own initiative or at the request of one of the parties to hold a hearing to hear the expert's observations, giving the parties the opportunity to hear and discuss the content of his report and to examine any document based on his report. He shall be appointed by him to express his opinion on the matters dealt with in the report of the expert appointed by the arbitral tribunal, unless the parties agree otherwise.

The fees and expenses of the expert appointed by the arbitral tribunal under this article shall be borne by the parties, as determined by the arbitral tribunal.

Article 35: Testimony

The arbitral tribunal may hear witnesses, including experienced witnesses, through modern means of communication that do not require their personal presence at the hearing.

Article 36: The power of wisdom to order the presentation of evidence

1. The arbitral tribunal may, on its own initiative or at the request of a party, request the assistance of the Court for any evidence.

The Court may, within the limits of its powers, order the execution of the request and in the presence of witnesses before the arbitral tribunal, in order to present and make oral statements, or to produce documents or any other evidence.

The application shall be submitted to the President of the Court.

(A) convict any witness who fails to appear or refuses without legal justification to answer to the penalties provided for by the legislation in force in the State;

B) The judgment by which a third party has been instructed to produce a document in its possession that is necessary to adjudicate the dispute.

(C) Order the judicial delegation.

- The civil procedure (regulation of the pre-arbitration law) did not contain similar provisions.

Egyptian Law No. 27 of 1994 on the Arbitration of Civil and Commercial Goods included articles containing similar (and perhaps similar) regulations to these provisions stipulated in articles 25:38.

(Check the book table in the headings.

"The interruption, suspension, fall and abandonment of the dispute in the arbitral proceedings, the place and time of the arbitration sessions" and "the power of the arbitrator to prove, delegate an expert, hear witnesses, keep lines and conduct the decisive oath, to take due account of judicial recognition, the language of the proceedings, public hearings)

Arbitration procedures in court decisions:

Seat of arbitration: -

If the Code of Civil Procedure does not provide for the invalidity of the arbitration, if the place of arbitration is not specified in the document, any objection to the contested decision on this ground will be rendered unfounded.

(Appeal of the Federal Supreme Court No. 360 out of 24 - hearing of 21/12/2004 at the Technical Office, 26 p. 2646)

- Article 28 of the Arbitration Act provides that the arbitral tribunal has the power to meet at any place it deems appropriate to conduct any arbitration proceedings, including an inspection. The arbitral tribunal may appoint one or more experts to submit a written or oral report to be proved in the minutes of the hearing. In accordance with the provisions of article 25 of the Code of Procedure and article 31 of the BC Proof of the invalidity of the inspection carried out by the arbitral tribunal without the presence of a clerk writing the related work, whereas this was not required by Act No. 27 of 1994 on arbitration and that this invalidity influenced the verdict on the basis of the invalid inspection concluded at the conclusion of the judicial power. The reasons are defective.

(Appeal of the Egyptian Court of Cassation No. 4721 of 73 B.C. - session 27/12/2007)

- Article 28 / 2.1 of the Arbitration Act No. 27 of 1994 stipulates that the parties to the arbitration may agree on the place of arbitration in Egypt or abroad.

(Appeal of the Egyptian Court of Cassation No. 4721 of 73 B.C. - hearing of 27/12/2007)

As stated in article 36 of the same Act concerning the experts' report, it stipulated that the arbitral tribunal could appoint one or more experts to submit a written or oral report to be proved in the minutes of the hearing. The Law on Pleadings and Article 31 of the Law on Evidence of the Invalidity of the Interrogation Conducted by the Arbitral Tribunal without the presence of a clerk writing a report of the proceedings relating thereto, which was not required by Arbitration Law No. 27 of 1994 and which affected the verdict because it was based on the invalid inspection by the judiciary. The judgment contested that a defective one.

(Appeal of the Egyptian Court of Cassation No. 4721 of 73 B.C. - hearing of 27/12/2007).

- Pursuant to the provisions of article 28 / 2.1 of the Arbitration Act No. 27 of 1994 - according to which the parties to the arbitration agreement at the place of arbitration in Egypt or abroad, in the absence of an agreement, the arbitral tribunal designated the place of arbitration, taking into account the circumstances of the case and the ability of the parties.

(Appeal of the Egyptian Court of Cassation No. 4721 of 73 B.C. - hearing of 27/12/2007).

Language of arbitration in court decisions:

Although the meaning of Article 8 and the first and second paragraphs of Article 29 of Law No. 27 of 1994 on the Arbitration of Civil and Commercial Articles, the arbitration shall be conducted in Arabic, unless the parties agree or the Arbitral Tribunal does not determine another language, which applies to the language of the notes or written statements. However, if one of the parties to the dispute continues its arbitration proceedings, knowing that there has been a violation of a clause of the arbitration agreement or a provision of the law that can be accepted to contravene it without objection, this will be considered as an objection to the violation.

(Appeal of the Egyptian Court of Cassation No. 109 of 71 BC - session 22/12/2008)

The arbitrator's right to delegate an expert without calling or hearing the parties:

Exemption of arbitrators in accordance with the original rules of procedure before the courts, except in cases provided for in the Code of Civil Procedure and procedures agreed by litigants, as well as procedures relating to litigants, hearing their defenses and allowing them to present their documents. In the performance of his duties, he shall request the assistance of his assistants and persons under his control.

(Federal Supreme Court - Appeal No. 438 of the hearing of year 23 of 12/7/2004 - Technical Office p. 1922)

- The expert shall give an opinion, which has not been requested by the parties or shall submit documents proving a right without the Arbitral Tribunal requesting it, and not through the Federal Court. - Call No. 297 of 20 - Session 14/5/2000 - Technical Office. 764)

Confidentiality of arbitration sessions:

"The philosophy of arbitration is confidentiality and this is one of the issues that distinguishes arbitration from the ordinary judicial system, because in the ordinary judicial system, the court is open, but the law prohibits the court from closing its doors only on the judicial order, that is... Why? Why?

Because opponents address the arbitrator and not with the intention of winning against each other, they go to court to put an end to the dispute between them and to maintain existing commercial relationships that can be attributed to a father for too long for a son, and do not want to sacrifice them,

Therefore, the origin of the confidentiality of the arbitration and the judgments are published, books speak about it and anyone who can obtain a copy of the judgment and publish only the judgments of the arbitral tribunal is not published only with the agreement of the parties, and who wishes to publish it to notify that he will publish the judgment,

Judges tended to publish arbitral awards for scientific purposes in order to allow professors who write in arbitration to clarify the arbitrators' decisions, which the committee rejected on the grounds that confidentiality was the basis of the arbitration.

This is without prejudice to the right of the parties - if there is no embarrassment in public and in publications - to hold the arbitration in public and to publish the verdict. "

(Dr. Mohsen Shafiq during the People's Assembly debates on Egyptian Arbitration Law)

- Arbitration is an exceptional way to settle postponements using traditional dispute resolution methods. Act No. 27 of 1994 on arbitration in civil and commercial matters, including the rules of arbitration procedure, from its creation to the full implementation of the arbitrator's decisions, stipulated that his explanatory statement to the same Act stated that the rules of civil and commercial procedure did not achieve the desired objective of arbitration through the prompt settlement of disputes. The provisions of article 28 of the Arbitration Act invited the arbitral tribunal to meet at any place it deemed appropriate to carry out any arbitration proceedings, including inspection. The minutes of the inspection shall be submitted by the Registrar to the President of the Arbitral Tribunal, even if the legislator so wishes, in order to stipulate it expressly, in accordance with article 36 of the same law concerning the experts' report. In violation of the present contested decision, and ruling that the arbitral award is null and void on the basis of the provisions of Article 25 of the Code of Procedure and Article 131 of the proof of the nullity of the examination carried out by the arbitral tribunal without the presence of a clerk writing the corresponding works,

Although this was not required by Arbitration Act No. 27 of 1994 and this invalidity affected the verdict on the basis of an invalid inspection concluded by the judiciary, the verdict challenged on these grounds will be imperfect.

According to article 25/6 of the UNCITRAL Arbitration Rules, it is the arbitral tribunal that accepts or rejects the evidence presented, the existence or absence of a link between the subject matter of the dispute and the importance of the evidence provided. The arbitral tribunal, like the courts. Having appealed against the judgment, he contested this consideration and decided to reject the applicant's payment on the ground that the arbitral tribunal was the supreme expert.

He revealed the reason for his reluctance to rule on the expert's rationing solely to the content of the file, the text is unfounded.

(Appeal of the Egyptian Court of Cassation No. 196 of 74 before JC - session 23/2/2010)

Arbitration procedures for judicial decisions:

Articles 13, paragraph 2, and 53 of the Arbitration in Civil and Commercial Matters Act No. 27 of 1994 stipulate that recourse to the courts in respect of a dispute that is the subject of an arbitration agreement shall not prevent the opening or continuation of the arbitral proceedings or the award of the arbitral award; This provision is null and void when a vice-default is rendered defective in accordance with the conditions specified exclusively in Article 53 above, which does not include the issuance of an arbitral award in a dispute before a court. Possible incompatibility between court decisions and the body Arbitration about a particular conflict.

It is decided that post-agreement arbitration proceedings - instead of the judiciary - shall commence from the day on which the defendant receives the request for arbitration concerning the disputed right of the plaintiff, unless the parties agree on another date.

This is what the street stated in article 27 of Act No. 27 of 1994 on arbitration in civil and commercial matters, which codified what was done before the entry into force.

According to the provisions of the second paragraph of Article 13 and Article 53 of Act No. 27/1994 on Arbitration in Civil and Commercial Matters, the introduction of recourse to the courts for a dispute covered by an arbitral agreement does not prevent the opening or continuation of arbitral proceedings; The pronouncement of the arbitral award or the nullity of this judgment if it is rendered void of an invalid defect in accordance with the conditions set out exclusively in the text of Article 53 above, which includes the pronouncement of the arbitral award in the context of a dispute before the courts exclusively within the meaning of Articles 55, 58/2 - a The same provisions of the law remove the suspicion of a possible contradiction between the provisions of the simulator and the arbitral courts for a particular dispute.

It is permissible to modify the applications of the procedure before the arbitral tribunal:

The arbitration is limited to what the arbitrators have decided to submit to the arbitral tribunal, to be agreed in the contract of contract to submit all disputes arising out of or resulting from the arbitration.

(Federal Supreme Court - Appeal No. 449 of 21 BC - Hearing of 11/4/2001 Technical Office Q 23 p. 706).

Chapter Five

Arbitral Award

Article 37: Application of the law of will to the subject matter of the dispute

1. The arbitral tribunal shall apply to the subject matter of the dispute the rules to be agreed between the parties, unless they are contrary to public policy and morality, unless the substantive rules are respected.

2. If the parties agree to subordinate their legal relationship to the provisions of a model contract, international convention or any other document, these provisions and their arbitration provisions shall apply, provided that they do not violate public policy and the morals of the State.

Article 38: Power of the arbitral tribunal to determine the law applicable to the subject matter of the dispute.

1. If the parties do not agree on the legal rules applicable to the subject matter of the dispute, the arbitral tribunal shall apply the substantive rules of the law which it considers most relevant to the subject matter of the dispute.

2. In determining the subject matter of the dispute, the arbitral tribunal shall take into account the terms of the contract in question, the current customs of the type of transaction and the manner in which the parties have conducted the transactions.

3. The arbitral tribunal may not rule on questions of justice and equity without being bound by the provisions of the law, unless the parties have expressly authorized or authorized it to reconcile.

Article 39: Provisional and partial provisions

1. The arbitral tribunal may make interim or part-time judgments before making an award ending the dispute.

2. The provisional provisions of the arbitral tribunal shall be enforceable before the courts and shall be executed upon the order of a request issued by the President of the Court or his authorized representative.

4. The award shall be justified unless the parties agree otherwise or the law applicable to the arbitral proceedings does not require the reasons for the award.

5. The arbitral award shall include the names and addresses of the parties, the names and addresses of the arbitrators, their nationalities and addresses, the text of the arbitration agreement and a summary of the claims, declarations, documents and just cause of action of the parties, if such mention is due, the date and place of issue.

6. The arbitral award shall be deemed to have been made at the place of arbitration provided for in Article 28 of this Law, even if it is signed by the members of the arbitral tribunal outside the place of arbitration, regardless of the manner in which it is signed by the members of the arbitral tribunal or sent for signature by each member. Unless otherwise agreed by the parties.

7. Unless otherwise agreed by the parties, the award shall be the date on which the arbitrator signed the award if it was individual and, in the case of several arbitrators, the date of the last signature of the arbitrators.

Article 42: Date on which the judgment ends the dispute

1. The arbitral tribunal shall render the award ending the dispute in its entirety within the time limit agreed by the parties. In the absence of agreement on a specific date or on a means of determining that date, the award shall be made within six months of the date of the first session of the arbitral proceedings. Extension of the time limit, provided that the extension period does not exceed six additional months, unless the parties agree on a period longer than this period.

2. If the arbitral award is not rendered after the expiry of the period referred to in paragraph 1 of this article, the arbitral tribunal or one of the parties may request the tribunal to render a decision specifying an additional date for the issuance of the arbitral award or the termination of the arbitral proceedings, if necessary, and extend that period. On such terms as it deems appropriate, its decision in this regard shall be final, unless the parties agree otherwise.

3. If the court issues a decision to close the arbitral proceedings, either party may apply to the court initially competent to hear the case.

Article 43: Priority decision

If, during the arbitration proceedings, a matter within the jurisdiction of the arbitral tribunal or contested by a forgery is presented in a document submitted to it or if criminal proceedings are instituted for its falsification or any other crime, the arbitral tribunal may continue to examine the subject matter of the dispute if it considers that the settlement of the matter or the falsification of the document will not be necessary to decide the subject matter of the dispute, otherwise it shall suspend the proceedings until a final judgment is rendered, which shall result in the suspension of the date fixed for the arbitral award and shall be counted from the day following the day on which the arbitral tribunal is notified of the disappearance of the reason for the suspension.

Article 44: Declaration of Arbitral Award

Subject to the provisions of Article 47 of this Law, the Arbitral Tribunal shall proclaim the award to all parties by delivering to each of them an original or signed copy of the Arbitral Tribunal within fifteen (15) days from the date of the judgment.

Article 45: The arbitration procedure is completed

1. The arbitral proceedings shall end with the publication of the judgment ending the entire dispute by the arbitral tribunal.

2. The arbitral tribunal shall terminate the proceedings in one of the following cases:

(A) If the parties agree to terminate the arbitral proceedings in accordance with the provisions of the law

(B) If the arbitrator leaves the dispute, unless the arbitral tribunal, at the request of the arbitrator, decides that it is in the interest of continuing the proceedings until the dispute is resolved.

(C) If the arbitral tribunal considers for any other reason that the continuation of the arbitration is not feasible or impossible.

- The Code of Civil Procedure (Pre-Arbitration Legal Organization) contains provisions relating to the date on which the judgment was rendered, the mode of delivery of the judgment, the conduct of the deliberation before it is issued, its wording, the date and place of publication of the available data and the methods of appeal (article 217).

- Egyptian Law No. 27 of 1994 on arbitration in commercial and civil articles contained provisions almost identical to those of the Law (6 of 2018) on arbitration in articles 39:51 of the Law.

The explanatory memorandum to Egyptian law states that "the procedure shall be finalized by the arbitral award; Title V shall deal with the judgment, beginning with the statement of the law applicable to the subject matter of the dispute and stipulating that the law of the will shall be chosen by the parties in accordance with the logic of freedom.

This solution is supported by modern case law. It is based on two levels of arbitral jurisdiction. It first chooses the law best suited to the case, but does not apply its substantive rules but the conflict rule, then this rule leads the court to the law applicable to the case and adopts the model law for this graduation. The Court of Arbitration is authorized to apply directly the substantive rules of the law which it considers most appropriate to the case.

In this section, a number of basic rules, in particular:

Approve the agreement that the arbitral tribunal has the right to settle the dispute in accordance with the rules of justice without complying with the provisions of any law (article 39/4).

Based on the jurisdiction of the arbitral tribunal to the law and the arbitration agreement.

It is decided that while arbitration is an asset, contractors have the right to use it to examine any dispute that may arise between them which was the jurisdiction of the State courts, which implies that the jurisdiction of the arbitral tribunal when considering the dispute, although this depends mainly on the rule of law, which has allowed the exclusion of the jurisdiction of the judiciary. In each case, we will rely directly on the agreement of the parties, who may agree to appoint an arbitrator or arbitrators in accordance with the conditions they determine, to settle the dispute between them and to choose the rules applicable to the arbitral proceedings and those applicable to the subject matter of the dispute by determining the place of arbitration and the language in which it is used. ,

These are covered by most of the provisions of the Arbitration Act No. 27 of 1994 and are considered complementary to the will of the parties to the arbitration and are applied only when they do not comply with the provisions of specific provisions relating to the basic guarantees of the dispute to be followed by the public interest, since the arbitral award is a chapter of the dispute. The jurisdiction of the State's judiciary.

(Appeal No. 2050 of the Egyptian Court of Cassation for the year 75 BC) - hearing of 12/6/2007)

The agreement of both parties on the work of the Arbitration Rules of the Regional Centre for International Commercial Arbitration in Cairo, which determines their determination to determine the applicable law and the mandate of the arbitral tribunal in its application, as well as the commercial standards and principles of justice that govern them. The arbitration concluded between the applicant company and the applicant company referred to in Article X of the Parties shall agree to resolve any dispute between them by mutual agreement by arbitration with the Regional Centre for International Commercial Arbitration in Cairo and by arbitration in accordance with the procedure in force at the Centre. Core and the majority arbitration decision is final and binding on the parties,

Arbitrators have the broadest powers to apply laws, commercial customs and principles of justice between the two parties, which means that the parties to the arbitration have freely determined the law applicable to the arbitration existing between them. The application of the United Arab Emirates Civil Transactions Act, which is the law of the State of the applicant company, as the law of the State in which the contract was concluded and performed. The arbitral tribunal shall decide on the lack of jurisdiction after concluding that the contract of the disputed agreement is a separate contract from the contract of 4/4/1980 as regards the difference between its parties. In the present case, after each of the parties had submitted its defense and documents, and found that the compensation resulting from the implementation of the agreement concluded between the parties resulted from the implementation of the agreement concluded between them, its decision would be in accordance with the will of the parties and would therefore not have exceeded the limits of its mandate and would not be imposed by invalidity.

(Egyptian Court of Cassation Appeal No. 145 of 68, hearing in British Columbia on 28/5/2007)

In the event of disagreement on the applicable legal rules, the substantive rules of the law most relevant to the dispute shall apply:

The decision - and as stipulated in article 39 of Law 27 of 1994 - on arbitration in civil and commercial matters, stipulates that, when the arbitrators have agreed on the matter in dispute, the arbitral tribunal shall apply the agreed legal rules to it. If the arbitrators agree to apply Egyptian law, this body shall apply the branch of law most applicable to the question of arbitration.

(Appeal of the Egyptian Court of Cassation No. 86 of 70 in British Columbia, hearing of 26/11/2002)

The decision - within the jurisdiction of the Court of Cassation - and in accordance with article 39 of the Arbitration Act No. 27 of 1994, according to which, when the two arbitrators agree on the subject matter of the dispute, the arbitral tribunal shall apply to the Court the agreed legal rules, if they agree to apply the law of a State. The arbitral tribunal may apply the substantive rules of this Act to the dispute without the conflict of laws rules, unless the parties to the dispute otherwise agree. If they were limited to the simple law of the State without any particular branch, the arbitral tribunal applied the branch of law which, in its view, was most relevant to the subject matter of the dispute, since its error in the definition of that section was not an exclusion from the law of arbitrators, but a factual error in the application of the law.

(Egyptian Court of Cassation Appeal No. 15091 for the session of the year 80, 27/12/2011)

Deliberation before arbitral award

(The main body of the book reviews the item entitled deliberation between the members of the arbitral tribunal and the majority of opinions)

Arbitration proceedings in which the arbitrator is required to comply only with the basic litigation proceedings, unless he is allowed to reconcile, shall not be bound by them, except as regards public policy. If the status of any of them changes or if they die, the arbitral award must be returned to the procedural document so that it can be completed and the proceedings before the new body can be completed. The application to set aside the arbitrators' verdict was decided exclusively by the legislator in three cases, including the publication of the verdict in the presence of certain arbitrators and in the absence of others without authorization.

(Federal Supreme Court - Appeal No. 556 of the 24th session 19/4/2005 Technical Office XY 833)

The lack of motivation to refrain from signing the verdict shall not be considered null and void unless the plaintiff proves that the purpose of refraining is to prevent himself from verifying a deliberation before rendering the verdict.

(Egyptian Court of Cassation - Appeal No. 88-515 for the 73rd session of 9/2/2010)

Drafting of the arbitral award, its case, signature and declarations in court decisions:

- Revision of the book in the moral elements and arbitral award (judgment writing) -

Signature of the arbitrators - what the judgment should include).

Originally, all judgments must be reasoned, but some laws do not require a causal link, including English law. The judgment has only the operative part of the judgment, but if the judge writes his reasons, this is not part of the judgment and does not count on appeal and there are disputes in which arbitration does not work. It is conceivable that the cause of the arbitration in the class is as if the dispute revolved around the type of cotton sold, the arbitrator decided it once the inspection (and did not have to cause) (Dr. Mohsen Shafiq in the discussions that took place at the People's Assembly on article 42 of the Egyptian Arbitration Law).

- The arbitrators believe that it should include a copy of the arbitration agreement to ensure that it is issued within the limits of their authority arising from the will of the parties. An example of a defective reason for the invalidity of the arbitral award due to its absence from the image of the arbitration document, despite compliance with the provisions of civil procedure under article 212 on the subject.

(Federal Supreme Court - Appeal No. 224 of 2014 - hearing of 26/11/2014)

- The arbitrator's judgment does not apply to him, which applies to the judgment which deemed it necessary to submit a draft and an original to him, the arbitrators filed the file of the arbitral award signed by all members of the Committee. Notice of death On a no basis.

(Federal Supreme Court - Appeal No. 427 of the 2009 hearing of 28/10/2009)

Judgment of the arbitrators. Failure to include all statements to be included in the judge's judgment. It must include, in particular, a copy of the arbitration document, summaries of the litigants' statements and documents, the reasons for the judgment, the date of entry into force, the date of its publication, the place where it was rendered and the details provided by the arbitrators.

Its work will be limited to the examination of the procedural aspects set out in Articles 212, 216 exclusively of civil proceedings.

(Federal Supreme Court - Appeal No. 67 out of 26 hearings 23/5/2004 Technical Office Q 26 p. 1306)

- The arbitrators must include a copy of the arbitration document, if it appears in a separate document, or of the arbitration clause, if it appears in the contract. To the arbitrators during the dispute

(Federal Supreme Court - Appeal No. 438 of 23 - hearing on 12/7/2004 Technical Office Q 26 - p. 1922)

Failure to release the clerk of the court by filing the arbitral award with the original of the arbitration document and documents.

(Federal Supreme Court - Appeal No. 22 of 22 - Hearing of 03/03/2002 - Technical Office S22 - p. 539)

- The arbitrator's failure to rule on any of the issues raised in the arbitration clause or his or her verdict may be ambiguous with which it cannot be implemented.

(Federal Supreme Court - Appeal No. 32 of 23 - Hearing of 8/6/2003 Technical Office Q25 - p. 1476)

- Material errors in the judgment of the arbitrators must be corrected by the competent court in the prescribed manner.

(Federal Supreme Court - Appeal No. 9 for year 20 - hearing 13/2/2000 - Technical Office Q 22 - p. 196)

The absence of the arbitral award for reasons not related to public policy:

While the appeal was brought on two grounds, the applicant mourns the second ground of the contested judgment, which is contrary to the law and poorly motivated. 3, 53 of the Arbitration Act No. 27 of 1994 after the documents did not allow the parties to the arbitration not to cause, but the contested verdict did not set out or respond to what the appellant had raised in this regard, although it was a fundamental defense to the defect and should be revoked.

Although this obituary notice is false, it appears from the documents that the appellant personally attended the hearing before the Court of Appeal on January 15, 1996 and cancels the minutes of the hearing, indicating that the appellant agrees with the cause of the death notice. Article 43 of the Arbitration of Civil and Commercial Articles Act No. 27 of 1994 authorized the agreement to exempt the arbitral tribunal from the judgment it had rendered. He first raised it before the Court of Cassation and sacrificed contested provision of allegedly this reason is unacceptable.

(Appeal of the Egyptian Court of Cassation No. 5539 of 66 BC - Session of 11/7/1998)

Causing the arbitral award:

It was established in the documents that the applicant's claim was based on the invalidity of the arbitral award against him because he had settled the dispute concerning the arbitration agreement binding him to the appellant, contrary to the previous judgment delivered on 27/04/1991 in Case No........... ... which he had established against others with the validity and effectiveness of the original contract dated 10/10/1984, which included the purchase of the land in dispute with extradition and intervened by the applicant against him by affirming that he was the owner of the property and ruled on his claims and rejected the object of the intervention of the disputed persons. 14/3/1998 that it contained nothing indicating that the applicant renounced this judgment in his favor. authentic judgment wise not to prejudice the former final published with regard to authoritative judicial decisions disputes that are superior to considerations of public policy

In the event of failure and settlement of the dispute, the right of the disputed person on the ground in question and preventing him from being subject to the execution of the judgment rendered in his favor in the above-mentioned proceedings, then he will have lost the authenticity of the previous judgment in the same dispute between the two parties.

If the contested judgment does not discuss this defense and ultimately dismisses the appellant's appeal, it will be vitiated by errors in breach caused by the error in the application of the law.

(Appeal of the Egyptian Court of Cassation No. 1626 of 74 BC - Session 20/4/2006)

- A review of the arbitration agreement concluded on 16 April 1995 between the parties to the appeal shows that it did not provide for the arbitral tribunal to be authorised to reconcile in order that it may rule on the subject of the dispute in accordance with the rules of justice and equity without complying with the provisions of the law in accordance with the provisions of paragraph 4 of the article. 39 of the Law No. 27/1994 on Arbitration in Civil and Commercial

Matters, and it was established by the arbitral award that it did not apply the rules of justice and equity in the dispute, obeying the contested decision on this ground "violates the law or is prejudicial in its application. In the causality of not responding to what I have stuck Anyone who applies the rules of justice and equity of the arbitral tribunal, although he is not allowed to end the dispute, will be misled and his judgment will not be vitiated by a defect of form motivated by an unknown generalized statement. Let this judicial system do what it takes to respond to them without breaking it.

(Appeal of the Egyptian Court of Cassation No. 5539 of 66 BC - hearing on 11/7/1998 S49 - p. 539)

Data relating to the arbitral award: -

The provision contained in the third paragraph of article 43 of the Arbitration in Civil and Commercial Articles Act No. 27 of 1994 stipulating that "the arbitral award shall include... and a copy of the arbitration agreement...", but indicates that the legislator's objective is positive The proof of this affirmation in the judgment is to verify the arbitrators' verdict within the limits of their powers derived from the arbitration agreement, in the interests of the parties. This will change the fact that the arbitration agreement was filed in favor of the arbitral award with the arbitral award The letter of the tribunal provided for in article 9 of the Arbitration Act referred to in its article 47;

Because the judgment must go without saying by supplementing the conditions of his health so that he does not accept to supplement the lack of material data in any other way.

(Egyptian Court of Cassation overturning the hearing of 18/12/1997 Q 48 - p. 1495)

- Considering that, for the third aspect of the reason given in support of the fact that the arbitration decision does not include the copy of the arbitration agreement insofar as it is free to file the contract it contained, and that the Egyptian law on arbitration stipulated that the arbitration decision would be valid, it would be null and void. As this obituary is not valid, it confuses the arbitration clause with the arbitration clause, although both express the same meaning as the arbitration contract, i.e. the consent of the parties to resort to arbitration to settle all or part of the disputes set out in this contract. The arbitration clause must always precede the establishment of the dispute, whether it is independent of itself or contained in a particular contract. It is therefore inconceivable to include a specific subject of the dispute that has not yet been raised and that the parties will not be able to predict exclusively and in advance.

Consequently, the legislator did not require that the arbitration clause contain a specific subject matter of the dispute, as stipulated in article 39 of the Egyptian Arbitration Act No. 27 of 1994, unlike what is decided - within the jurisdiction of this court - with respect to participation in the arbitration as an independent agreement. The Egyptian legislator, in article 10 of the above-mentioned law, stipulates that the agreement must specify the matters covered by the arbitration, failing which it is null and void. As such, it appeared from the documents and codes of the contested judgment that the agreement between the parties on the use of arbitration was preceded by the dispute between them and took the form of the arbitration clause set out in the first paragraph of Article 13 of the dispute contract "any dispute between the parties concerning the application or interpretation of the terms and conditions of this contract shall not be settled amicably and shall be submitted to arbitration in accordance with the rules of the International Chamber of Commerce in Paris.

The arbitral award stipulated the text of this clause in its codes, which the street sought filled. There was no objection to the consideration of any of these issues or to the assertion that the arbitral award was made on matters not covered by the arbitration agreement or that it exceeded the limits of this agreement. The contested judgment This consideration of the obituary to the foregoing is unfounded.

(Appeal No. 7307 of the Egyptian Court of Cassation for the year 76 B.C. - hearing of 8/2/2007)

Copy of the arbitration agreement or the texts of a declaration of verdict on the merits:

The text of article 43, paragraph 3, of the Arbitration in Civil and Commercial Matters Act No. 27 of 1994 indicates that the legislator intended that this declaration - the image of the arbitration agreement - should contain in the judgment evidence of the verdict rendered by the arbitrators within the limits of their power. Arbitration, the care of the parties to the dispute, is therefore a fundamental statement necessary for the validity of the judgment, leading to a breach of the purpose for which the legislator is required to prove the decision leading to the invalidity, and does not change the fact that the arbitration agreement is attached to the arbitral proceedings, as it must be arbitration. In itself, it meant the completion of his health conditions in accordance with the Enough principle. Self-dispositions, so that does not accept the absence of who complete the kernel in any other way than data.

(Appeal of the Egyptian Court of Cassation No. 10635 of 76 B.C. - hearing of 27/2/2007)

The copy of the arbitral award is received and published in court decisions:

The memorandum of the Egyptian Arbitration Law stated that "it is essential to prohibit the publication of the arbitral award without the consent of both parties.

- The result of what the appellant denies on the other side of the second ground is that the contested verdict did not invalidate the arbitral tribunal's award, even though it included a judgment of what the litigants did not request.

Although this obituary is due to the fact that article 7) of paragraph 3 of annex 6) of the arbitration procedure is annexed to the arbitration procedure, it is permissible for the arbitral tribunal to publish the arbitral award without the parties to the dispute having to give their consent. The arbitration, and the contested judgment respects this consideration, the obituary is sacrificed on an unfounded basis.

(Appeal of the Egyptian Court of Cassation No. 3161 of 64 BC - session 10/3/2009)

Date and decision of the arbitral award in court decisions:

The explanatory memorandum to the Egyptian Arbitration Law indicated that the speed of finalizing the procedures for issuing the arbitral award was one of the characteristics of the arbitration system that made it preferable to traders and businessmen. This consideration allows the arbitral tribunal to continue the proceedings despite the appeal of a decision and when the proceedings choose reasonable and not excessive dates in the palace, and perhaps the only situation in which the legislator is willing to respect the time limits is article (45). I put to the time limit rule of control time may be higher for both parties after the end of the request for expiry of the procedure and authorization for them to raise the dispute to the judiciary State His original mandate.

- The first paragraph of article 45 of Act No. 27 of 1994 promulgating the Law on Arbitration in Civil and Commercial Matters provides that the arbitral tribunal shall decide the dispute within the time limit agreed by the parties. In the absence of agreement, the judgment shall be delivered within twelve months of the date of the commencement of the arbitration proceedings. In any event, the arbitral tribunal may decide to extend the time limit provided that the time limit for the extension does not exceed six months, unless the parties agree on a time limit exceeding that which indicates that the legislator has obliged the arbitral tribunal to render its decision terminating the dispute within the time limit agreed by the parties. If they do not agree on the time limit, they shall deliver their judgment within twelve months with the right to extend that time limit or the agreed time limit, an additional time limit not exceeding six months, unless the parties agree to extend it further and the legislator does not stipulate the validity of the dispute agreement. The date shall be before the arbitral tribunal or the extension shall be for a specified period of time. Therefore, it is not precluded from agreeing with the expert appointed by the arbitral tribunal to extend the date of the arbitration until the end of its work and until the arbitral tribunal has rendered its judgment in the dispute.

(Appeal of the Egyptian Court of Cassation No. 3669 for the year 68 BC - hearing 15/12/2010)

Agreement to extend the duration of the arbitration implicitly:

- The decision to extend the duration of the arbitration as expressed shall implicitly benefit from the presence of the parties before the arbitral tribunal and the discussion of the case after the time limit.

(Appeals No. 1041, 1145 for the year 74 BC - meeting 13/4/2010)

The arbitral tribunal shall be required to render its award in arbitration within six months from the date of the first hearing and the parties may agree, explicitly or implicitly, to extend this period. It is permissible to authorize the arbitrator within a certain period of time to pay for the invalidity of the arbitrator's judgment when the court is considering ratifying it because of the fall of the arbitration document within the prescribed period.

(Federal Supreme Court - Appeal No. 71 of 20 - Hearing of 12/12/1999 - Technical Office S21 - p. 13)

Conclusion on whether or not to extend the date of arbitration - from the authority of the court of first instance once it has established its jurisdiction for justifiable reasons of origin in sufficient documents for a campaign

(Federal Supreme Court - Appeal No. 64 of 22 of the hearing 19/11/2002 Technical Office Q 24 - p. 2146)

(Federal Supreme Court - Appeal No. 43 of year 23 - hearing 13/4/2003 - Office at Q 25 - p. 854)

- The right of the Tribunal to extend the term of office of the arbitrators for such period as it deems appropriate to settle the dispute at the request of one of the parties to the arbitration or the arbitral tribunal.

(Appeal of the Federal Supreme Court No. 266 for the year 2009 - hearing of 21/10/2009 at the Technical Office Q 31, p. 287)

- The arbitration provision is free to set a date for termination or arbitration - Article 210 of the Code of Civil Procedure is not null and void.

(Federal Supreme Court - Appeal No. 22 for year 22 - hearing 3/3/2002 Technical Office Q 24 p. 529)

Arbitration litigation Legal claim Obsolescence

Articles 483 and 484 of the Civil Transactions Act stipulate that the time limit for not deciding a case in general is interrupted by legal proceedings and by any legal action taken by the creditor to enforce his right or if he exercises his right to it as long as the debtor and the respect of a right are respected. The case is brought before the ordinary judiciary, namely the courts in general or the courts of justice, such as arbitral tribunals, and therefore the filing of a request with the arbitral tribunal for the settlement of the dispute under the arbitration procedure is considered to be a legal action within the meaning of the above-mentioned definition.

(Federal Supreme Court - Appeal No. 188 of 23rd hearing of 29/10/2003, Technical Office Q 25, p. 2065)

The effect of force majeure on the arbitration clause:

- The introduction of a case of force majeure would not waste the agreed arbitration clause, but would only involve the suspension of the effective date set for the submission of the dispute to arbitration if it had a fixed date.

(Court of Cassation of Egypt - Appeal No. 406 of 30 BC) - hearing of 17/6/1965 AD 16 - p. 778)

Arbitration costs

Article 46:

1. Unless otherwise agreed by the parties, the arbitral tribunal shall assess the costs of the arbitration, including the fees and expenses incurred by any member of the arbitral tribunal

for the performance of his or her duties, as well as the costs incurred by the arbitral tribunal for the appointment of experts.

2. The arbitral tribunal shall bear all or part of the costs referred to in paragraph 1 of this article, at the request of one of the parties, to modify the assessment of their fees or costs in the light of the effort made, the nature of the dispute and the arbitrator's experience.

3. The Court cannot be asked to reconsider the amount of the costs if there is an agreement to determine them.

Refrain from postponing the judgment in the event of non-payment of costs

Article 47:

1. Without prejudice to the right of the arbitrators to appeal to the parties for their fees and costs, the arbitral tribunal may refuse to deliver the final arbitral award to the parties if the costs of the arbitration are not fully paid.

2. If the arbitral tribunal refuses to deliver the award in accordance with the provisions of paragraph 1 of this article, either party may request the Court, after the declaration of the other parties and the arbitral tribunal, to oblige the arbitral tribunal to deliver the award to the parties, after having paid all the fees and expenses requested by the arbitral tribunal. Or those determined by the Court in accordance with Article 46 of this Law.

- The Civil Procedure (Pre-Arbitration Judicial Organization) Act did not contain a similar provision.

No judgment in the event of non-payment of fees:

- The claimant invokes his agreement with the Arbitration Commission and the Centre not to commit more than his share of the fees before the arbitration and the delivery of the arbitral award. This does not contradict the legal provisions on civil proceedings and settlements, insofar as the need to submit a copy of the arbitral award does not prevent the arbitration center from collecting fees, expenses or fees as a precondition for granting the image of the arbitral award in accordance with the regulations. The arbitration procedure was in accordance with its provisions.

(Federal Supreme Court - Appeal No. 546 for the 22nd session of the Bureau on 12/11/2002 to the 24

Confidentiality of arbitrators' judgments

Article 48:

The arbitrators' decisions are confidential and may not be published, or in part, without the written consent of the parties. The publication of the decisions relating to the arbitral award should not be considered as a violation of this principle.

Interpretation of the arbitral award

Article 49

1. Once the arbitral award has been made, the arbitral tribunal no longer has the power to rule on the matters dealt with in the arbitral award. The parties have not agreed on any other procedures or time limits and the interpreter must notify the other party of this request before submitting it to the arbitral tribunal.

2. If the Arbitral Tribunal considers that the request for interpretation is justified, it shall render its decision in writing within thirty days of the date on which the request is filed with the Tribunal, which period may be extended by fifteen days if it considers it justified.

3. A judgment rendered in interpretation shall be deemed to be complementary to the arbitral award it will interpret and to which its provisions shall apply.

Correction of material errors by arbitration

Article 50:

1. The arbitral tribunal shall correct the written or mathematical errors in its judgment by a decision taken ex officio or at the request of one of the parties after the announcement of the other parties. The request must be made within 30 days of receipt of the arbitral award, unless the parties rectify the judgment within thirty (30) days of the delivery of the judgment or present the request for rectification, as the case may be.

2. The correction decision shall be rendered in writing by the Arbitral Tribunal and communicated to the parties within fifteen (15) days from the date on which it was rendered.

3. A rectification judgment shall be deemed to supplement the arbitral award and its provisions shall apply.

(For these provisions, see comments on sections 37:45 of the Act

No. 6 of 2018 concerning arbitration.

Article 51: Additional Arbitral Award

1. Any party may request the Arbitral Tribunal, within thirty (30) days of receipt of the arbitral award, to issue an additional arbitral award in any claims made during the proceedings and omitted by the arbitral award.

2. If the Arbitral Tribunal considers that the request referred to in point (1) of this Article is justified, it shall deliver its judgment within 60 days of the filing date of the request and may extend this period by thirty (30) days.

3. An additional arbitral award shall be considered as complementary to the award and its provisions shall apply.

4. If the Authority does not issue an arbitral award in accordance with the provisions of this article and articles 49 and 50 of this Law, the party concerned shall make a request to the Court.

- The Civil Procedure (Pre-Arbitration Judicial Organization) Act did not contain a similar provision.

Egyptian Law No. 27 of 1994 on the arbitration of civil and commercial articles contained a provision similar to article 51 of the Code:

(1) Either party to the arbitration may, even after the expiry of the date of the arbitration, request the arbitral tribunal, within thirty days of receipt of the arbitral award, to issue an additional arbitral award in claims filed during the proceedings and omitted by them.

2. The arbitral tribunal shall be formed within sixty days from the date of filing of the request. The explanatory memorandum of the Egyptian Arbitration Law stipulated that one of the basic rules for approving the request for the issuance of an additional arbitral award in the applications submitted during the proceedings was to omit the arbitral award in accordance with the conditions set out in article 51. It goes without saying that it applies to the additional provision containing the same provisions as the original arbitral award.

It should be noted that arbitrators may agree to choose the same arbitral tribunal because the request for an additional arbitral award within the meaning of this text is in reality a request for arbitration of any ignored request.

Article 52: Binding force of the arbitral award

An arbitral award rendered in accordance with the provisions of this Law shall be binding on the parties.

Article 53: Objection to the arbitral award

1. An objection to an arbitral award is admissible only by filing an action for a declaration of invalidity before the court or at the time of the hearing of the application for ratification of the award. The applicant must justify one of the following reasons:

(A) the absence of an arbitration agreement, the invalidity of the agreement or the termination of its duration in accordance with the law to which the parties were subject or in accordance with this law, in the absence of a reference to a specific law;

(B) At the time of the conclusion of the arbitration agreement, one of the parties was incompetent or incompetent in accordance with the law governing its capacity.

(C) The person does not have the capacity to dispose of the contested right in accordance with the law governing his or her eligibility, as provided for in Article 4 of this Law.

(D) If one of the parties to the arbitration is unable to present its defence because it has not made a valid statement regarding the appointment of an arbitrator or the arbitral proceedings, or as a result of the violation of the dispute by the arbitral tribunal or for any other reason beyond its control.

(E) If the arbitral award excludes the application of the law that the parties have agreed to apply to the subject matter of the dispute.

(F) If the arbitral tribunal is constituted or an arbitrator is appointed in a manner contrary to the provisions of this Act or the agreement of the parties.

(G) If the arbitral proceedings are null and void and the arbitral award is rendered after the expiry of the prescribed period.

(H) If the arbitral award has decided on matters not covered by the arbitration agreement or has exceeded the limits of this agreement, however, if the parties to the arbitral award may be separated from those parts of the award that are not submitted to it. Invalidity only concerns the last parts.

2. The Court shall rule on the nullity of the arbitral award on its own initiative if it finds any of the following elements:

(A) that the subject matter of the dispute is one of the matters that cannot be arbitrated;

B - Violation of the arbitral award to public order and public morals in the State.

Article 54: Application for annulment of the arbitral award

1. The judgment rendered by the court in an action for annulment is considered final and the appeal is admissible only by cassation.

2. An application for a declaration of invalidity of the arbitral award shall not be heard after thirty (30) days from the date of the award made to the applicant.

3. The award annulling the arbitral award shall entail the annulment of all or part of that award, depending on whether the annulment is totally or partially invalid.

4. Unless otherwise agreed by the parties, the arbitration agreement shall remain in force in accordance with the provisions of this Law after the annulment of the arbitral award, unless the annulment is based on the absence of the agreement itself, its termination, its invalidity or its inability to enforce it.

5. An application for a declaration of invalidity shall not prevent the acceptance of an application for a declaration of invalidity.

6. The Tribunal, which is required by the arbitral awards to suspend the cancellation proceedings for a period not exceeding sixty (60) days, if it considers it appropriate at the request of one of the parties, in order to give the arbitral tribunal the opportunity to take any action or modification in the form of the award that would remove the grounds. Revocation without affecting its content

Article 55: Enforcement of the arbitral award

1. Any person wishing to enforce an arbitral award shall submit a request for ratification of the award and order its enforcement to the President of the Court, together with the following:

The original or a certified copy of the judgment

Copy of the arbitration agreement

Translation of the arbitral award into Arabic certified by a recognized organization, if not published.

A copy of the minutes of the filing of the judgment in court.

2. The President of the Court or his representative shall order the ratification and enforcement of the arbitral award within sixty (60) days from the date of filing of the request for ratification and enforcement, unless he establishes the existence of one or more grounds for

invalidity on the basis of the justification of one of the cases mentioned above. Article (1) of Article (53) of this law.

Article 56: Suspension of the execution of the arbitral award

1. The filing of an action for annulment of the arbitral award shall not result in the suspension of the execution of the judgment. However, the court hearing the invalidity of the arbitral award may order the suspension of enforcement at the request of one of the parties if the request is based on serious grounds.

2. The Court shall decide on the stay of execution within fifteen (15) days from the date of the first scheduled hearing.

3. If the court decides to suspend enforcement, it may order the applicant to provide a guarantee or financial guarantee.

Article 57: Appeal against the enforcement of the arbitral award

The decision of the court ordering the enforcement of the arbitral award or refusing to enforce it may be appealed to the competent court of appeal within thirty (30) days from the day following the day of the announcement.

- The Code of Civil Procedure contained provisions governing some of the provisions of the previous articles (arts. 15, 16 and 17).

Egyptian Law No. 27 of 1994 on arbitration in civil and commercial articles also contained provisions similar to article 52: 58.

- The arbitral award does not accept the appeal or request for reconsideration even if one of its cases is completed, or challenged on appeal, and the request for a declaration of invalidity referred to in the second paragraph is not a means of challenging judgments, because the influence of the contractual nature of the agreement is the source of the arbitrator's power to open the way. The invalidity proceedings against the arbitral award, provided for in Articles 52 to 54 of the Law and applicable to any arbitral award rendered as from the date of its entry into force on or after 22 May 1994, shall be subject to the rules of the arbitral act annulled. Arbitration with authorization for reconciliation and m The place of invalidity is then an Egyptian arbitral judgment, i.e. it is rendered in Egypt, even if the arbitration proceedings are conducted in accordance with the Egyptian Arbitration Law, the proceedings are subject to the provisions of the Egyptian Arbitration Law, whether with regard to the filing date or the competent court, in accordance with the principle of the territorial jurisdiction of Egyptian courts. The issuance of an arbitral award in a given country confers jurisdiction on the courts of that State to examine the invalidity of that decision; Egyptian courts have jurisdiction to claim the invalidity of the arbitral award rendered in Egypt, even if the parties have agreed to submit it to a foreign law or the rules of an arbitration center.

Or it has been rendered in an international commercial arbitration that has no connection with the legal system. Egyptian only, with the exception of the publication of the verdict in Egypt (see what Professor Fathi Wali said in his reference - arbitration law in theory and practice - the first edition in 2007 - knowledge of facilities, p. 451 and beyond.

It is also prohibited to seek the annulment of an arbitral award rendered during the dispute before the end of the arbitral proceedings and after appealing the closure of the dispute, with the exception of temporary judgments rendered under the general sharia in the Code of Procedure and under article 212 of the Code of Procedure.

The explanatory memorandum to the Arbitration Law in Egypt states that:

The arbitration phase ends with the delivery of the judgment. The post-judgment phase then begins, during which two topics discussed in Sections VI and VII emerge one after the other.

Theme 1: Special invalidity of the arbitral award Because this judgment, although it does not accept the appeal in the manner provided for in the Code of Civil and Commercial Procedure, is subject to appeal against the invalidity in the cases listed in Article (53) exclusively, and it was noted in his appointment that it is in conformity with the cases of invalidity provided for in Article 5 of the New York Convention mentioned above.

Article 54, paragraph 6, of the Arbitration Act 6 of 2018 included a new provision allowing one of the parties to the arbitration to request the court seized of the invalidity of the arbitral award to suspend the annulment proceedings (procedure) for a period not exceeding sixty days granted by the arbitral tribunal. A procedure or change in the form of the judgment which removes the grounds for setting aside without affecting the content of the judgment shall be available to the court which ratified the arbitral award without the annulment court in the event that it has relied on the failure of the arbitral tribunal to rule on the ambiguity of its judgment. In either case, it can restore it. For a decision of the arbitral tribunal to consider what has been neglected or clarify the ambiguity encountered, review the decision of the Federal Supreme Court Appeal No. 32 out of 23 hearing 8/6/2003 Technical Office Q 25 - p. 1476)

However, the legislator authorized the parties to the proceedings, when they filed an application for a declaration of invalidity, to request that the verdict be restored to the arbitral tribunal in order to rectify what they considered to be a invalidity, which the defendant could retain in the invalidity proceedings by using the grounds provided by the defendant in order to avoid the annulment of the arbitral award. In addition to achieving the objective of arbitration in the prompt and unfettered resolution of ordinary disputes and to avoid any loss of time, effort and money spent until the verdict, which could end the invalidation of the trial, the ball is supposed to create a new control of the parties over the invalidation claims and give them the possibility of Discoloration Allows the arbitral tribunal to remedy this nullity and removes its grounds when it does not affect the content of the decision, the legislator ensures that this possibility is under the control of the court which examines the action for invalidity, which is better able to know what may lead to invalidity without prejudice. The content of the provision and what can be corrected without prejudice to that by giving it the power to respond to that request if it considers it appropriate or not to respond when it considers it inappropriate derives from its assessment for action or modification in the form of a provision the deletion of which would result in the invalidity of its effect. The content of the provision is so restrictive The procedure and the modification of the form of the judgment, which would remove the grounds for annulment, for example, the judgment will be devoid of any indication of the place of arbitration, its composition or composition, the date on which the award was made and any other formal declaration of judgment. A statement of the arbitration document or the absence of an investigation into the confrontation rule between the parties, which will be resolved by a judicial treatment of this provision.

Invalidity of the arbitral award in judicial decisions

- Judgment of an arbitrator declaring a composite interest The litigant may request the annulment of article 216 of the Code of Civil Procedure, for example in the context of an arbitrator's decision stipulating a composite interest.

(Appeal of the Federal Supreme Court No. 11 for the year 23 - hearing 19/5/2002 Technical Office Q 24 p. 120)

- The invalidity of the arbitrators' judgment shall be limited to the error made in the proceedings and defects referred to exclusively in Article 246. Subject to the violation of the right of defense, any dispute raised by one of the parties to the arbitration against the judgment of an arbitrator, which is not related to the previous cases, the rules of evidence, or the discretion or omission of the court, did not make it possible to determine the merits of the dispute, Or the adequacy of the reasons for the judgment route are not acceptable.

(Federal Supreme Court - Appeal No. 831 of 25 - Hearing of 23/5/2004 - Technical Office Q 26, p. 1306)

(Call No. 273 for year 25 - session of 25/12/2006 - Technical Office Q 28 - p. 238)

- The publication of the arbitrator's judgment on behalf of His Highness the Head of State is not mandatory.

- The fact that the appellant has not disclosed which foreign documents are not translated into Arabic on the basis of the arbitrator's judgment and its consequences on his jurisdiction, the text in this respect is unacceptable.

An example of a valid reason for ratifying an arbitral award.

(Federal Supreme Court Appeal No. 518 of 2010 - hearing on 12/1/2011)

- Arbitral decision to acquire the authenticity of the verdict after its pronouncement, which is still only until its disappearance, although its implementation remains subject to ratification by force. An application for a declaration of invalidity is limited to the cases mentioned in the law exclusively.

(Federal Supreme Court - Appeal No. 92 for year 25 - hearing 8/6/2003 Technical Office Q 25 - p 1489)

Claims for ratification of arbitrators' decisions - the authority of the court of first instance must not exceed the limits of control of the procedural aspects of the award.

(Federal Supreme Court - Appeal No. 335 of year 293 Commercial - Hearing of 28/01/2014)

Invalidity proceedings may not be instituted before the end of the arbitration dispute.

Article 22 of the Civil Code stipulates that[the rules of jurisdiction and all questions relating to procedure shall apply to the law of the country in which the action is brought], these rules of procedure not authorized by Egyptian law shall prevail over the agreement of the parties on the award of the arbitration. Arbitration proceedings relating to the arbitration rules of one of the arbitration organizations or centers, including the Cairo Regional Arbitration Centre, and judgments rendered in the course of the arbitration proceedings and not ending the dispute may not affect security solely by ending the dispute in accordance with all the procedural rules. Article 22 of the Arbitration Act 27/1994, which decided that it was not permissible to bring an action for annulment of the arbitral tribunal's award in the defense case. With regard to lack of jurisdiction, including defenses based on the absence of an arbitration agreement or on the fall or invalidity or non-inclusion of the subject-matter of the dispute, with the exception of the arbitral award ending the dispute in its entirety, including the need to apply this rule of jus cogens on procedures for the examination of the arbitral proceedings.... Rules of procedure prevail A group of the Cairo Regional Arbitration Centre stated that the argument that the arbitral tribunal did not have jurisdiction in the various forms mentioned above and the argument that the arbitral tribunal was not authorized to accept the arbitral proceedings because of the lack of status of the defendant in order to prevent the arbitral tribunal from deciding the case in question. The same rule is set out in article 22 of the Arbitration Act 27/1994, which cannot be invoked to annul a decision refusing to accept the application for non-acceptance of the case because of the absence of judicial status, except with the end of the arbitral dispute. Result p The Court of Cassation may supplement these grounds in such a way as not to invalidate it, nor to deny the description of its decision not to accept the trial in court in order to bring it before the court, its validity is its inadmissibility without it being necessary to mention it. In the operative part of this provision.

Failure of arbitral justice to apply and interpret the law

As established in the documents, the parties to the arbitration agreed to apply Egyptian law without specifying a branch, the arbitral tribunal applied the provisions of civil law and commercial law, which are branches of Egyptian law, as it considered them to be the most applicable with regard to the arbitration, another is only an error in the application of the law and therefore leaves no possibility of bringing a claim for invalidity.

Article 53 of the Arbitration in Civil and Commercial Matters Act No. 27 of 1994 stipulates that the author of the determination of invalidity is inadmissible, and it is not permissible to contest the invalidity on any ground other than that set out in that article. This was the applicant's defense contained in the obituary notice centered on the arbitral award in question and not in the cases of invalidity provided for in Article 53 of the above-mentioned law. The contested judgment dismissing this defense would have been in accordance with the true rule of law.

(Appeal of the Egyptian Court of Cassation No. 1041, 1145 for the year 74 BC - hearing 13/4/2010)

Article 53/1-a- Nullity of the arbitration agreement

- Decision in the jurisdiction of that court - that arbitration is an exceptional means decided by the legislature to resolve postponements on the basis of the normal procedures of the dispute and the guarantees provided by it and is therefore inevitably limited to the willingness of the arbitrators to submit to the arbitral tribunal and to the law prescribed in the second paragraph of Article X of Law No. 27 of 1994, which includes the arbitration agreement in the event that the dispute has been filed against it before a judicial authority, specifically for matters covered by the arbitration or otherwise null and void. Including what I have reported in a If the arbitration agreement is invalid or if the arbitral award is settled in matters not covered by the arbitration agreement or exceeds the limits of this agreement, and in the second case, if the arbitral award contains something that is contrary to public policy. As such, it was established that the applicant based his claim on the invalidity of the arbitral award against him that he had settled the dispute concerning the arbitration agreement binding him to the appellant, contrary to the earlier judgment of 27/4/1991 in Case No. 6826 of 1990, the Civil Court of Mansoura Elementary What it had established against others on the validity and effectiveness of the original contract dated 10/10/1984, which provided for the purchase of the land in dispute with extradition and had intervened against it by the applicant by asserting its ownership of the property and rejecting the subject of the intervention of the persons challenged against it. 3/1998 that it did not contain any evidence that the appellant had waived this right. The arbitral tribunal should not prejudice the final verdict rendered in the dispute with regard to the authenticity of judicial decisions that transcend public policy considerations. Had the contested judgment failed to consider this defence and ultimately dismissed the appellant's appeal, it would be vitiated by errors in the case that would have resulted in an error in the application of the law. It must be cancelled for both of these reasons without the need to review the rest of the grounds for appeal.

(Appeal of the Egyptian Court of Cassation 1626 out of 74 BC hearing 20/4/2006)

Invalidity shall be annexed to the parts relating to matters not submitted to arbitration 35/1

It is decided that the judiciary is the final word in both the grounds and the operative part, and the provision of article 53/1 of the Arbitration Act - the preceding statement - that "an application for a declaration of invalidity of the arbitral award shall only be accepted in the following cases (a)... (F) If the arbitral award is separate in matters not covered by the arbitration agreement or exceeds the limits of this agreement, however, if the parties to the arbitral award may be separated from those of the non-arbitral matters, the invalidity shall be null and void only in the latter.

(Appeal of the Egyptian Court of Cassation No. 86 of 70 BC - session 26/11/2002)

- If the Arbitration Act No. 27 of 1994 authorizes the text of the second paragraph of article 53, paragraph 2, of the Court to hear ex officio the invalidity of the arbitral award rendered by the judiciary if the provision contains something that is contrary to public policy in Egypt and the violation of what the law provides For the arbitration process and the violation may be that the judiciary in violation of public policy in Egypt is not sufficient to violate the rule of jus cogens under Egyptian law.

(Appeal of the Egyptian Court of Cassation No. 1790 of the year 75 s - 12/03/2011)

Decision to annul the arbitral award for violation of public policy of its judiciary with benefits exceeding the maximum limit of 277 civilians and not to show the amount and extend the invalidity to the rest of the verdict despite the possibility of separating the part relating to the invalidity.

The contested verdict resulted in the invalidity of the arbitral award for violation of public order in Egypt, when it ruled that interest exceeding the maximum limit set in Article 227 for civilians did not specify the amount of interest (LIBOR + 3%) and whether it exceeded the prescribed legal limit. Otherwise, it can be said that this is contrary to Egyptian public policy, marred by irregularities, as well as to the extension of the invalidity to the other parts of the other judgment of the arbitral tribunal, even if it can be separated from the parts declared invalid, which has led to the error in the application of the law.

(Egyptian Court of Cassation Appeal No. 810 for the 71st session of 25/1/2007)

Authentic judgments of arbitrators and their effects.

It is decided that, although the original rule provides that once the verdict has been validated, it is up to the court to prevent it from resuming consideration of the issue in which it has ruled on any subsequent case in which the same dispute arises. In a case already heard, for a period indicating that he was waiving his right, his effect on the judicial centers that had settled his opposition for his opponent at a later date should not be considered as a consequence of the judgment he had contributed to render in accordance with the fundamentalist rule that whoever What was his share, he replied, was scheduled In the Court of Cassation, the arbitrators' decisions, like those of the judiciary, are valid from the moment the order is issued, which remains in force as long as the verdict is rendered. It must limit its examination to the merits of the case, in the context of the case mentioned in the judgment in cassation, and the parties must not return to the debate on the matter.

(Egyptian Court of Cassation Appeal No. 76 for the year 73 BC - hearing 13/3/2007)

- If it is stated in the documents that the decision No........ Cairo appeal rendered on 23 February 2000, confirming the preliminary decision dismissing the appellant's appeal before being challenged against him, the invalidity of the arbitration clause contained in the contract and the appeal and inadmissibility of the arbitration if it received exceptional amounts of social security and taxes, which fall within the jurisdiction of the courts, are limited to the judiciary because they are linked to public policy, because the dispute between the parties did not concern the payment of these amounts, but was limited to determining their commitment, including the use of arbitration to decide and whether this judicial power had the force of law. What is the difference between separation and so on Om in this case what can not be with him to raise this conflict again in the trial that lie, the death notice of this face is unfounded.

(Appeal No. 1910 of the Egyptian Court of Cassation for the year 75 BC) - hearing of 27/12/2011).

Suspension of the execution of the verdict and application for a declaration of invalidity:

The application for enforcement of the judgment will not be accepted if the filing date of the application for a declaration of invalidity has not expired in the first paragraph of Article 58 of Act No. 27 of 1994 on arbitration in civil and commercial matters. The arbitral award expired, stating that the statement of reasons indicated the right to win the case in arbitration in the application for enforcement of the judgment in which the expiry of the ninety-day period for bringing the action for invalidity expired. In order not to remain negative after being challenged by the opponent The arbitral awards are enforceable as soon as they are published because they do not accept the appeal by one of the means of appeal provided for in the Code of Procedure, except that the application for annulment of the arbitral award may be made in accordance with the conditions set out in article 5/2/1 of Act No. 27 of 1994. However, the court may order a stay of execution if the plaintiff so requests in his procedural file and the request is based on reasonable grounds, in accordance with article 57 of the same law. The case in which the justification for waiting for pain to pass He loses his legal title.

(Appeal of the Egyptian Court of Cassation No. 10792 for the hearing of the years 65 BC of 5/6/2008)

Possibility of winning an arbitration case during the execution of the judgment:

The lesson to be learned from the interpretation of texts is about goals and meanings, not words and buildings; defining the right layout in the text requires research on the purpose and purpose dictated by the text. An application for enforcement of the arbitral award shall not be accepted if the date of filing of the invalidity of the arbitral award has not expired. The date is prohibited from me from the r T the arbitration ruling in favor of his right to request the original implementation directly from the agent remains negative after being attacked by his opponent to establish a case of invalidity.

(Appeal of the Egyptian Court of Cassation No. 10792 for the hearing of the years 65 BC of 5/6/2008).

The New York Treaty, after its entry into force, is the applicable law.

- Article 296 of the Code of Civil and Commercial Procedure provides that the enforcement of judgments and orders issued in a foreign country may be ordered under the same conditions as those provided for by the legislation of that country for the enforcement of Egyptian judgments and orders issued there. Article 298 defines the conditions to be verified before issuing the order to execute the foreign order. Article 301 of the conclusions, in which the legislator concluded the chapter on the enforcement of foreign judgments, orders and sureties, provides that the promulgation provided for in the preceding articles shall be without prejudice to the provisions of treaties concluded or concluded between the Republic of Egypt and other States. However, the legislator violated this principle in section 301. The above arguments stipulate that, in the case of a treaty, the treaty will, after its entry into force, be the applicable law in this respect. Had it contradicted the provisions of the above-mentioned law, Egypt would not have acceded to the Convention. Concerning the recognition and enforcement of the provisions of the arbitrators on 8 June 1959, adopted by the United Nations Conference on International Commercial Arbitration, held in New York from 20 May to 10 June 1958 and enacted by Presidential Decree No. 171 of 1959 and entered into force in Egypt Accordingly, article 3 of the 1958 New York Convention provides that each Contracting State shall recognize the authenticity of the arbitral award and order its enforcement in accordance with the rules of procedure. Monitoring in the desired territory Execution and in accordance with the conditions set out in the following articles, that the implementation complies with the procedural rules in force in the territory in which the implementation is required, taking into account the simplest procedures and excluding the most severe procedures, it is true that the rule of law has been applied to the fact of the trial and that the obituary is sacrificed on an unfounded basis.

(Appeal No. 945 of the Egyptian Court of Cassation for the year 69 BC - hearing 8/5/2008)

The text of article 198/1 does not include the conclusions of the New York Convention.

Article 301 of the Code of Procedure, by which the legislator concluded the chapter on the enforcement of foreign judgments, orders and sureties, provided that, if there was a treaty between Egypt and other States concerning the enforcement of foreign judgments, the provisions of those treaties should be applied and that Egypt had acceded to the 1958 New York Convention on the Recognition and Enforcement of Foreign Arbitral Awards.

As regards eligibility - the applicant insisted on the inadmissibility of the arbitrator's judgment, provided that the finance lease, which included the arbitration clause on the basis of which the judgment had been rendered, was not automatically convened, which means that the arbitral award was rendered without an arbitration agreement. The above-mentioned rental agreement, provided in an official translation of the documents, stipulates that the clause provides that the law applicable to this agreement is Swedish law and that any dispute arising from its interpretation or execution shall be submitted to arbitration in Sweden in accordance with the provisions of the Swedish Arbitration Act. It is Swedish law as the law chosen by the parties to govern the initial contract contained in the arbitration agreement in its terms, and it is the last word on the existence of this contract and the related arbitration agreement, in terms of the existence of consent and convergence of the acceptance of the affirmative and the binding force of the affirmation, as well as the conditions necessary for the acceptance of the affirmation Without the Egyptian civil law adopted by the appellant's defence in this regard - and both did not provide any evidence of the Swedish law mentioned until the court was guided by its rules This affirmation, contrary to the original according to which the judgment of foreign arbitrators is supposed to be rendered on the basis of a legally valid arbitration agreement, was preliminarily judged in favor of the contested judgment and is in the process of verifying the obligations to publish the annex to the arbitrators' judgment subject to the executive's formulation. As the arbitration agreement is based on the arbitration clause contained in the finance lease, it will have corrected the law in its result and will not invalidate it simply by failing to disclose its act of law or by failing to respond to a legal defense of the litigants. In his statement, he may also set out the facts established in the appropriate legal manner, provided that he only takes into account what has been obtained by the court of first instance. The obituary for this reason will not be valid.

(An Egyptian court rejected the appeal 2660 for the year 59 session of 27/3/1996 Technical Office 47 c 1 s 107 p. 558)

Request for enforcement of a foreign arbitral award not subject to the provisions of Egyptian law on arbitration in Egypt:

If the convicted person requests the enforcement of a foreign arbitral award not subject to the provisions of Egyptian law on arbitration in Egypt, he shall institute proceedings in accordance with the usual procedures in accordance with the provisions of the Egyptian procedural law "Articles 296 et seq. Republican Decree No. 171 of 1959 of 2/2/1959, entered into force on 8/6/1959

(Egyptian Court of Cassation appeal 913 for the 73rd session of 23 February 2010)

The provisions of articles 235-236-238 of the Code of Civil Procedure stipulate that the provisions of treaties between the United Arab Emirates and other States are applicable to the enforcement of decisions rendered by foreign courts as national legislation. Included in these international treaties or conventions before ordering the ratification or implementation of these provisions in the State. One of the conditions set out in the judicial cooperation agreement between the United Arab Emirates and the State of France is that the decision is enforceable and not subject to ordinary appeal in the country of origin. This means that the ICC seal on the pages of this document is not endorsed and that they are exempt from any certified document proving that the award is enforceable and not subject to appeal in the country of origin.

Therefore, the appellant's appeal in recognition of the arbitral award to be ratified is inadmissible.

(Federal Supreme Court - Appeal No. 764 of 24 Hearing 7/6/2005 Technical Office Q27, p. 1526)

Chapter VI Final provisions

Article 58: Charter of arbitrators and their laws

The Minister of Economy publishes the Charter of Arbitrators in coordination with the State arbitration institutions.

2. The Minister of Justice or the head of the competent judicial authority shall establish the lists of arbitrators chosen from among them in accordance with the provisions of Article 11 of this Law.

Article 59 - Scope of the law

The provisions of this Law shall apply to any arbitration existing at the time of its application, even if it is based on a previous arbitration agreement, provided that the procedures followed in accordance with the provisions of any previous legislation remain valid.

Article 60: Deletion of arbitration articles in the Code of Civil Procedure

Articles (203) to (218) of Federal Law No (11) for the above-mentioned year 1992 are repealed, provided that the procedures in accordance with it remain valid.

2. Any provision contrary to the provisions of this Act is repealed.

Article 61: Dissemination and enforcement of the law

This Law shall be published in the Official Gazette and shall enter into force one month after the date of its publication. The law was promulgated on 17 Sha'ban 1439 Hijri corresponding to 3 May 2018 and entered into force one month after the day after its publication.

Examples of Emirati judgments

In the event of an appeal from an arbitral award

No. (1): If the defendant appears before the courts at the first hearing and does not make the arbitration clause, the judicial authority will decide.

Agreement on arbitration, which means that litigants cannot resort to justice - with the exception of - the court may examine and judge the case if the defendant or his representative is represented at the first hearing and does not comply with the arbitration clause. Sentenced in solidarity - its effect.

Considering that the applicant institution mourns the contested judgment against the law and that, consequently, a lawyer for the first applicant attended the first hearing scheduled for the hearing on 16 June 1992 without respecting the arbitration clause,

Therefore, the claimant's right against this payment will be lost and will not be modified if the third claimant does not appear at the first hearing, then his lawyer appears at the specified hearing before the plenary chamber to which the complaint has been referred and if he complies with the arbitration clause at that hearing. The opponent is the husband of the second applicant and, at the first hearing, his lawyer asked for time to submit a power of attorney.

If the contested judgment contradicts this consideration, the court will not accept the case because of the arbitration clause stating that the dispute will not be divided. To comment on the appellant's appeal list against them in the appeal and leave the heart of the matter, the judgment is imperfect enough to be overturned.

2. As this notice of death is counterproductive, the provision of article 203, paragraph 5, of the Code of Civil Procedure in the section on arbitration stipulates that "if the parties to the proceedings agree to arbitrate a dispute, it cannot be referred to the courts. At the first session, the case may be considered and the arbitration clause shall be considered null and void, indicating that the original is the inadmissibility of the litigant's dispute when he has agreed with his opponent to settle his disputes by arbitration.

However, if the dispute is brought before it, the court may examine and decide the case if the defendant or his representative is brought before the court during the first session during which the litigant is brought before the court. Each of them has its own objections and other common objections,

This is based on the idea of mutual prosecution while providing an advantage to the remaining debtors who must be jointly and severally convicted, without the cases in which the conduct of one of them has caused damage. The applicants against them did not appear at the first session before the Sharia Chamber of the Court of First Instance on 11/5/1992.

At the hearing on 16/06/1992, the first appellant's lawyers were present and requested time to present an agency to the third appellant and provide him with copies of the documents filed by him.

During this session, the Sharia Department took the decision to refer the case to the Trade Department.

At the first hearing scheduled for 22/10/1992, the third applicant's lawyer was present against him and his act was certified by him on 11/10/1992. This was the first hearing in which a lawyer represented the third applicant

He filed a defense in which he opposed the examination of the case in court, confirming the arbitration clause stipulated in the contract in support of the case. Failure to accept the case for this reason will encourage the rest of the defendants in the case (the first to be challenged) to suspend this reason to all, and if the verdict of the contested conclusion of this correct result

He ruled in favor of the preliminary judgment appealing after accepting the trial because of the arbitration clause, as it did not violate the law. He did not require his request for the arbitration to take place in Dubai.

If the documents are vacant and the arbitration cannot take place at the agreed place, the disputed judgment will not have violated the law when I drafted the text of the agreement and rejected the claimant's request for arbitration in Dubai.

1. Considering that the action is dismissed.

(Discrimination - Dubai - Appeal No. 61 of 1994, "Rights" hearing of 13 November 1994)

Conditions for extending the arbitration clause to third parties

Judicial principles in arbitration in the United Arab Emirates

The Dubai Court of Cassation establishes a legal principle by adopting the idea of reciprocal prosecution

The validity and extension of the effect of the arbitration clause and the arbitration agreement for those who have not acceded to it before the courts

The Dubai Court of Cassation rendered on 13/11/1994 Appeal Judgment No. 61 of 1994, "Rights" presided over by Dr. / Mustafa Kira, the most important implication of this decision is that the court has established a new legal principle or if it is true to take a new turn for the judiciary In accordance with the provisions of Article 203/5 of the Code of Civil Procedure, the complainant is not required to adhere to this payment, the court has adopted the idea of reciprocal proceedings. Between the joint and several debtors and carried out his actions as soon as the adhesion to the payment not to hear the case the existence of the arbitration clause.

The mutual pursuit between the solidarists is based on the idea that each solid debtor acts as a deputy and representing other solidary debtors, in a way that provides them with a benefit and not a prejudice. This idea first emerged as the French codification and then adopted by the Egyptian codification.

Following the judgment of the Dubai Court of Cassation in question, we note that this judgment, as we have already mentioned, has given a new direction to the Emirates judiciary with regard to extending the effect of compliance with the arbitration clause by one of the parties to those who have not joined the dispute.

Under article 203/5 of the United Arab Emirates Code of Civil Procedure, the section on arbitration provides that the parties to the dispute may not resort to justice when the parties to the dispute have agreed to resolve it by arbitration, but the court may consider the dispute if it is submitted to it and the respondent does not comply with the condition. The arbitration stipulated by the contract during the first session and, considering the provisions of this provision, we find that it contains two very important elements from a legal point of view, we highlight them in a brief and simplified.

First, the court clarified the meaning of the term "first hearing" in the text of article 203, paragraph 5, of the Code of Civil Procedure, in the sense of the hearing at which the litigant appears before the court and not the first hearing in the dispute. For any reason whatsoever for several hearings, this does not invalidate the right of the litigant to defend the payment in the presence of the arbitration clause as long as the first hearing he attended is the session during which the arbitration clause is held, even if the proceedings were earlier. This reduces the rigidity of the payment. The provision of this article stipulated that this payment had to be accepted at the first meeting.

Secondly: the court adopted the idea of reciprocal proceedings between the joint and several debtors and applied them as well as their actions in payment of the existence of the arbitration clause by one of the parties to the dispute in the case without adhering to the rest of the parties who are entitled to adhere to this payment and the extension of its incidence, if a contract is concluded between several parties guaranteeing a solution. Disputes between them by arbitration,

A dispute was filed before the ordinary judiciary and did not resist the argument that the arbitration clause had not been heard at the first session. In accordance with the idea of reciprocal proceedings, each party was included in the contract in which it provided for the arbitration clause, and then became a debtor or co-creditor between them.

With regard to compliance with this clause once the dispute is submitted to the judiciary, each of them has the right to maintain this payment as well as other objections or defenses common to them. The rest of the litigants were to be convicted during the proceedings, not what caused them harm or increased their burden.

The arbitration clause, if included in a multilateral contract, if one of them adheres to this clause once the dispute is brought to court, for the benefit of other persons who have not adhered to this payment, because of the common defenses between them, on the other hand it is advantageous for those who have not respected it. Do not consider the case of the existence of the arbitration clause even if he did not maintain this clause in court.

Finally, this provision marks a turning point in the history of the UAE judiciary, as it established a new legal principle to overcome the impact of adhering to the payment of the existence of the arbitration clause and extending it to those who have not adhered to it on the basis of the idea of mutual prosecution.

So it's a question of

This approach represents new trends in the world of arbitration that are jointly established by the judiciary so that the principles and rules of arbitration are complemented and follow the judicial approach.

N ° (2): Arbitral award rendered abroad by a foreign arbitrator to ratify it before a court and become an executive act.

Arbitration decision - rendered by agreement between the parties outside the court - ratified by the competent court - arbitration award rendered outside the State by a foreign arbitrator - follow the procedures provided for in article 235 of the Code of Civil Procedure after ratification and considered as an executive act.

While article 213/2 of the Code of Civil Procedure stipulates that "when an arbitration takes place outside the court, the arbitrators must provide a copy of the award to each party within five days of the arbitral award being made. At the request of one of the parties to the usual review procedures, it is stated that the arbitral award rendered pursuant to the agreement of the parties outside the court must be ratified by the competent court, whether the decision was taken by an arbitrator inside or outside the State,

Because the text is general and specialized only in evidence and the difference between them is that if the arbitral award is made outside the country by a foreign arbitrator, it must be ratified and following the procedures provided for in articles 235 of this law.

The rules for the execution of the judgment or decision will only be applied after its publication and will be considered as an executive act.

(Abu Dhabi - Federal Supreme Court - Appeal No 202 for the 25th year of the Supreme Judiciary - Public hearing held on Sunday 16 Rabi II 1427 H corresponding to 14/5/2006)

N ° (3): Ratification of a judgment by a court of no jurisdiction resulting in the invalidity of the judgment

Ratification of the arbitral award - of the competent court - Selection criteria for the court competent to ratify the arbitrators' decision.

1. The court competent to rule on an arbitral award shall be convened by the court competent to hear the case, whether the arbitration takes place before the court or by agreement of the parties outside the court.

2. Article 31 of the same law stipulated in the third paragraph that the jurisdiction of the articles of the court of the court of the court where the defendant is located is that of the domicile of the defendant, the court in which all or part of the agreement was concluded or the court in which its agreement is to be enforced. Indicates that, where there are several

places of performance of the agreed commercial article, some of this work has been carried out by more than one court and none of these courts had jurisdiction to hear a case involving a dispute relating to the performance of the parties' obligations under that commercial article. Real estate made by the contractor with own materials or workers, which are considered commercial, if located in more than one place, the court in which one of these places is located has jurisdiction to hear the case and, according to the general rules, the choice of the plaintiff, These places where the pain was made A contract has been determined by one or more contracts between the same liabilities.

While it was established in the trial that the applicant and the disputed person had entered into several contracts, each agreed to refer the dispute between them concerning the contract to the arbitral tribunal constituted in accordance with the provisions of those contracts. These contracts have been performed in several emirates, including the emirate of Sharjah, and jurisdiction is attributed to the performance of such contracts in one of the UAE courts where the obligations of the parties to these contracts, including the Sharjah court, have been fulfilled. All contracts are referred to the arbitral tribunal that rendered its decision in the dispute. The jurisdiction to hear the case is ratified by one of the above-mentioned courts, including the Sharjah court. In a trial to ratify the decision of the above-mentioned arbitrators,

If the contested judgment contradicts that examination and determines that the Sharjah Court of First Instance does not have jurisdiction to examine the case on the ground that the person competent to do so is the Ras Al Khaimah Court in which the headquarters of the disputed company is located, the judgment must be incorrect in the application of the law to be annulled.

(Abu Dhabi - Federal Supreme Court - Civil Cassation - Appeal No. 252 of the 26th year of the Supreme Judiciary - at the public hearing held on 6 Rabi Al-Akher 1428 H corresponding to 23/4/2007)

N ° (4): When requesting the award, the court must not be subject to its content or its degree of compliance with the law.

The grounds for invalidity are exclusively provided for by law. The Court of First Instance will not be submitted to arbitration objectively and to the extent that it complies with the law when considering the request for ratification. Allows the parties to discuss, defend and comment. Pronunciation.

The case of invalidity of the arbitrator's judgment - and in accordance with the jurisdiction of this court and Article 216 of the Code of Civil Procedure - refers to the arbitrator's decision as a legal act and is based on an error in the procedure without calculation error and that the defects that the plaintiff can invoke the mentioned article exclusively not to be measured, which relates either to the arbitration agreement or to the arbitration dispute and any defects relating to the arbitration agreement and the ground for invalidity of the arbitrator's judgment, is the delivery of the judgment without an arbitration document, or on the basis of a false document, or has fallen within the time limit, or if the arbitrator on h Dodd of the document or contravenes a rule of public policy, but those concerning the arbitration dispute and which also result in the invalidity of the arbitrator's judgment are specified in the article mentioned in the cases of arbitrators who have not been appointed in accordance with the law or issued by some of them without being authorized to rule in the absence of others or not The confrontation principle in dispute, violation of the right of defense, invalidity of the verdict or invalidity of the proceedings has an impact on the verdict, any dispute raised by one of the parties to the arbitration must challenge the judgment rendered by the arbitrator and must not be related to previous cases or must be related to an estimate. Arbitrator of the dispute or invalid or sufficiently invalid The reasons for his judgment are inadmissible, in the sense that the court of first instance, when considering the request for ratification of the arbitral award, cannot objectively object to that decision and to the extent to which it complies with the law. The arbitral tribunal established that, after the parties appeared, each party gave each party time to present its exhibits and to present its defenses and observations. It then examined all aspects of the defense raised and examined in the light of the documents presented and the statements of the witnesses it heard. The Commission is charged with commission for 96/97, i.e. AED 322 733, and for witnesses and documentary evidence establishing that its commission for the Adma project is 10% and not 5% as indicated in the contract, and that the amounts it held - in this respect - are within its rights and in accordance with this percentage, and the appellant is not entitled to claim.

He then ordered him to pay him MAD 322,733 and interest at the rate of 12% per annum from the end of the month until payment and to reject his counterclaim. If the appellant invokes grounds of appeal, even if they are formulated in nullity and have an impact on the arbitrators' verdict, it is in fact a new presentation of the subject matter of the dispute, which is notified in article 216 of the above-mentioned Civil Procedure Act, if the contested verdict respects this examination. It decided to ratify the arbitrators' verdict and dismissed the counterclaim. The invalidity of the obituary notice on grounds of appeal is unfounded.

(Abu Dhabi - Federal Supreme Court - Appeal No. 56 for year 27, Supreme Judicial - Commercial Cassation - in public hearing held on Sunday, April 23 in Rabi'Al-Akher 1427H, corresponding to 21/5/2006)

N ° (5): Appointing authority The parties consult each other when appointing the arbitrator and the judiciary does not become competent.

Disagreement between the parties on the following points: Appointment of arbitrators - Appellate authority - Consultation on the appointment - Decision to appoint without consultation - Appeal to justice for the appointment of an arbitrator.

1. Under articles 203 and 204 of the Code of Civil Procedure, if the parties agree to settle any dispute that may arise between them in the performance of the contract concluded between them, and if they have not agreed on the persons of the arbitrators or on one or more of the accredited arbitrators He has resigned, revoked or revoked his decision or prevented him from intervening between the parties to replace it. At the request of one of the litigants, the judgment is not subject to appeal. This is the case and in accordance with article 12 of the Rules of Procedure for Conciliation and Commercial Arbitration at the Abu Dhabi Commercial Conciliation and Arbitration Centre, it has been decided that bodies will be formed... Arbitration in accordance with the requirements of the parties and their agreements, and if the parties are unaware of the duration of the training or appointment of the members of these bodies, or do not include the names of the members of these bodies, the Director

General of the Centre - after consultation with the parties to propose the constitution of these bodies, and the parties to make known this proposal Publicity.

2. If the Director General of the Centre receives no objection within the period referred to in point (1), the proposal of the Director General of the Centre to establish the Authority or to appoint its members shall be deemed to be an acceptance by the parties. Authorizes him to respond to the above-mentioned bodies.

If a party objects to the establishment of the Authority within the time limit specified in point 1), such objection shall be submitted to the Arbitration and Arbitration Committee of the Abu Dhabi Chamber of Commerce and Industry for decision by a final and binding decision of the parties. The final decision of the Customs and Arbitration Committee in Abu Dhabi depends on compliance with the above-mentioned procedures. It was established that the director of the center against which the second appellant had brought the case before the Customs and Commercial Arbitration Committee directly to select the likely arbitrator without consulting the parties to the arbitration.

He dismissed the objection without following the procedure provided for in the aforementioned article and the applicant was therefore entitled to appeal to the competent court to hear the dispute relating to the arbitration with a view to the appointment of such an **arbitrator. The judgment rendered in this respect may under no circumstances be appealed.**

(Abu Dhabi - Federal Supreme Court - Appeal No. 206 of 27 Supreme Court - Civil Cassation - in public hearing on Tuesday, December 25 in Dhu al-Qaida)

N ° (6)

The arbitral award shall have an authoritative order

This prevents the judiciary from considering the dispute unless it refuses to ratify the arbitral award.

The arbitrators' judgment shall have the validity of the order issued upon its publication.

It is decided that the verdict rendered by the arbitrators shall have the validity of the order issued upon its publication. In the latter case, the judgment has no authoritative precedent for review on the merits at the request of the parties before the judiciary as the holder of general jurisdiction.

(Abu Dhabi - Federal Supreme Court - Appeal No. 236 for 27 January of the Supreme Judicial Year - Civil Cassation - in public hearing on Tuesday 11 April 1426 H corresponding to 13/12/2005)

N ° (7)

The appellant's refusal to sign the arbitration document shall not affect or lead to nullity.

The agreement on arbitration must be in writing -

There is no particular form of writing - the agreement of the parties - the date of arbitration of the first session - the application of the legal text - the delivery of the judgment before the expiry of the six-month period - to affect it - the Court of Cassation corrects the error in the legal relations -

The arbitration document signed by the applicant against her and the arbitrator - sent to the applicant for signature - refusal to sign - the invalid application is received.

1. Arbitration is an exceptional way to resolve a dispute by departing from the ordinary dispute and the guarantees it guarantees. It is inevitably intended for what the arbitrators' willingness is to present to the arbitral tribunal.

Article 203(1) of the Code of Civil Procedure generally allows contractors to require that, in a basic contract or subsequent agreement, any dispute that may arise between them in the performance of a particular contract be subject to one or more provisions.

In accordance with the second paragraph of this Article, the arbitration agreement may only be drawn up in writing, even with regard to commercial documents. This may not be proven by testimony, even if it is sufficient to recognize or swear an oath. It is not necessary to write in the form of an agreement or mutual legal declarations or letters between the parties pleading approval of the arbitration or a letter from the litigant to the court stating that, since the arbitration procedure was set up as from 31/3/1999, 11/4/1999 AD The Abu Dhabi Commercial Conciliation and Arbitration Centre has requested the appellant company to select the individual arbitrator from the list of arbitrators registered with the Centre. Ms Habib is an arbitrator on the list of arbitrators sent by the Centre, which she confirmed in her letter of 9/5/1999, in which she also replied that she was not entitled to continue the arbitration proceedings. The appellant accepted the arbitration and his attachment to what was said because of the obituary, regardless of the opinion expressed therein, is unproductive and therefore unacceptable.

2. Although the appellant qualifies the second ground for contesting the contested decision, it contravenes the law and the error in its application. The dispute must be held within a maximum period of six months from the date of receipt of the arbitrator's mandate.

3. As this obituary is not valid, article 203/1 of the Code of Civil Procedure authorizes contractors to accept, either in the main contract or in a subsequent agreement, to settle their dispute by arbitration, in accordance with special conditions and procedures that have not violated public policy or applicable legal provisions. If the parties to the dispute agree to entrust arbitration to a specific permanent organization or centre, this implies agreeing to respect the rules of that organization or centre, in particular with regard to procedures, and taking into account the speed of the characteristics of the arbitration system that have made it preferable. The legislator sets a time limit for the issuance of a judgment The arbitration of the parties may request after the expiry of the closure of the proceedings and authorization for them to raise the dispute to the judiciary State His original mandate.

In accordance with the previous article of the ADCCI Rules, the appointment or extension of the date of the arbitrators shall be subject to the agreement of both parties, unless the latter specifies this period within a maximum period of six months from the date of receipt of the assignment.

Any action after this period shall be deemed to have no effect on the parties unless the leave is notified in writing. As such, the parties have agreed in the arbitration clause referred to in point 25 that the duration of the arbitration shall be six months from the date of the first arbitration session, which was set at 1 p.m. on 23/11/1999 in the minutes of the Centre located in the Chamber's building.

The verdict was delivered on 17/5/2000 during the agreed period, it is not invalid and, since the contested judgment applied the procedural rules set out in the Code of Civil Procedure, the six-month period from the date of the first hearing was taken into account. The dispute, whose outcome is correct, is not compromised by false legal relationships in its cases. The Court of Cassation can correct this error and refer it to the appropriate database without reversing it. Therefore, the appeal against the judgment for this reason is unproductive and therefore unacceptable.

The third party considers that the third ground for judgment is an appeal against the law and error in its application. If the contested judgment does not include a copy of the arbitration clause and its judgment does not include the content of this activity, it will be vitiated by a defect due to its revocation.

5 - As this obituary is not valid, it appears from the examination of the documents that the arbitral award included an arbitration document signed by the applicant against him and the arbitrator on 13/5/2000 after JC. It was sent to the appellant for signature but refused to sign it. In addition, the judgment also includes a summary of the dispute and a summary of the litigants' statements and exhibits. If the contested judgment rejects the judiciary, it will be at the heart of the law and the judgment on this ground will be unfounded.

6. In the foregoing, the action is dismissed.

(Abu Dhabi - Federal Supreme Court - Appeal No. 891 of year 27: Supreme Court of the Judiciary - Commercial Cassation - in public hearing on Saturday 21, Jumada I 1427 H, corresponding to 17/06/2006)

Number (8)

The judgment which determines the existence of the arbitration clause and its effect may be appealed separately

The request for non-acceptance of the existence of an arbitration clause - payment of incompetence - may be appealed against the judgment rendered before the resolution of the dispute was issued - the duration of the appeal being sixty days.

It is decided that the argument of non-acceptance of the existence of the arbitration clause will be considered as the argument of the lack of jurisdiction of the State to settle the dispute from the jurisdiction of the judiciary to the arbitral tribunal. Considering that the applicant has argued before the Court of First Instance not to accept the contested request on the basis of the provisions of section 46 of the general conditions of the contract, according to which the settlement of the dispute through the Compensation and Arbitration Committee, which is part of the Standing Committee on Projects,

The court of first instance refused to pay and ruled on the merits. On appeal, the Court of Appeal declared that the contested judgment was set aside and that the case could not be brought before the courts because of the arbitration clause, but was overturned by Appeal Judgment No. 377 of 24 BC. After this cassation, the Court of Appeal ruled on the appellant's 2001 appeal 150 for the year 2001. The appellant sought the annulment of the contested judgment because of the existence of the arbitration clause. The arbitration clause, which is one of the provisions concerning jurisdiction,

It may then be appealed in accordance with the provisions of article 151 of the Code of Civil Procedure. The duration of the appeal is sixty days, in accordance with article 176 of the Code of Civil Procedure No. 11 of 1992, as amended by Act No. 30 of 2005.

Has been marked on the draft judgment of the adviser / Ali Ahmed informing him of the date of the next session of 19/2/2006 m. He also attended Mr. Rashid Ali's last session on the complainant. On appeal from this judgment on 19/10/2006, it will be filed after the legal date,

It is therefore unacceptable to lift it after the deadline.

(Abu Dhabi - Federal Supreme Court - Appeal No. 421 of the year 28 Supreme Judicial - Public hearing in civil cassation held on Monday 28 Rabi al-Akher 1428H corresponding to 14/5/2007)

Summary of the judgments of the Dubai Court of Cassation

Payment of non-acceptance of the case due to the arbitration clause

(1) An appeal may be lodged against the judgment rendered by the competent court, provided that the competent court does not have the right not to accept the case because of the arbitration clause, such as objections to jurisdiction, the judgment rendered in the dispute concerning this payment. Mandate of the judgment in the trial.

(Call No. 152 of 2004 - Labor Call Session, 27/2/2005)

2. Advocacy not to accept the case of accepting arbitration. Such as defenses of incompetence leading to the court's refusal or decision on the matter, implicit jurisdiction to hear the case cannot be challenged on independence grounds if it does not modify the whole dispute, unless the court has jurisdiction to hear the case.

(Call No. 56 of the 2005 session "Commercial Call" 10/10/2005)

Arbitration agreement

1. The reference in the contract to the settlement of any dispute arising between the contractor and the employer in accordance with the General Conditions of Procurement (FIDIC) is sufficient to report the agreement of the parties to the arbitration without the need to indicate in the contract the details of this condition.

(Appeal No. 100 of 2004, Civil Appeal Session, 9/1/2005)

2. Arbitration. What it is Arbitration Agreement. His ways. It is not permissible to extract evidence of the arbitration from the mere silence of one of the parties in response to the offer of arbitration made by the other party or the implementation of what has been presented to it by that party, unless this proves its acceptance of the arbitration. The arbitration agreement will have the competence to dispose of the disputed right and will not be subject to the theory of the apparent situation.

(Call No 220 of 2004 -'Commercial Call' - Session 17/1/2005)

3- Director of the limited liability company. Eligibility to accept arbitration on its behalf and to calculate it within the limits of its activity. Other persons are permitted to hold a special power of attorney on his behalf by way of agreement at arbitration.

(Call No. 220 of 2004, session "Commercial Call", 17/1/2005)

4 - The arbitration contract concluded by the unauthorized agent is relatively invalid in favor of the client without his opponent. Thereafter, only the client has the right to confirm the invalidity of the arbitration agreement, in violation of this error in the application of the law.

(Appeal No. 209 of 2004, Civil Appeal session, 20/03/2005)

5. Agreement on arbitration. What it is Arbitration will only take place if it is proven that the common will of the contracting parties will be exempted from arbitration. The inadmissibility of an arbitration agreement cannot be implicit

(Appeal No. 64 of 2005, Commercial Appeal hearing, 18/04/2005)

Arbitration and agreement. What is each of them? An express assignment in the original contract of the document containing the arbitration clause shall be considered as an agreement on arbitration, if the assignment is expressed at the time of adoption of this clause. General reference to the texts of the document without attribution of the arbitration clause, not to be extended to arbitration.

(Call No. 174 of 2005, "Commercial Call", session of 19/12/2005)

7- The existence of annexes or schedules to the contract. Not requiring the parties to sign it only stipulates in the contract that it is part of the contract they have signed. The bug included the inclusion of an exception clause as an arbitration clause. Not be valid unless you sign such attachments.

(Call No. 174 of 2005, "Commercial Call", session of 19/12/2005)

Arbitration document

The fall of the arbitration document

The fall of the arbitration document beyond the time limit for the delivery of the judgment. Not related to public order. It must be explicitly respected by the interested party of both parties to the arbitration before the arbitrator or a court or to request its invalidity.

(Call No. 322 of 2004, session "Commercial Call", 11/4/2005)

Appointment of arbitrators

1. Judgments of the Court of Appeal relating to the inadmissibility or admissibility of the action and which do not focus on the appointment of arbitrators, challenged by discrimination, are admissible.

(Call No. 273 of 2004, Commercial Call Session, 5/3/2005)

2- The agreement of the contractors on arbitration. The right of each of them to have recourse to the courts to appoint arbitrators in the event of a dispute between them. Jurisdiction of the court to appoint a particular arbitrator. There is no way to appeal this judgment. M.P. 203, 204 civil proceedings.

(Call No. 273 of 2004, Commercial Call Session, 5/3/2005)

Adhere to the arbitration clause

1- The waiver of the arbitration clause, explicitly or implicitly, is admissible. The waiver must be a clearly disclosed procedure that leaves no doubt as to the willingness to waive this condition. Draw this. The authority of the court of first instance.

Appeal No 100 of the 2004 Civil Appeal Hearing of 9/1/2005

2. A party who invokes the arbitration clause at the first hearing must oppose its litigant's appeal. No objection to this hearing, the effect of which is the merits of the case. First meeting. It is the session during which the defendant is represented by a person or agent who has proved his or her presence.

This does not change the fact that the court is not competent in terms of quality, qualification or local examination.

(Appeal No. 39 of 2005, Civil Appeal Session, 25/9/2005)

Scope of the arbitration

1. The arbitration is limited to what the parties have agreed to submit to the arbitrator. This does not prevent both parties to the dispute from causing or being directly related to the subject matter of the dispute.

Deferred benefits are associated with the principal amount of the debt. Arbitration agreement of the parties to the dispute concerning a monetary obligation. Its scope for deciding on the application of late payment due

Appeal No. 322 of the "Commercial Appeal" hearing for the year 2004 of 11/4/2005

2. Arbitration may not be conducted in connection with seizure and execution procedures, nor with the claims necessary for its validity. Exception, agreement on the jurisdiction of the arbitral tribunal. The law stipulates, in the context of seizure proceedings, that a specific action must be brought. It may only be submitted by the competent court without the arbitration body, unless otherwise agreed.

(Call No. 204 of 2005, session "Commercial Call", 2/7/2005)

Payment by reference to arbitration

Independence cannot be challenged in judgments rendered in the course of the proceedings and does not put an end to the dispute. The exception Article 151 Civil proceedings. Advocacy not to accept the case of accepting arbitration. What it is The judiciary rejects it or the judiciary in this matter. It is not permissible to challenge independence except for the whole dispute, unless the tribunal has jurisdiction to rule on the case.

(Call No. 174 of 2005, "Commercial Call", session of 19/12/2005)

Arbitration clause

Include the arbitration clause in an independent arbitration contract, which is not necessary. The adequacy of the arbitration agreement in the contract concluded between the parties.

(Call No. 39 of 2005, session "Commercial Call", 16/04/2005)

2. Obligations of the lessor during the chartering of the vessel. What is the relationship between the lessor and the lessee is governed by the ship's charter. To do so. If such a discrepancy exists with the bill of lading, Signature of the shipper of the ship's charterer on the charter contract in which the arbitration clause is mentioned. He must comply with this condition even if the bill of lading is exempt from it.

(Call No. 179 of 2004 "Commercial Call" and Call No. 184 of 2004 - Session 14/5/2005)

3. Indicate in the arbitration clause that it will apply to the partners of the company with regard to any dispute or litigation between them concerning the management of the company and its accounts. The lawsuit must be brought between the partners on this subject and the company must not be a party to this dispute. Its effect Its competence has no effect in activating the effect of the arbitration clause. To do so. The arbitrator decides on the merits of this legal action and does not fall within the jurisdiction of the Court.

Call No 56 of 2005 - Commercial Call Session 10/10/2005

Arbitration examination

Arbitrators are required to swear an oath to witnesses before hearing their testimony, even if litigants do not object before them to violate this procedure. In violation, the arbitration procedure is invalid. It does not prevent the acceptance of the invalidity by waiving the right of the pleader before the arbitral award. The opponent may declare this invalidity before the court.

(Call No. 322 of 2005, session "Commercial Call", 10/12/2005)

2. Provide in an arbitration clause that the arbitral tribunal is authorized to reconcile.

Once the arbitral tribunal is obliged to make conciliation efforts first between the parties before commencing arbitration, it is no longer advantageous until the document indicates so.

(Call No. 325 for the 2005 commercial call session, 10/12/2005)

Arbitration procedure

The arbitrator shall invite the parties to appear before him, hear and consider their defence and allow them to submit documents, whether the arbitrator has undertaken to rule on the arbitration or is authorized to reconcile. Offence, nullity of the judgment. M.P. Civil proceedings. The opponents have failed. Do not fall into the principle of confrontation.

(Appeal No. 133 for the year 2004, "Civil Appeal" hearing, 27/3/2005)

The arbitrator's response

Request for arbitrator's reimbursement. It must be submitted before the arbitrator's decision or the closing of the argument. This applies to arbitrations conducted by or outside the Court.

Bug it. Ask the next arbitrator to return his sentence. The confirmation of the arbitrator's judgment has no effect on the price of the shares before the court.

(Call No 220 of 2005, Commercial Call Session, 17/10/2005)

D - Arbitration order

Extension of the arbitration date for other periods. It is permissible to accept it expressly or implicitly or by authorizing the arbitrator in his report. The court may extend this time limit by a period it considers appropriate whenever one of the parties or the arbitrator so requests. The condition to extend the date of the arbitration, the duration of the arbitration extended to the previous period. Continuous presence of the parties to the arbitration before the arbitrator and not adhering to any of the falls from the arbitration document. The effect of considering the duration of the connected arbitration.

(Call No. 322 of 2004, session "Commercial Call", 11/4/2005)

Judgment of the arbitrators

First: Judgment

Judgment of the arbitrators. It must include a copy of the arbitration agreement. Include the provisions of the agreement. No need. It is permissible to specify its content, including the agreement on arbitration, without derogating from its provisions.

(Call No. 39 of 2005, session "Commercial Call", 16/04/2005)

Second: approval of the arbitrators' judgment

1- The approval of decisions of arbitrators under the jurisdiction of national courts consists in ratifying decisions of arbitrators rendered in the United Arab Emirates only, without decisions of arbitrators rendered in a foreign country, whether or not such decisions can be ratified in the country where they were rendered. Contained in the chapter on the enforcement of judgments, orders and judgments rendered by arbitrators in a foreign country.

(Appeal No 218 of 2004 - Civil Appeal Session 15/5/2005)

2. Ratification of the arbitrators' judgment. The Court has the power to interpret the terms of the arbitration agreement and to determine the extent to which the arbitrators have left the terms of the arbitration document unattended by the Court of Cassation, provided that this does not deviate from the meaning of the terms of those terms.

(Call No. 225 of 2005, session "Commercial Call", 10/12/2005)

3. Approval by the court of the arbitrators' judgment. He has no objection to objectifying it and its compliance with the law. The reason for this is to include in their judgment a copy of the arbitration agreement and a summary of the parties' statements and exhibits, as well as the reasons on which they based their opinion on the dispositive, so as not to contravene a rule of public policy. Authorized for causation. This applies to the evidence procedure.

(Call No. 225 of 2005, session "Commercial Call", 10/12/2005)

Thirdly: authentic judgment of the arbitrators

Judgment of the arbitrators.

Earns the validity of the order once it has been issued. Effect Prevent opponents from returning to the debate on the issue on which the judgment was rendered, even in the presence of legal or factual evidence that had not previously been presented.

It is permissible to take legal action against his disability if his conditions are met

(Call No. 325 of 2005, session "Commercial Call", 10/12/2005)

Fourth: appeal against the arbitrators' judgments

The appeal may not be lodged or replaced. 204 Civil proceedings. This should not be extended to the court by refusing to appoint the arbitrator, if it refuses to replace him or to settle the defenses related to the invalidity of the parties' statement or to what may arise between them as to the status of the parties in the trial or any of the preliminary issues that depend on the determination of the arbitrator's appointment.

(Call No. 260 of 2004, Commercial Call Session, 25/4/2005)

Fifth: Invalidity of the arbitrators' judgment

1. The arbitrator shall invite the parties to appear before him to hear their inquiry, thereby allowing them to submit documents, whether the arbitrator is required to rule on the arbitration or is authorized to reconcile otherwise. Invalidity of the judgment. Article 216 Civil proceedings.

The opponents have failed. Do not fall into the principle of confrontation.

(Appeal No. 133 for the 2004 Civil Appeal Hearing held on 27/3/2005)

2. The arbitrator may be sued for misconduct and may initiate proceedings against him or her in accordance with the normal procedures for filing the case. Disputes concerning the invalidity of the arbitral award with regard to its fees and the costs of the arbitration. Permits

(Call No. 225 of 2005, session "Commercial Call", 10/12/2005)

3. Removal of the arbitrator. It is permitted when all litigants agree to dismiss him or her after his or her appointment, either by appointment or through the court. Evidence of intentional negligence in this case in the work under the arbitration agreement, despite a written warning. No need. This does not preclude one of the litigants from making a request for a referral as long as he or she proves his or her agreement with the other parties to the dispute.

(Appeal No. 7 of 2005, Civil Appeal Hearing, 12/6/2005)

Arbitration of Arab-European Chambers of Commerce

We continue to examine some of the international arbitration systems: the system of conciliation, arbitration and experience of Arab and European chambers of commerce has been adopted by seven European Arab chambers: Belgian Arabic, Luxembourg Arabic,

French Arabic, Greek Arabic, Greek Arabic, Italian Arabic, Portuguese and Swiss. It must be implemented from 10 January 1983

This system includes a supreme arbitration board, arbitration commissions for joint chambers of commerce and the notary's secretariat.

When international arbitration centers were established in the last century, foreign arbitrators - where no Arab personality was prepared - were qualified to serve as international arbitrators. Arab countries have tended to encourage the inclusion of prominent Arab personalities to act as international arbitrators.

On the basis of these considerations, the Arab-European Arbitration Centre was established in Paris.

It is a combination of Arab and European expertise, and the bodies of this center are jointly shared by both parties. One of them is the author of these lines.

Thus, the Arab side in the conflict finds an Arab arbitrator close to it in thought and roots and understands its interests on the ground. Without hindrance, dispel Arab businessmen's suspicions that foreign arbitrators favor the foreign party.

It is the responsibility of the Supreme Council of Arbitration to ratify the arbitration document.

Fourth: Competence of arbitration boards in Arab-European chambers:

- The competence of each arbitration board in the Arab-European Chambers is that specified in Article (8) of the Law.

The foreign party must be a national of the State in which the arbitral tribunal is located.

2. The foreign party must be a permanent resident of the State in which the seat of the Council is located or be In this state, it has its main business center.

3. The contract is directly based on the dispute with the territory of the State in which the arbitration board is located.

(See details and criticisms of the text: Study of the Arab-European arbitration system - Advisor Ahmed Munir - Issuance of the Council of Saudi Chambers of Commerce and Industry - 14, 15).

The jurisdiction of the Arbitration Board is also based on the agreement of the parties to the dispute to settle the dispute rather than constituting an arbitral tribunal to examine the dispute, Article 8 of the Statute stipulates that the Arbitration Board shall submit its own jurisdiction to the Supreme Arbitration Council.

- The second competence of Article (10) is to resume the work of recording the minutes of the sessions of the Supreme Council and the implementation of its decisions, which are shared with the Secretary General of each Arab-European chamber in the organization of the Arbitration Council. The third competence of the agent is that it is the body to which requests for arbitration are submitted and distributed.

The principle of this provision is that the representative examines the requests in an ostensible manner to verify that they are correct and complete data and that the parties to the conflict belong to Arab and European nationalities.

The power of the arbitration board to extend the time limit for hearing the case and reviewing the judgment before it is formally rendered:

- Article 23/10 stipulates that the arbitral award must be rendered within 90 days of the date on which the notary referred the matter to the arbitral tribunal.

Once the draft judgment has been completed, the Arbitration Board shall be subject to the examination of Article 24/4 of the Statute, for the purpose of verifying the integrity of the proceedings and respect for the rights of the defense, without interference in the dispute.

Article 25/2 stipulates that the arbitral awards rendered by the arbitration bodies set up at the Arab-European Arbitration Centre shall be final and may under no circumstances be contested.

As the parties to the dispute have already accepted the Arab-European arbitration system, they have waived their right to appeal the arbitral award.

The system of Arab-European Chambers of Commerce contains rules for conciliation, arbitration and experience.

Conciliation begins with a request to be submitted to the trustee and to deposit an amount for the costs of the proceedings to be calculated according to a fixed rate. This request shall be forwarded to the Secretary-General, who shall request the other party to the dispute to reply within ten days. If the conciliation fails, the attempt fails and the amount allocated to the costs of the proceedings is refunded to the claimant after deduction of the cost of this step. When pluralism, they take their decisions unanimously. If the conciliator has the opportunity to reach an agreement, he or she has prepared a conciliation report and sent it to the parties for approval within a specified period. It may then submit proposals to the parties on the basis of which they seek a solution. The documents and information presented during the conciliation procedure are considered confidential and the conciliator is obliged to protect them and not to disclose them to anyone.

With regard to arbitration, which is generally the most important thing in international disputes, the plaintiff submits his request to the notary, it is necessary that one of the parties be Arab and the other European or of another affiliation if it has direct or indirect relations with the Arab countries. The request for arbitration must be submitted to one of the chambers participating in this system, which will be forwarded to the notary secretary, who will forward the request to the competent counsel for the purpose of monitoring the procedure and forward a copy to the other party. The parties may agree on the composition of the arbitral tribunal. If such an agreement does not exist, the notary secretary shall ask the parties to inform the secretariat of the board within thirty days of their opinion on the appointment of one or three arbitrators.

The defendant must submit his observations and defense within thirty days of notification of the application against him. He must also submit his documents within this time limit and must be filed.

If the defendant makes his own requests, the plaintiff is advised to respond within thirty days.

Each party shall select an arbitrator if the arbitral tribunal is tripartite. The third arbitrator, who presides over the court, was appointed by agreement of both parties or by the board that appointed him. Either party may not appoint an arbitrator, in which case the Board shall do so. The arbitral tribunal is competent to rule on questions of jurisdiction raised by one of the parties, called jurisdiction.

The arbitration procedure shall be conducted in accordance with the rules laid down by law or in accordance with the rules agreed between the parties.

The arbitrator may apply such rules as he deems appropriate to achieve an early, economic and final settlement of the dispute. The parties expressly decide to waive any appeal or recourse to the Court on any question of law raised or raised in the course of the proceedings.

The arbitrator or arbitrators will conduct the arbitration proceedings, which will be subject to the rules of public policy in the country where the arbitration is conducted, unlike what we have seen with the rules of the World Bank's International Centre for Settlement of Investment Disputes.

The arbitrator may first summarize his or her mission and present it to the Board and the parties.

If the arbitrator is invited to hold hearings, he or she must comply with their request.

He may hold such hearings alone and the arbitrator may continue to hear such hearings despite the absence of any person.

The parties to the extent that the announcement was made in time and does not provide any explanation as to why there was no reason within a reasonable time.

The arbitrator must render his decision within 90 days of the date on which he referred the arbitration file to him, which may be extended with the approval of the Board of Directors and rendered unanimously or by a majority (two to one). The Commission is deemed to be coveted by the arbitrator or to interfere with the arbitral proceedings, which may draw the arbitrator's attention to substantive or procedural issues that it considers to be raised.

The judgments shall be final and shall be executed in good faith by the parties. The Council shall exercise its good offices to facilitate the enforcement of judgments rendered in accordance with this Law, provided that the competent authorities of the country where enforcement is refused enforce it.

The parties may choose to submit the dispute to the bodies that govern the Arab-European Chambers of Commerce and to apply the UNCITRAL Arbitration Rules (UNCITRAL Rules).

If correspondence is exchanged by telex, it shall be deemed valid if the addressee indicates that it has been received or if the sender confirms it by registered letter with acknowledgement of receipt.

The system of Arab-European Chambers of Commerce has also specified how.

By conducting an expertise through these chambers, each party may ask the notary's secretariat to appoint one or more experts at its own expense. The expert shall prepare a reasoned report, but this report shall not bind the arbitral tribunal and shall not affect the obligations of the contracting parties. The other party may request a second opinion and the experience may be gained in proceedings before the arbitration or for itself for the purpose of establishing the case or assessing its value.

The fees of conciliators, arbitrators and experts are calculated on an hourly or daily basis and depend on the adequacy of each of them, the complexity of the case and any other factors affecting the estimate. Also in arbitration fees and expenses. The system of Arab-European Chambers of Commerce has been developed in three languages: Arabic, French and English, with all texts to be adopted in the same way. In the event of disagreement on interpretation due to different language versions, the Supreme Council shall decide on the matter at the request of the arbitrators or the parties. Translations into other languages can be extracted from the French text. This system came into force after its approval by the Boards of Directors of three Euro-European Joint Chambers of Commerce.

There is no doubt that the existence of this system is a powerful factor for growth and prosperity in trade relations between Arab countries and other countries of the world, particularly European countries.

The following are a number of cases of arbitration in the UAE

Isolating agent

Parties to the conflict

* - West Germany / UAE

* - System of dealing with foreign contractors only through a local contractor

* - Does this system lead to the existence of a new company or the relationship is considered an agency

* - Government error in disbursement to the local contractor despite the dangers of the foreign contractor, which is the original contractor.

The UAE has established a system of government housing and contracted to establish the required housing with a Western German company. The UAE system does not allow the contracting of a foreign contractor unless he has a local partner or agent from the country, so the German company was forced to agree with another local company to provide the required legal form. In the government tender under this agreement, the amounts due to the German company became deducted its share and received the rest. The company was supplying the local labor and provide some of the equipment, machinery and equipment it has for use by the German company as it was doing some work assigned to it. This was the case from January 1977 to May 1979, when disputes between the two companies started because Al-Khaleejia did not fulfill its obligations and enter into local judicial disputes with the German company. The latter notified the Gulf Government to refrain from paying any dues to the Gulf Company and to issue exchange bills starting from this time. To the German company alone.

The Gulf government did not implement the German company request and continued to spend a period of time to the Gulf company, which forced the German company to submit an arbitration request against the Gulf government, where the contract between them included the arbitration clause of the International Chamber of Commerce and provides that the contract is subject to the subject of Gulf law and arbitration In Geneva, the arbitral tribunal was composed of a Swiss president. The two members were not chosen by the nationality of each party as usual. The German company chose an arbitrator from Austria, while the Gulf state chose an arbitrator who works as a lawyer in France and of French nationality. The Gulf government notified that the German company is not the contracted party, but the contracted company is a company consisting of the German and Gulf companies and not the German company to demand disbursement of money alone, but it must be for the company consisting of the two companies has paid the government to the new company amounts owed to it It has been doing before since the start of the contract, the German company is demanding the payment of invoices numbers 26,27,28, which is due after the outbreak of the dispute and these invoices are no different from the previous invoices from number one to No. 25 and proof that the Gulf company is a partner in the amounts Anba's expense is the obligation to receive the amounts and it is mentioned in the original contract and the country's regulations do not allow to deal with it. Final judgments have been issued by the national judiciary in the Gulf state that the German company is not a party to the tender, but the new company formed with the Gulf company is considered a party to it. .

The German company replied that the Gulf company is not a partner but a local agent working for them for a fee and that there is no ruling from the national judiciary in the Gulf state denies the contractor contractor in the tender. There was no dispute before the national judiciary between it and the Gulf government over the validation or denial of this status and all judicial disputes to which it was a party, especially with private sector parties rather than the government. The role of the arbitral tribunal began to discuss aspects of the dispute, where it was addressed in the following manner:

1. Arbitrators first questioned whether the application of the Gulf law means the application of its texts only or the application of judicial rulings in the State. Therefore, the Authority began to determine the extent of binding the judgments of the national judiciary in the Gulf State to the arbitral tribunal. To determine this, reference should be made to the rules of private international law. As arbitration takes place in Geneva, the Commission considered that it is committed to this research in the same manner as any Swiss court, that is, it determines the answer in light of the provisions of Swiss law. Swiss law stipulates that previous judicial decisions are also binding and Swiss law considers this matter as a procedural matter.

2. Accordingly, the arbitral tribunal examined the judgments issued by the local judiciary on which the Government of the Gulf is based and determined the conditions which must be met in these judgments - also in accordance with the laws of Switzerland, namely, that the previously adjudicated proceedings were between the same parties and the reason In considering the above judgments, the arbitration panel found that the parties in the previous cases were not the Gulf government among them, but the German company with the Gulf company in one case and the German with another person in another case. the parties . The location and the reason for each of these cases was different. The first involved wages of unpaid workers and the second was a provisional seizure of the German company by the Ministry of Public Works. All this is different from what is before the arbitral tribunal.

- The arbitration panel then discussed the relationship of the Gulf company with the German company because this point is the basis of the decision whether the government has been injured or missed in not paying to the German company has decided that there is no new legal person and no new company made by the two companies While the contract speaks of participation and partners, on the other hand, the Gulf company did not offer its existing machines as a stake in a company, but it does not exist. One of the articles of the law of agencies issued in the Gulf state in 1970 stipulated that the services agent is limited to facilitate the relations between the owners of the company and its employees with local authorities and assist them in obtaining facilities and employment and take the procedures for obtaining visas and residence and issuing licenses For the activities of the company and all services requested by the company and the services agent is not responsible for the activities of the company and the services agent is not responsible for the activities of the company and this text shows the relationship of the Gulf company with the German company, which falls within the scope of Air only and is not a partner in its operations and there is no provision in the contract between the two companies that it is irrevocable and that the German company holds at any time to isolate the local agent.

4 - The Gulf government raised that the German company did not inform them in writing about the suspension of disbursement to the local agent, the Gulf company, only after it deserved the amounts claimed and sent to the bank that maintains the account of the Gulf company, but the arbitral tribunal decided that the rule in Swiss law is that such notification does not It must be in writing unless stipulated in the contract and not in the law of the Gulf State contrary to this provision and can therefore be said that the writing was not required to report the removal of the agent and that the written notification sent by the German company had been preceded by a verbal message communicated by the delegate The German letter to the engineer in charge of the government to supervise the implementation of the project in charge of considering the disbursement of amounts to the contractor and this oral message was sufficient to prevent the disbursement to the agent, especially as the engineer had mentioned in his written correspondence. To the bank to stop cashing it to the agent.

5 - The Gulf government also indicated that the removal of the local agent is not the will of the German company alone, but must be approved by the Gulf government. However, the arbitration panel did not take this payment and said that the agency contract between the two Gulf and German companies was stipulated that German law applies to this contract and the German law in this matter stipulates that the principal may dismiss his agent without the consent of this agent or the consent of a third party.

6 - The Gulf government also claimed that the German company was able to stop the payment of amounts to the agent by notifying the bank that received those amounts to refrain from

disbursement to him, but the arbitration said that there is no such obligation on the German company.

7. The German company demanded interest on the amounts owed to it by 12% per annum, but it was found that the contract of contract stated that the amounts that are overdue pay interest at the rate of 6% per year and therefore the arbitral tribunal adopted this price.

8. The Arbitral Tribunal also found that invoice No. 26 had been paid to the agent prior to verbal or written notice from the German company.

As for invoices 27.28, the Gulf government erred in the performance of its value to the agent and that value had to be paid to the German company. Therefore, the arbitral tribunal decided to oblige the Gulf government to value these invoices, half of the arbitration and arbitration expenses, and the defense costs of the German company.

The decision of the engineer in the terms of FIDIC

Parties to the conflict: Kuwait / UAE

Topic: Construction of roads

Contract: FIDIC terms are part of the agreement

The subject of the dispute: 1- The nature of the decision of the engineer and how to appeal it.

2. The appeal may not be addressed to the Engineer, but to the Secretariat of the Supreme Court of Arbitration and send a copy to the Engineer.

3. Payment of non-jurisdiction

4. Is it possible to refer to the engineer after the completion of his work?

5. Compensation.

A Kuwaiti contractor contracted with the Municipality of the United Arab Emirates to establish roads. The contract included the appointment of a project engineer to supervise the implementation and the parties will refer to it. The contract stipulates that both parties are subject to the FIDIC (International Federation of Consulting Engineers) terms. The case of the Kuwaiti contractor is that the cost of his operation has increased significantly as a result of the many amendments made by the municipality far more than the stipulated in the contract and this increase is estimated at more than six million He made a claim to the municipality, which did not meet him. He applied to the consultant engineer for the operation.He decided that he was entitled to about three and a half million dirhams owed by the municipality, and the contractor demanded that amount.

The contractor was based on his claim that the decision of the engineer is considered final as long as no one of the parties objected to it within ninety days of notifying the parties. In case of objection, such objection shall take the form of an arbitration request with the International Chamber of Commerce. It has not submitted an arbitration application within the said period and the decision of the Engineer shall be final and binding.

The contractor asked the municipality to pay any of the aforementioned amount (three and a half million dirhams.

The municipality paid the contractor's claim with many defenses. The sole arbitrator responded to these defenses, an arbitrator from the Kingdom of Jordan, who was holding hearings of the case in Amman.

1- The contractor is not a party in a contractual relationship, he is of Kuwaiti nationality, while she contracted with a commercial industrial establishment bearing a name similar to his name and because there is no contractual bond between them, the arbitral tribunal shall not be competent to hear the case. However, he works in the UAE and has registered his name as a contractor and that he adds the name of the facility to his name to show his work in trade and contracting, thus the arbitrator ruled that he is competent to consider the dispute because of the arbitration clause in their contract.

2- The municipality argued that the decision of the engineer exceeded the limits of his competence. The engineer had finished his work and left the UAE when the contractor submitted his application to him. Therefore, he had no jurisdiction at this time to issue a decision on this request and the arbitrator did not accept this defense. The decision entrusted to him shall be valid.

3- The municipality also challenged that the decision of the engineer was not a decision in the right sense, but merely a recommendation and did not specify a certain amount, but gives a rough estimate or basis for understanding between the two parties. .

The arbitrator responded to this defense that the decision of the engineer does not need a formula in fact actually a recommendation and this is always his nature, which does not become a final decision and binding only to accept them, there is nothing in this change of nature or diminish its impact and if the municipality does not accept this decision It has to follow the path it had before it to challenge, namely arbitration.

It does not affect the value of the decision of the engineer from the legal point of view that he has been directed to other than the correct address of the contractor.

4 - The Municipality also maintained that the decision of the Engineer was not issued within the period specified for him, which is ninety days from the date of submission of the application to him, as his decision arrived five days after the end of that period.

When the arbitrator examined this payment, he decided that the lesson was not the arrival of the engineer's decision to the parties before the end of the ninety days, but the lesson of the issuance of the decision during this period. Arrival by mail five days after the end.

5- The municipality challenged the engineer's decision that it is not final or binding because it objected to it two months after its issuance by sending this objection to the engineer (one of the foreign consultancy offices). The arbitrator responded to this point after a long consultation with the consultants of both parties and a number of specialists - that the determination of the period for the issuance of the decision of the engineers and the duration of the appeal is intended to speed up the resolution of the problems related to the contracting, and therefore appeal to the decision of the engineer and not to accept the announcement of this objection to Eng. Following the provisions of Article 67 of the FIDIC conditions by submitting an arbitration request against the decision of the Engineer within 90 days from the date of notification thereof, and sending a copy of this application to the Engineer, if this is not done within that period, the decision of the Engineer shall be final and binding because there shall be no objection to it. An objection to the engineer and not to inform him of the intention to submit an arbitration request because the engineer is not the body through which the arbitration is held, but it turns out that the request for arbitration to the Secretariat of the Court of Arbitration at the International Chamber of Commerce during the ninety days referred to and inform the engineer and the secretariat informs the other party to arbitrate to submit It is inconceivable that the objector only expresses his objection with the engineer and his intention to enter into arbitration without taking the arbitration procedures, this would disrupt the settlement of disputes, which is incompatible with the intent to put these periods, which is the speed of adjudication and as long as the municipality did not take arbitration procedures within the specified period It shall be deemed to have accepted the decision of the Engineer.

6. The municipality raised another objection regarding the legitimacy of the benefits and requests not to be judged because they are contrary to Islamic law.

With the final decision of the engineer, it became necessary to judge the amount of the engineer and obligate the municipality to pay the contractor with his interests by 11% annually, thus ruling the arbitrator obliging the municipality to pay an amount of three and a half million dirhams (approximately) including interest since May 79 to March 82. Date is calculated and added to that amount until the date of payment.

The arbitrator distributed the expenses of the arbitration equally between the two parties and each party carried the expenses of his defense before the arbitrator. The arbitrator could make all expenses incumbent on the municipality on the grounds that it had lost the entire case and exempted the contractor who had spent all his requests.

Waiver of something from the convicted to others

In 1975 a deal was made to supply cement from a small English company to the United Arab Emirates. The English company did not produce the required Portland cement but bought it to supply it. Therefore, it contracted with a German company to buy the contracted quantity of fifty thousand tons with an increase or decrease of ten percent according to the seller's choice. The English company has contracted with the German company to supply at a price of forty-six and a half dollars per ton and was agreed with the UAE government to sell it to them at sixty dollars per ton, ie there is a profit of thirteen dollars and a half dollars per ton.

The buyer asked the seller to provide him with a bank guarantee letter in which a bank undertakes to pay a certain amount if the seller fails to fulfill his obligation to supply and the seller requests the buyer to open a letter of credit with a bank undertaking to pay the value of the goods when submitting the shipping documents to him. Between the UAE and the English company, where the letter of guarantee to be equivalent to three percent of the value of the transaction and to open a documentary credit for the English company.

The parties did not fulfill their commitments. The UAE did not open the documentary accreditation. Therefore, the English company could not supply the cement. At the same time, the UAE issued a decree requiring the ships wishing to unload their cargo to declare it to it two months before entering its waters.

The position of the UAE government is that with the delivery of the arbitration clause in the contract, it denies the right of the English company to compensation and denies the existence of the price at which the English company bought from the German company and says that the English company did not provide the agreed letter of guarantee.

At the commencement of the arbitration, the International Court of Arbitration at the International Chamber of Commerce shall determine on the proposal of the Secretariat the amount of the expenses that must be deposited with the Chamber to start the case. The court estimated the required expenses from the English company at fifty-five thousand dollars. It has a modest financial system and no arbitration system for legal assistance to the poor, so the English company tricked to get the money to start the arbitration and agreed with a company from New York and another person (whose name appears to be from an Islamic country) to share with them the spending. On this case in order to succeed they share with them the amounts sentenced by a certain percentage has been released a contract thus submitted to the arbitrators appointed to consider the dispute and the terms of this contract are summarized as follows:

The American company pays the arbitration fees, which are fifty-five thousand dollars and also shares the burden of other expenses with the English company and the third partner, including attorneys' fees and expenses in a certain percentage stipulated in the contract, but concealed in the image submitted to the arbitral tribunal. Reconciliation between the original parties, whereby the English company receives its compensation directly from the UAE after the American company has paid the arbitration expenses, so it set a condition that allows it to appoint a counsel from its party to defend the case and bear its expenses in its share and when it is appointed. This consultant takes the wishes of the other parties (the English company and the individual partner) but does not abide by these desires and in return divides the amount resulting from the follow-up of the UAE and not the amount resulting from the judgment in the case alone) Between the three with the deduction of the share of which one of them has failed to pay in expenses.

The American company was also apparently afraid to us that its role in the case appears negative or weak does not deserve the proportion stipulated in the contract, which is a reason to challenge it, so it made in this contract for itself a positive role by appointing a counselor also submitted to the defense on the other hand to work on its part If the dispute arises in connection with this contract, the American Arbitration Association shall be competent to examine it in accordance with the laws of the State of New York. The American Company shall have the right to transfer its rights in this contract to third parties. Arbitration expenses were paid in accordance with this contract. The UAE appointed one of its sons and the English company appointed an English arbitrator. The two arbitrators agreed to choose an English chairman of the arbitral tribunal. The Arbitration Court agreed to this and Paris determined a place for arbitration. There is no reason for them to move to Paris, and it is enough for the parties to move to them in London.

The jury examined what each party had done, and where the required letter of guarantee was worth $ 90,000, the arbitrators questioned whether the English company could provide such a guarantee, but it turned out that the company had agreed with the German company that would supply Portland Cement to provide it. It has a letter of guarantee in the amount of 93 thousand dollars and submitted this letter to its bank and asked him to issue a new guarantee letter for the benefit of the African government and this letter was actually issued on the way Back guarantee This method is familiar in the documentary credits, but the company transferred here to the field of letters of guarantee

As a result of this research and investigation it was confirmed that the English company had already submitted the required letter of guarantee contrary to what was claimed by the African government, as well as the arbitrators discovered that the contract submitted to the English company and the United Arab Emirates appeared to be new and not contemporary to the time of contracting in 1975 and the court concluded The parties have prepared this contract on the occasion of their intention to enter into arbitration.

The arbitrators found that the United Arab Emirates has proposed a non-compliance with the agreed terms in favor of the English company and thus did not fulfill its obligation in the contract. The English company deserves compensation for this equal to the difference between the purchase price and the selling price of 13.5 dollars per ton. That there is a profit in the international market up to this limit, but the arbitrators have investigated the search of his health and yet they deducted from him a quarter of dollars for each ton and this amount is the cost of transferring credit because the credit that was opened by the United Arab Emirates company would make a transfer to the company only Manet to pay the price of cement and the cost of conversion for each quarter of dollars paralleled tons and this is deducted from the profit and net be adjudged for each ton is 13.25 dollars multiplied by 50 thousand tons, becomes the total is 662.5 thousand dollars.

The English company has also not been able to dispute this amount as the contract states that the quantity is 50,000 tons, with an increase or decrease of ten percent, according to the seller's choice. It has chosen to supply a 10 percent increase, or 55,000 tons. Five thousand, but the arbitrators did not agree and said that all correspondence on the implementation of the contract and the letter of guarantee only talked about fifty thousand tons.

The English company was also demanding compensation for delays in implementation and the judges found no such compensation.

The arbitrators divided the arbitration expenses by 80% on the United Arab Emirates and 20% on the English company. According to the arbitrators, the interest is based on the fact that the amount is denominated in dollars and that they rely on interest rates on the interest rate on Euros. Ten years (ie from the date of the conflict began in 1976) and extracted the average interest rates was 11.25% per year, and applied this price to the amount sentenced.

The arbitrators rejected the agreement between the American company and the English company and its other partner on the grounds that there are precedents in English law to invalidate such agreements and should not be recognized, including Gril v. Levy in 1864 and Wylo v. Smithson in 1919. The contract means that no one has the capacity to receive the sums except the English company.

The defense of the United Arab Emirates handed the arbitrators a few months before the proceedings of the arbitration in a sealed envelope, asking them not to open it until after the mother has finished preparing the verdict and before making a decision about the expenses. The English firm's lawyer offers the UAE much less compensation than it actually did. It seems that the defense of the UAE wants to say that this amount was offered before the arbitration and therefore the English company bears the bulk of its expenses but the arbitrators said that due to the small This amount for the convicted, they would have been free to rule on the expenses to dismiss it for a small amount but they can not and reduced for this reason to reduce the proportion committed by the African government in the expenses and made it 8% as provided.

Multinational companies before arbitration

Children always follow the nationality of their parents, but in the field of large companies, there is another main objective is that the companies born by these companies enjoy nationalities other than the nationality of the mother company and the nationality of its sisters, for economic, financial, tax and sometimes political and even colonial reasons. The birth of a mother company or sisters in the field of responsibility for the implementation of these contracts and give an example of this case.

A group of multinational companies belonging to one mother has set up a factory in the UAE based on two contracts signed by a person as a representative of some of the companies of this group, but in details pointed out the role of each of the fledgling companies in its implementation technically and the first contract is related to the establishment of the factory. These contracts are part of a series of contracts between this country and the international group of companies.

In reading the contracts, the arbitrators noted that the identification of the parties was very flexible and that the drafting requirements governing the mention of the parties did not take into account sufficient data. In some of these contracts, the signatory was the representative of the International Group of Companies. This was repeated several times, confirming that it was not limited to the signatory companies. However, there are references to the contrary in some of these contracts, such as the use of the singular when talking about signing the contract.

The arbitrators considered that there is no need to weigh these statements, but must resort to the will of the parties themselves, as there is no doubt that the Government of the United Arab Emirates was intended to deal with a full range of international companies represented in its president, who signed the two decades in dispute and was shown to be the person who Manages and drives this large industrial group and all the papers submitted by the two parties confirming that the deal is taking place between a state and a group of fledgling companies, even if the expressions of internal suitability in the group required that some of its members be entrusted with the implementation of the project. Therefore, it is not permissible for some companies in this group to protect behind one provision or another to escape from the scope of liability and the arbitration clause is also comprehensive for all its members.

The responsibility of all members of the group of companies does not contradict the principle of narrow interpretation of the requirement of arbitration because the review of the negotiations between the parties led the arbitrators to believe that all members of the group are bound by these contracts where it was clear that their intention to do so during the drafting of the contracts and the arbitration clause and the interpretation of the will of the parties in this way. A close relationship with the theory of the apparent agency where the group's president and representative appeared as a spokesman for all its members and the arbitrators added to this two other elements, one is the spirit of contracts, which derives their will to submit to arbitration and the second is the real economic that is In the unit of a number of companies within the framework of an international unit, these two elements do not themselves decide to submit to arbitration, but they are taken only as elements to guide them in the interpretation of an existing arbitration clause and enter into the assessment of the element of economic realism that the members of the group not signed a realistic role in the implementation of the contract in some parts This confirms the direction of their will to contract.

The issue of the legal system on which arbitrators decide the dispute as well as the point of responsibility for parts of the factory that were technically flawed and led to disruption of production were also raised in this case.

With regard to the first point (legal system), it was clear that the parties refer in their memorandums and pleadings to French law, suggesting the generally established principles in the area of conflict of laws. This method gives arbitrators freedom of choice as long as they are not bound by a particular legal system. International arbitration in the place of arbitration (Geneva was the seat of arbitration in this case), as well as in countries related to the subject matter and subjective elements that establish the link between the subject matter of the case and a particular legal system.

In practice, it was noted that companies dealing with countries in international contracts are usually keen to choose a legal system other than the contracting state system whenever possible because it avoids many difficulties and disputes and this is why one of the contracts chose French law (while there were British, American and Canadian companies The other contract did not refer to the selection of a particular legal system and therefore the arbitrators favored the application of French law to the whole case based on complementing the objective elements with the subjective or personal elements in the analysis of the relations of the parties.

With regard to the responsibility for the supply of parts of the factory with technical defects, this entails the prosecution of the seller party, the international group of companies, the provisions of liability for defects of something sold in French law, which generally tends to consider the supply process in this case involves fraud by the seller and this fraud The seller considers that he intentionally and intentionally committed this mistake and the supply of defective parts on the other hand is a breach of an obligation to achieve a certain purpose or result, an obligation that the seller is not discharged except by proving the existence of a foreign cause that led to the non-fulfillment of his obligation such as Force majeure, or actually by others, is something that the international group of companies could not prove, so the arbitrators had to decide to compensate them for the delay, disruption of production and for the real implementation at their expense.

Continuous commissions in construction operations

When the cases of bribery and the exploitation of influence were proven, even if they proved what the arbitrators hesitated to convict them in civil terms, in the case that we are presenting, the facts have been established by the recognition and approval of the perpetrator. As follows :

There was a group of companies that are preparing real estate constructions on a large scale in agreement with another group of companies working in the form of a joint venture and the implementation of the required buildings. A key partner who supervises the buildings and consultants himself in accordance with an editorial contract between him and the group.

Mr. X felt that he could earn twice as much as he could from the supervision contract with the group. He agreed with the joint venture that executes the buildings. He also advises them in exchange for secret commissions he receives from them at the expense of the interests of the owners of the buildings. This series of contracts is concluded at the end of the execution of the buildings with a final contract that ensures that it is subject to the Swiss Contracts and Obligations Act and that if a dispute arises, it will be submitted to the ICC arbitration. / X to convince the group to pay to the joint venture and the prices offered by it.

Mr. X did this and the joint venture companies received their dues as they wanted and Mr. X asked them to pay him the percentage stipulated in the last decade.

The joint venture maintained that the last contract was absolutely null and void because it seriously affected the rights of a third party, the group represented by Mr. X.And this agreement is an agreement on bribery and the exploitation of influence and hidden commissions, which are all prohibited in Swiss law which is applicable to this contract because of the existence Text it into it.

Mr. X maintained that he was in the process of reviewing quantities, quality, and other material work that did not require the Secretariat's duty to the group he represented and that he had not done anything that affected the interests of that group and that he was doing the joint venture work that was not related to his interests with the group, such as consulting on matters Tax and matters relating to its activity with other companies.

The arbitrators considered that what Mr. X claims is not true. The contract between him and the group is one of the most important contracts of the Secretariat and the engineers are bound by strict professional obligations towards those who assign them work. Swiss law requires that contracts that affect the duty of the Secretariat be invalidated.

The arbitrators confirmed the damage done by Mr. X to the interests of the group and cited two examples:

First, it was a pledge to the joint venture to get them the sums they requested in full. He knew that the companies involved in the joint venture were willing to give a discount on the prices of the materials they provided, but instead of getting this discount for the benefit of the group and instead of asking for a greater discount rate for the group. He persuaded the group to pay the prices provided without deduction, causing damage and the joint venture reported that the second example was that they agreed to complete the buildings according to the levels of country (a) and they cost a lot. Implemented for buildings Tactful levels (b) without a reduction in the agreed price, and thus the joint venture achieved a great gain.

Therefore, the plaintiff consultant engineer has no right to claim the secret commissions in the last contract because it seriously affects the rights of a third party and contrary to good manners. His defense because the joint venture has benefited from the illegal and participated in it and is contaminated by illegality, so there is no less than the obligation to bear the expenses of his defense as a penalty for his bad faith.

It remains that the group has the right to refer another claim to the consulting engineer for violating the duty of the Secretariat and the joint venture to lure the engineer and entice him with money to betray the Secretariat and demanding compensation for it and the price differences that were paid illegally.

I hope to see in this judgment the engineer points out in his defense that these commissions are familiar in some countries of the Middle East and he saw the arbitrators say in the reasons of their judgment that they do not pay attention to what is happening in the countries of the Middle East because the engineer is committed to the European level.

Enforcement of arbitration provisions in UAE law

First, distinguish between two situations in general

UAE law distinguishes in the filing of a judgment between an arbitration agreement that is made through the court and arbitration that takes place outside the court. During the consideration of this judicial dispute, the parties agree to refer it to arbitration and the Court shall so decide.

The second means arbitration, which takes place on the basis of a prior arbitration agreement outside the judicial system so that the dispute is not before the court.

Accordingly, it can be said that the judicial dispute about the validity or non-application of the arbitration agreement so that the court determines its validity and therefore rejects the case is not a form of arbitration through the court as long as the subject of the dispute is originally an arbitration agreement, the arbitration is considered out of court even if the It has been referred to arbitration by a judicial decision as a result of the dispute over the arbitration agreement. Nor is it considered arbitral through the court if the role of the court is to appoint arbitrators based on prior arbitration agreement between the parties.

Second: Arbitration through the Court

What is to be deposited is only the first arbitration, which is done through the court. The origin of the judgment and the origin of the arbitration agreement with the minutes and documents must be deposited with the Registry of the court originally competent to hear the dispute. Also, in the case of UAE law, this should be filed with the Court of Appeal if the case is already pending before this court and the arbitration agreement was agreed upon during this time. We note here that the Court of Appeal in this case is competent to consider ratification or annulment of the judgment on T Qatar law.

This deposit must be made within the fifteen days following the issuance of the judgment, which is the same period in Qatari law and what is also said about the provisions of this period in Qatari law also applies to UAE law.

A copy of the award shall also be filed with the number of parties to the arbitration in order to notify them of the award within five days of its filing.

After filing, the clerk of the court shall prepare a record thereof, which shall be submitted to the judge who was considering the dispute in the event that he is no longer in his position for any reason.

Article 213

(1) Dubai 403/2003 discrimination on 13/3/2004

(1) In pursuance of the stipulation that the case may be filed against an arbitrator who fails to call his or her duty to file the judgment with the court within the period specified for this (Dubai Discrimination 21 Date 11/3/2001 No. 12 p 214)

Thereafter, a hearing shall be determined within fifteen days and shall be communicated to the parties. The purpose of the hearing shall be to ratify or disbelieve the judgment based on one or more pleading sessions to which the parties are invited. The court shall hear their statements, defenses and other trial proceedings. .

During the hearing of the ratification of the verdict, the convicted person may request his annulment and consequently refuse to execute on the basis of one of the reasons for invalidity provided for in Article (216) of the law as stated above for the invalidity of the arbitral award. The court's decision to approve or invalidate the arbitration award shall be subject to appeal Ordinary appeal and lack of (discrimination) according to the Code of Procedure and according to the periods stipulated in the General Rules, but the judgment of the Court of First Instance shall not be subject to appeal if the arbitrators are authorized to conciliate, the litigants have expressly waived the right of appeal or the value of the dispute does not exceed ten. Thousands of dirhams.

After the case is seized, the court may consider that a defect in the judgment can be avoided before the verdict is confirmed or overturned. In such a case, UAE law permits the court to reinstate the arbitrator to issue a supplementary or clarifying judgment in two first cases - to consider omitted matters such as the plaintiff's requests. The arbitrator shall decide on an application and omit to address the second application and shall not issue a positive or negative judgment to clarify the judgment if it is not specified to the extent that it can be implemented, such as giving the buyer the option of paying the rest of the price or refunding the goods in exchange for refunding the price paid or settling a dispute between a Saudi company. And other diagonal in Arbitration made in the UAE to pay a sum of money in riyals without indicating whether the currency is Saudi or Qatari.

We see the application of the principle of re-judgment of the arbitrators as referred to not only in the ratification of the verdict as evidenced by the apparent text, but also during the filing of an original claim to invalidate the verdict, the wisdom of the text in one case and no difference between them and each lead in the same way, but in a different way. Ratification may lead to the outcome of rejection, which means in effect the annulment of the ruling and the request for nullity may be doomed to rejection, which means ratification of the verdict in practice

(1) See also Federal Supreme Court in Abu Dhabi, appeal 233 on 12/12/1999 year 20 p 1265

(1) Article (214) of the UAE law, see also paragraph 647 above

(2) The application of this see the Supreme Federal Court in Abu Dhabi, appeal 32 for the year 22 BC dated 8/7/2003 25 p 1476

(1) Compare the distinction of Dubai 126 dated 27/5/2001, number 12 p 487, which states that the arbitrators may not be re-sentenced for consideration of the issues that have been omitted in the matter except during the consideration request for ratification when this request is submitted to the court

The arbitrator shall issue a supplementary or explanatory judgment within three months from the date of being notified of the decision of the court or any other period deemed appropriate by the court. The period prescribed by law is six months, of which the duration prescribed by the court may be extended by the parties' express or implied consent for any other term.

The principle in the UAE law in terms of re-arbitration of the arbitrators has a corresponding in Qatari law with the difference in at least one substantive point in the UAE law may not be re-sentenced to the arbitrator only in the cases referred to earlier, while in the law of Qatar for any defect with the court that It is better before making the final decision to overturn the verdict or not to revoke the verdict to the arbitrator to fix this defect, whether formal or objective.

After the new verdict is supposed to be submitted to the court hearing the invalidity verdict, which has already restored the verdict to the arbitrator, then it is also assumed that the new verdict will be added to the original verdict for adjudication together as a verdict or revocation. Based on the new judgment, such as the issuance of the new judgment outside the deadline or exceeding the task specified in the court decision.

UAE or Qatari law did not face the imposition that it is difficult or difficult to return the arbitrator to the arbitrator for any reason such as his death or illness, or because he did not meet the legal conditions in the arbitrator, or that the arbitrator was a foreigner and traveled to his country after the issuance of the judgment. In order to solve this problem, we see that several issues are determined in these two laws first - that the court may not appoint an arbitrator on its own to consider a part of a case that was before it, but that the third party decided it arbitrarily. An alternative arbitrator if they find it appropriate, assuming If the alternative arbitrator cannot be appointed as such, the court shall only have to reopen the case file at the request of the party concerned. The arbitrator shall rule on the debt without mentioning the subject of interest, in which case the parties shall only resort to a new arbitration concerning the second interest or the court shall decide to overturn the judgment in whole or in part.

Third: Arbitration outside the Court

As for the second type of arbitration, ie arbitration that takes place outside the court, the judgment shall not be deposited with the Registry of the court, but the arbitrator shall deliver a copy of the judgment to each party within five days of its issuance. There shall be no legal effect on the non-delivery of the judgment during this period.

Once the award has been handed over to the parties to the arbitration, either of them may apply to the competent court for annulment or ratification. If two applications are submitted, one for ratification and the other for annulment, the lawsuit shall include one suit or one of them shall be suspended pending the other in accordance with the general rules. To raise the argument of non-ratification or, in a more correct sense, to invalidate the judgment on the basis of one of the invalidity cases stipulated in Article (216) of the law. In case of ratification of the judgment by a final decision, the judgment shall be implemented like all other judicial decisions.

(1) Dubai 403/2003 discrimination on 13/3/2004

(2) See also the Federal Supreme Court in Abu Dhabi appeal 279 on 14/12/1997 year 19 p 816 and in particular this is not a reason for the annulment of the ruling (discrimination Dubai 111 dated 7/6/1998 No. 9 p. 496) See also The above is paragraph 682/1

(1) Federal Supreme Court 92 on 8/7/2003 Year 25, p. 1489

(2) Judgment of the Federal Supreme Court.

Federal Law No. (6) of 2018

On arbitration

We are Khalifa bin Zayed Nahyan, President of the United Arab Emirates

- Having considered the Constitution;

- Federal Law No. (1) of 1972 concerning the functions of the ministries and the powers of the ministers and its amendments.

The Federal Law No. (3) of 1983 on the Judicial Authority and its amendments;

- And the Federal Law No. (5) for the year 1985, issuing the Debit Transactions Law and its amendments.

- And the Federal Law No. (3) for the year 1987 issuing the Penal Code and its amendments.

- Federal Law No. (23) of 1991 on the organization of the legal profession and its amendments.

- Federal Law No. (10) of 1992 promulgating the Law of Evidence in Debit and Commercial Transactions and its amendments.

- And the Federal Law No. (11) for the year 1992, issuing the Procedural Debt Law and its amendments.

- Federal Law No. 35 of 1992 promulgating the Code of Criminal Procedure and its amendments;

- Federal Law No. (18) of 1993 on commercial transactions.

- And the Federal Law No. (1) of 2006 on the Law of Transactions and Electronic Commerce.

- Federal Law No. (6) of 2012 on the organization of the translation profession.

- Federal Law No. (7) of 2012 on the organization of the profession of experience before the judicial authorities

- Federal Law No. (2) of 2015 on commercial companies and its amendments.

- Based on the proposal of the Minister of Economy, the approval of the Council of Ministers, the Federal National Council and the ratification of the Federal Supreme Council;

We have issued the following law:

Chapter One

Definitions and Scope of Definitions Article 1

In the application of the provisions of this Law, the following words and expressions shall have the meanings assigned to each, unless the context otherwise requires:

Country: United Arab Emirates.

Arbitration: A means regulated by law through which a binding award is settled in a dispute between two or more parties

By the arbitral tribunal upon the agreement of the parties.

Arbitration Agreement: The parties agree to resort to arbitration whether such agreement was made prior to the dispute or

After him.

Arbitral Tribunal: The body formed by one or more arbitrators to adjudicate the dispute referred to arbitration.

Court: Federal or local appellate court agreed by the parties or being within

Arbitration jurisdiction.

Arbitration Institution: An entity or center established to regulate arbitration proceedings.

Authorized: Any natural or legal person the parties agree to grant any of the powers

Prescribed in accordance with this law.

Concerned party: The authority authorized to arbitrate or the court.

Parties: The arbitrator and the arbitrator against him no matter how many.

Arbitrator: The party initiating the request to commence arbitration proceedings.

The party against whom the arbitrator has initiated arbitration proceedings.

Scope of Law Article 2

The provisions of this law shall apply to:

Any arbitration conducted in the State unless its parties agree to submit it to the provisions of another arbitration law, provided that it does not conflict with the public order and morals of the State.

2. Any international commercial arbitration conducted abroad and the parties agree to submit it to the provisions of this law

3. Any arbitration arising out of a dispute concerning a contractual or non-contractual legal relationship regulated by the laws in force in the State except where a special provision is excluded.

International Arbitration Article 3

Arbitration shall be of an international character even if it takes place within the State in any of the following cases:

1. If the principal place of business of the parties is located in two or more different States at the time of the conclusion of the arbitration agreement, if one of the parties has several business centers, the course shall be the most closely related to the subject of the arbitration agreement.

2 if any of the following places is located outside the State in which the headquarters of the work of any of the Parties is located:

(A) the place of arbitration as specified in the arbitration agreement or indicated how it shall be determined;

(B) The place of implementation of a substantial part of the obligations arising from the commercial relations between the parties or the place which is closely related to the subject matter of the dispute.

3. If the subject matter of the dispute to which the arbitration agreement is concerned relates to more than one State

4. If the parties expressly agree that the subject-matter of the arbitration agreement concerns more than one State.

Chapter II

Arbitration Agreement Eligibility Arbitration Agreement Article 4

1. The arbitration agreement shall be concluded only by the natural person entitled to dispose of the rights or the representative of the legal person authorized to conclude the arbitration agreement, otherwise the agreement shall be invalid.

2. Arbitration may not be agreed upon in matters where reconciliation is not permitted.

- In cases where this law allows the parties to agree on the procedure to be followed to decide on a particular matter, each of them may authorize others to choose or decide on this procedure and is considered third party in this regard, any natural person or arbitration institution inside or outside the State.

4. The arbitration agreement shall not end with the death or expiry of a party and may be enforced by the legal successor of or against such party, unless otherwise agreed by the parties.

Article (5)

1. The arbitration agreement may be prior to the establishment of the dispute, whether it is independent of itself or contained in a specific contract concerning all or some of the disputes that may arise between the parties.

2. Arbitration may be agreed upon after the dispute has arisen, even if a lawsuit has been instituted before any court, in which case the agreement shall specify the matters covered by the arbitration.

3. Arbitration may be agreed through an assignment contained in a contract or any other document containing the arbitration clause if such assignment is clear in considering this clause as part of the contract.

Independence of the Arbitration Agreement Article (6)

1. The arbitration agreement shall be independent of the other terms of the contract and the invalidity, annulment or termination of the contract shall have no effect on the arbitration agreement it contains, if such agreement is valid in itself, except in respect of a contractor's incompetence.

(2) The payment of nullity, annulment or termination of the contract which includes the agreement on arbitration shall not entail the suspension of the arbitral proceedings and the arbitral tribunal shall decide on the validity of that contract.

Writing the Arbitration Agreement Article 7

1. The arbitration agreement shall be in writing, otherwise it shall be null and void.

2. The arbitration agreement shall be deemed to satisfy the conditions of writing in the following cases:

A- If it contains an editor signed by the parties or received in the exchange of letters or other means of communication written or made by electronic message in accordance with the rules in force in the State concerning electronic transactions.

(B) If he is referred in a fixed contract by writing to the provisions of a model contract, an international agreement or any other document containing an arbitration clause and the assignment is clear in considering this clause as part of the contract.

(C) If the arbitration is agreed upon during the hearing of the dispute by the competent court, the court shall issue its ruling confirming the arbitration agreement and shall leave to the litigants the arbitration procedures in the place and time determined and the conditions governing it and the judiciary as if the case is not.

(D) If the written memorandums exchanged between the parties during the arbitration proceedings or acknowledged before the courts, in which one party requests to refer the dispute to arbitration and does not object to that other party in the defense.

Settlement of Dispute Containing Arbitration Agreement Article (8)

1. The court to which a dispute in which there is an arbitration agreement is brought shall rule on the inadmissibility of the case if the defendant submits it before damaging any application or payment in the subject matter of the case, unless the court finds that the agreement on arbitration is invalid or impossible to enforce.

2. The filing of the lawsuit referred to in the previous country shall not preclude the commencement or continuation of the arbitral proceedings or the award of the arbitral award.

CHAPTER III ARBITRATION COMMITTEE Composition of the Arbitral Tribunal Article 9

1. The arbitral tribunal shall be formed by agreement of the parties by one or more arbitrators. If they do not agree on the number of arbitrators, the number shall be three unless the body concerned decides otherwise.

If the arbitrators are numerous, their number shall be considered and the arbitration shall be invalid.

Article (10)

In addition to the conditions agreed upon by the parties, the arbitrator shall be a natural person who is not a minor, is not interdicted or deprived of his civil rights due to bankruptcy unless he is rehabilitated or sentenced in any felony or misdemeanor violating honor or honesty To him mind.

2. The arbitrator shall not be a member of the Board of Trustees or the administrative body of the arbitral institution competent to organize the arbitral proceedings in the State.

3. The arbitrator shall not be of a specific race or nationality unless the parties or the law otherwise provide.

4. Any person notified of his nomination to take up the task of arbitration shall declare in writing anything that may raise doubts as to his impartiality or independence. Since his appointment and during the arbitration proceedings, he shall promptly notify the parties and other arbitrators in case of any circumstance that may give rise to doubts about his impartiality or independence. Independence, unless he had previously informed them of that circumstance.

How to Select the Arbitral Tribunal Article 11

1. The Parties may agree on the procedures to be followed for the appointment of the arbitrator (s) and the time and manner of their appointment.

2. If the arbitral tribunal is constituted by one arbitrator and the parties have not been able to agree on the arbitrator within fifteen (15) days from the date of submitting a written request by one of the parties to inform the other party to do so, the concerned party shall appoint him at the request of one of the parties. An appeal against such decision shall be accepted by any means of appeal without prejudice to the provisions of Article 14 of this Law.

3. If the arbitral tribunal is composed of three arbitrators, each party shall choose an arbitrator from its side, then the two arbitrators appointed shall agree on the selection of the third arbitrator and if one of the parties does not select an arbitrator from his party within (15) fifteen days following receipt of a request from the other party, or If the appointed arbitrators do not agree on the selection of the third arbitrator within (15) fifteen days following the date of the last appointment, the concerned party shall appoint him as a matter of urgency at the request of one of the parties. (14) of this law.

The concerned party shall observe in the arbitrator chosen by it the conditions required by this law and those agreed by the parties to ensure the appointment of an independent and impartial arbitrator.

5. In cases where the authorized party does not appoint the arbitrator in accordance with the procedures specified by the agreement of the parties or in accordance with the provisions of this law, in the absence of an agreement, any of the parties may request the court to take the

necessary action to complete the formation and appointment of the members of the arbitral tribunal. The matter is not subject to appeal by any means of appeal.

6. If an application is submitted to the party concerned for the appointment of an arbitrator, the applicant shall at the same time address copies of it to all other parties and to any arbitrator previously appointed in the same dispute and shall state briefly the subject matter of the dispute and any conditions required by the arbitration agreement of the arbitrator to be appointed and all steps That have been taken to appoint any perforated member of the jury.

7. The third arbitrator appointed in accordance with the provisions of this Article shall preside over the arbitral tribunal. This provision shall apply in case the arbitral tribunal is formed by more than three arbitrators.

8. The Court may, at the request of one of the parties, request any arbitration institution in the State to provide it with a list of arbitration specialists to be appointed by the Court, after payment of the fees prescribed by the arbitration institution by the party submitting the application and considered as part of the costs of arbitration.

Article 12 Arbitration Proceedings

Any decision in the arbitral proceedings involving more than one arbitrator shall be taken by a majority of the members of the arbitral tribunal unless the parties agree otherwise.

However, decisions on procedural matters may be made by the arbitrator presiding if the parties or other members of the arbitral tribunal so permit.

Breach of the arbitral tribunal selection procedure Article (13)

If the parties violate the arbitrators' procedures they have agreed to or have not originally agreed upon, or the appointed arbitrators do not agree on an order to be agreed upon, or the failure of others, including the authorized party, to perform the duties entrusted to them in this regard, A Party has requested that the requested action be taken unless the agreement provides for another means of completing the procedure and the appeal is not admissible in any other way.

Article (14)

1. The arbitrator may not be dismissed unless circumstances arise that raise serious doubts about his impartiality or independence, or if the conditions agreed upon by the parties or provided for in this Law are not met.

2. A request for the restitution of an arbitrator appointed by him or of whom he has been appointed shall not be accepted by any of the parties except for a reason determined after such appointment has been made.

3. A request for restitution shall not be accepted by those who have already submitted a request for restitution of the same arbitrator in the same arbitration for the same reason.

Article (15)

The parties may agree on the procedures for the return of the arbitrator, otherwise the following procedures shall be followed:

1. The party who intends to return an arbitrator shall announce the request for reply in writing stating the reasons for the request and shall send a copy thereof to the other members of the arbitral tribunal who have been appointed and to the other parties within (15) fifteen days from the date of the notification of the applicant. The arbitrator or the positive circumstances of the reply.

2- If the requested person does not grant his return or the other party does not approve the request for a reply within (15) fifteen days from the date of the arbitrator's announcement of the request for reply according to the provisions of Article (24) of this law, the applicant may submit his request to the concerned party within (15) five. Ten days from the end of the fifteen days mentioned and the concerned party shall decide on the request for reply within (10) ten days. Appeal against that decision shall not be accepted by any means of appeal.

3. Notifying the arbitrator of the request for restitution or filing the application with the concerned party shall not entail the suspension of the arbitration proceedings. The arbitral tribunal, including the arbitrator required to be returned, may continue the arbitration proceedings and issue the arbitral award even if the concerned party has not decided on the application.

4. The departure of the arbitrator from his mission or the agreement of the parties to dismiss him shall not be deemed to constitute any grounds for reply.

5. If the concerned party decides to return the arbitrator, it may decide the fees and expenses it finds suitable for that arbitrator or to recover any fees or expenses that have been paid to him.

Termination of the Arbitrator's Mission Article (16)

1.If the arbitrator is unable to perform his mission, or fails to perform his mission, or interrupts his performance, which leads to unjustified delay in the arbitral proceedings or intentionally neglects to work under the arbitration agreement despite declaring all means of communication and communication in force in the State, and he does not resign or the parties agree to dismiss him. The concerned party may, at the request of any of the parties, after hearing the statements and defense of the arbitrator, terminate his mission and the decision thereon shall not be subject to appeal.

2. The power of the arbitrator shall be personal and shall end with his death, disqualification or loss of a condition of appointment. The death or expiry of the person who appointed the arbitrator shall not cancel the arbitrator's authority, unless the parties agree otherwise.

Appointment of Alternative Arbitrator Article 17

1. If the arbitrator's mission is terminated by a decision of dismissal, removal, removal or any other reason, a substitute shall be appointed in accordance with the procedures followed in the selection of the arbitrator whose assignment has ended.

2. The parties may, after the appointment of an alternative arbitrator, agree to retain any of the previous proceedings and determine the scope of that. If the parties are unable to reach an agreement in this regard, the reconstituted arbitral tribunal shall determine whether any of the previous proceedings is deemed to be valid and the scope thereof. A decision of the reconstituted arbitral tribunal shall have the right of any of the parties to challenge the

proceedings before the restructuring of the arbitral tribunal on any grounds arising prior to the appointment of the alternative arbitrator.

General Jurisdiction for Arbitration Measures Article (18)

- Jurisdiction shall be convened to deal with arbitration matters referred by this law to the competent court in accordance with the procedural laws in force in the State and shall be the exclusive jurisdiction until the end of all arbitration proceedings.

2. The President of the Court may order, at the request of one of the parties or at the request of the arbitral tribunal, to take provisional or provisional measures, as he deems necessary, for existing or potential arbitral proceedings either before commencement or during the course of the arbitral proceedings.

3. Taking the measures referred to in the preceding paragraph of this Article shall not result in the suspension of the arbitral proceedings nor shall it constitute a waiver of the arbitration agreement.

4. If the President of the Court issues an order as provided for in paragraph 2 of this Article, the effect of this Order shall not be terminated in whole or in part except by a decision of the President of the Court.

Jurisdiction of the Arbitral Tribunal to Decide on its Jurisdiction Article (19)

1.The arbitral tribunal shall decide on any payment relating to its non-competence, including on the basis of the absence of an arbitration agreement, its invalidity or non-inclusion of the subject matter of the dispute.

2. If the arbitral tribunal determines in a preliminary decision that it is competent, any of the parties within (15) fifteen days from the date of its announcement thereof may request the court to adjudicate the matter and the court shall decide on the application within (30) thirty days from the date of the request. The arbitral proceedings shall remain pending the determination of this application unless the arbitral tribunal decides to continue it at the request of one of the parties.

3. The party who requests the continuation of the arbitration proceedings shall bear the expenses of the arbitration if the court rules that the arbitral tribunal has no jurisdiction.

Article (20)

1. The argument that the arbitral tribunal has no competence within a period not exceeding the time limit for submitting the defense against the arbitrator referred to in Article 30 of this Law shall be adhered to. The next session of the session at which such payment was made, otherwise the right shall be forfeited and the arbitral tribunal may in any case accept the late payment if it considers that the delay was for an acceptable reason.

2. The appointment or participation in the appointment of an arbitrator by either party shall not result in the termination of his right to make any of the defenses referred to in item (1) of this Article.

Temporary or precautionary measures Article 21

1. Subject to the provisions of Article 18 of this Law, unless otherwise agreed by the parties, the arbitral tribunal may, at the request of one of the parties or on its own initiative, order any of them to take such temporary or precautionary measures as the nature of the dispute may require.

(A) ordering the preservation of evidence which may be essential in the resolution of the dispute;

(B) take the necessary measures to preserve the goods forming part of the subject matter of the dispute, such as ordering them to be deposited with a third person or the sale of goods subject to damage;

(C) the maintenance of assets and funds through which a subsequent decision may be implemented;

(D) To keep the situation or return it to the way it was until the dispute is settled.

(E) ordering an action to prevent the occurrence of imminent or imminent damage or prejudice to the arbitral process or ordering a failure to take action which could cause damage or prejudice the arbitration.

2. The arbitral tribunal may require the applicant of provisional or provisional measures to provide sufficient security to cover the expenses of such measures and may also incur all damages resulting from the execution of such orders if the arbitral tribunal subsequently decides that it is not entitled to obtain them.

3. The arbitral tribunal may amend, suspend or cancel an interim measure ordered at the request of any party or on its own initiative in exceptional cases and by prior notification to the parties.

4. A party whose temporary measure has been ordered in its favor after obtaining the written permission of the arbitral tribunal may request the court to order the execution of the order issued by the arbitral tribunal or any part thereof within fifteen (15) days from the date of receipt of the request and send copies of any application. To obtain authorization or enforcement under this Article to all other parties at the same time.

CHAPTER IV ARBITRATION PROCEDURES

Introduction or intervention of new parties to arbitration Article 22

The arbitral tribunal may permit the inclusion or interference of a third party in the arbitration litigation, either at the request of one of the parties or the intervening party, provided that it is a party to the arbitration agreement and after giving all parties, including the third party, an opportunity to hear their statements.

Determination of the procedures to be followed Article (23)

1. Subject to Article 10.2 of this Law, the Parties may agree on the procedures to be followed by the arbitral tribunal to proceed with the arbitration, including subjecting these procedures to the rules in force in any arbitration organization or institution in or outside the State.

2. If there is no agreement to follow certain procedures, the arbitral tribunal may determine such procedures as it considers appropriate, subject to the provisions of this Law and without prejudice to the fundamental principles of litigation and international conventions to which the State is a party.

Declarations Article (24)

1. The provisions of this item shall apply unless the Parties agree otherwise:

(A) Any written communication received shall be deemed to have been received if delivered to the addressee in person, or delivered at his place of business or habitual residence or at the address of the parties known to the parties or specified in the arbitration agreement or in the document governing the relationship covered by the arbitration and if none of these addresses is known. After the necessary investigation, the written message shall be deemed to be received if it is sent to the last known place of business of the addressee, his habitual residence or postal address by registered mail, by courier companies or by any other means which provides written proof of delivery attempt. Fax or e-mail address already parties to use it in their dealings with each other or above one party declaration of the other party in his letters.

(B) The letter shall be deemed to have been received by the recipient on the day on which it is delivered as stated in this Law. A letter sent by fax or e-mail shall be deemed to have been received by the recipient on the date on which it appears on its data, provided that there shall be no evidence of an error. In any case, the receipt shall be deemed to have been received if it is received or sent before 6 pm in the country where the correspondence was received.

2- To calculate the periods according to this law, the period shall start from the day following the day on which the message was received or any other correspondence. If the last day of that period falls on an official holiday or a working holiday at the address or place of work of the addressee, the period shall extend to the first working day obtained. Public holidays or work holidays during that period shall be included in the calculation of that period.

3. The provisions of this article shall not apply to correspondence made through proceedings before the courts.

Waiver of the right to object Article 25

If one of the parties continues in the arbitration proceedings with the knowledge of a violation of the arbitration agreement or of a provision of this law which may be agreed to violate it, and no objection to this violation has been filed within the agreed date or within (7) seven days from the date of realization of the flag when there is no agreement. From him on his right to object.

Equality of Parties to Arbitration Article 26

The parties to the arbitration shall be treated on an equal footing and shall each have an equal and full opportunity to present and defend their claims.

Article 27

1. Arbitral proceedings shall commence on the day following the completion of the composition of the arbitral tribunal unless the parties agree otherwise.

2. A declaration of arbitration shall be deemed to be an action for the purpose of signing the provisional detention.

Place of Arbitration Article 28

1. The parties may agree on the place of arbitration.

2. The arbitral tribunal shall, unless the parties otherwise agree:

(A) to hold arbitration hearings at any place it deems appropriate to carry out any arbitration proceeding with the declaration of the parties well in advance of the date of the hearing;

(B) Arbitration sessions shall be held with the parties or deliberated through modern means of communication and electronic technologies. The Arbitral Tribunal shall deliver or transmit the minutes of the hearing to the parties.

Language of Arbitration Article (29)

1. Arbitration proceedings shall be conducted in Arabic, unless the parties agree otherwise.

2. The language agreed upon or specified shall apply to the arbitral proceedings and to any written memorandum submitted by the parties and any oral argument of the opinion of an arbitral award, decision or other declaration made by the arbitral tribunal, unless otherwise agreed.

3. Subject to the provisions of Federal Law No. 6 of 2012 on the organization of the translation profession, the arbitral tribunal may decide to attach to all or some of the written documents filing the case a translation into the language or languages used in the arbitration.

Statement of Case and Defense Article 30

1. Unless the parties agree or the arbitral tribunal decides otherwise, the arbitrator shall, within fourteen (14) days of the formation of the arbitral tribunal, send to the arbitrator against him, to each of the arbitrators, a written statement of his claim containing his name, address and the name of the arbitrator against him and to each of the arbitrators. A written statement of his claim including his name, address, the name of the defendant and his address, an explanation of the facts of the case, a determination of the issues in dispute and his claims, and any other matter required by the parties' agreement in this statement.

2. Unless the parties agree or the arbitral tribunal decides otherwise, the arbitrator shall, within fourteen (14) days from the day following receipt of the statement sent by the arbitrator referred to in the preceding paragraph of this article, to the arbitrator and to each of the arbitrators a written memorandum. The court may include any incidental or countervailing claims related to the subject matter of the dispute or may claim a right arising from it in order to pay the set-off, even at a later stage of the proceedings if the arbitral tribunal considers that the circumstances justify the delay.

3. Unless otherwise agreed by the parties, each party may modify or complete its claims or defenses, or file a counterclaim during the arbitral proceedings, unless the arbitral tribunal decides not to accept this in order to prevent delay in the adjudication of the dispute or

because it is outside its competence. Arbitration in its decision the principles of litigation and defense rights.

Documents in support of the statement of claim and defenses Article (31)

Each of the parties may attach a statement of the case or a defense memorandum, as the case may be, to copies of the documents on which it is based or to indicate all or some of the documents and evidence to be submitted while respecting the right of the other party to access them. The lawsuit in requesting the submission of the original documents or documents on which any of the parties are based and the right of the other parties to have access to them.

Breach of obligations by Parties Article 32

Subject to the provisions of Article (30) of this Law, unless the parties agree otherwise, the following shall be observed:

1. If the arbitrator fails to submit, without an acceptable excuse, the statement of the arbitral proceedings in accordance with the provisions of this Law and the parties agreed to follow the procedures, the arbitral tribunal may decide to terminate the proceedings if it is satisfied that there is excessive and unjustified delay on the part of the arbitrator in pursuing his claim and that the delay causes the impossibility of access. To a just or unfair solution against the defendant.

2. If the arbitrator fails to file a defense note, the arbitral tribunal shall continue the arbitration proceedings without regard as an acknowledgment by the arbitrator against the defendant's claim. The same ruling shall apply if the defendant does not present his defense in response to a counter-claim.

3. If one of the parties fails to attend a hearing or submits the required documents or performs any action without an acceptable excuse, the arbitral tribunal may continue the arbitral proceedings and conclude what it deems appropriate in light of the actions and breaches of that party, as warranted by the circumstances of the arbitral proceedings. A judgment in the dispute based on the elements of evidence available to it.

Holding Sessions and Presenting the Environment Article (33)

1. Arbitral hearings shall be confidential unless the parties agree otherwise.

2. Unless otherwise agreed by the parties, the arbitral tribunal may decide whether to hold oral pleadings to present evidence or to make oral arguments or to proceed with proceedings on the basis of merely submitting documents and other material evidence. The arbitral tribunal may decide to hold such hearings at a later stage. Appropriate procedures at the request of a party.

3. Sessions may be held through modern means of communication that do not require the parties to attend in person.

4. The arbitral tribunal shall notify the parties of the dates of the sessions scheduled to be held well before the date specified by the arbitral tribunal.

5. The parties may, at their own expense, seek the assistance of legal experts and agents of lawyers and others to represent them before the arbitral tribunal and the arbitral tribunal may request any party to provide proof of the authority granted to its representative in a manner to be determined by the tribunal.

6. The summary of the proceedings of each session of the arbitral tribunal shall be recorded in a record and a copy thereof shall be delivered to each of the parties.

7. Unless otherwise agreed by the parties, witnesses, including experts, shall be heard in accordance with the laws in force in the State.

8.The arbitral tribunal shall have the discretionary power to determine the rules of evidence to be followed and the extent to which the environment provided by any of the parties on the fact or opinion of the expert shall be accepted, assessed and may also specify the time, manner and form in which such environment shall be exchanged between the parties and how it shall be submitted to the tribunal.

The use of experts Article (34)

1. Unless the parties otherwise agree, the arbitral tribunal may decide to appoint one or more experts to present its report, determine its mission and duration and send a copy of its decision to the parties.

2. Each Party shall submit to the expert information relating to the dispute and shall be able to examine and examine such documents, goods, real estate or any movable or immovable property relating to the dispute. The arbitral tribunal shall decide on any dispute between the expert and a Party in this regard.

3. Before accepting his appointment, the expert shall submit to the arbitral tribunal and the parties a statement of his qualifications and a statement of his impartiality and independence. Any party shall inform the arbitral tribunal within the period specified by the tribunal in the decision if he has any objection to the appointment of the expert. The expert shall have a final decision in this regard.

4. No Party may object to the qualifications, impartiality or independence of the expert unless the objection is based on reasons known to that Party after that expert has been appointed.

5. The arbitral tribunal shall transmit to each of the parties a copy of the report of the expert as soon as it is deposited and shall provide them with the opportunity to comment on that report within the periods specified by it.

6. After submitting the report of the expert, the arbitral tribunal may decide on its own initiative or at the request of one of the parties to convene a hearing to hear the expert's remarks, giving the parties an opportunity to hear and discuss the contents of his report and to examine any document based on his report. A party shall be appointed to express its opinion on the matters dealt with in the report of the expert appointed by the arbitral tribunal, unless the parties agree otherwise. The provisions of Article 33 of this law shall apply to such procedures.

The fees and expenses of the expert appointed by the arbitral tribunal in accordance with this article shall be paid by the parties as determined by the arbitral tribunal.

Witness Testimony Article (35)

The arbitral tribunal may hear witnesses, including witnesses of experience, through modern means of communication that do not require their personal presence at the hearing.

Jurisdiction of the Court to Order Evidence Article 36

1.The arbitral tribunal may, on its own motion or at the request of one of the parties, request assistance from the Court to obtain any evidence. The Court may, within the limits of its authority, order the execution of the request and the presence of witnesses before the arbitral tribunal in order to present and give oral testimony or to produce documents or any other evidentiary material.

2. The application shall be submitted to the President of the Court and he may decide any of the following:

(A) Sentencing any witness who fails to appear or refuses without legal justification to answer the penalties prescribed in the laws in force in the State;

(B) The judgment that a third party be required to produce a document under his or her possession that is necessary to adjudicate the dispute.

(C) Ordering the judicial delegation.

Chapter V

Arbitration award

Application of the Administration Law to the Subject of the Conflict Article 37

1. The arbitral tribunal shall apply to the subject matter of the dispute the rules to be agreed upon by the parties. If it is agreed to apply the law of a particular State, the substantive rules shall be followed without the rules concerning the conflict of laws, unless otherwise agreed, provided that it does not violate public order and morals in the State.

2. If the parties agree to subject the legal relationship between them to the provisions of a model contract, an international agreement or any other document, such provisions and the arbitration provisions thereof shall apply, provided that they do not violate public order and morals in the State.

The authority of the arbitral tribunal to determine the law

Applicable to the subject matter of the dispute Article (38)

1. If the parties do not agree on the legal rules applicable to the subject matter of the dispute, the arbitral tribunal shall apply the substantive rules of the law which it considers to be most relevant to the subject matter of the dispute.

2. In determining the subject-matter of the dispute, the arbitral tribunal shall take into account the terms of the contract in question, the current customs in the type of transaction and the manner in which the parties have transacted.

3. The arbitral tribunal may not adjudicate on the subject matter of the dispute in accordance with the rules of justice and equity without being bound by the provisions of the law, unless the parties expressly agree or authorize it to conciliate.

Provisional and Partial Provisions Article (39)

1. The arbitral tribunal may render provisional judgments or judgments in part of the applications before issuing the judgment ending the entire litigation.

2. Provisional provisions of the arbitral tribunal shall be enforceable before the courts and shall be executed by order of a petition issued by the President of the Court or his authorized representative.

Arbitration Agreement Article 40

If the parties agree before a decision ending the dispute to settle the dispute amicably, they may request proof of settlement conditions before the arbitral tribunal.In this case, the parties shall issue an arbitration agreement containing the terms of the settlement and terminate the proceedings.

Article 41 Arbitration Award and Statements

1. The arbitral award shall be rendered in writing

2. The arbitral award shall be rendered by a majority of opinions if the arbitral tribunal is composed of more than one arbitrator and if the opinions of the arbitrators are divided so that the majority does not comply with it. The President of the arbitral tribunal shall render the award unless the parties agree otherwise. In such case, the dissenting opinions shall be written or attached and considered an integral part. Of judgment

3. The arbitrators shall sign the judgment. If any of them refuses to sign, the reason for not signing shall be stated and the judgment shall be valid if signed by a majority of the arbitrators.

4. The award shall be justified unless the parties otherwise agree or the law applicable to the arbitral proceedings does not require the reasons for the award.

5. The arbitration award shall include the names and addresses of the litigants, the names of the arbitrators, their nationalities and addresses, the text of the arbitration agreement and a summary of the litigants' requests, statements, documents, the operative part and the reasons thereof, if such mention is due, date and place of issue.

6. The arbitral award shall be deemed to be rendered at the place of arbitration in accordance with the provisions of Article 28 of this Law, even if it is signed by the members of the arbitral tribunal in person, or the award is sent for signature by each member individually or by electronic means unless the parties agree otherwise.

7. Unless otherwise agreed by the parties, the date of the award shall be the date on which the award was signed by the arbitrator if it was individual and in the case of more than one arbitrator.

Article (42)

1. The arbitral tribunal shall render the award terminating the entire litigation within the time agreed upon by the parties. The arbitration shall extend the period provided that the extension period shall not exceed six (6) additional months, unless the parties agree on a period exceeding that period.

2. If the arbitral award is not issued after the expiry of the period referred to in item (1) of this Article, the arbitral tribunal or any of the parties may request the court to issue a decision specifying an additional date for the award of the arbitral award or the termination of the arbitral proceedings if necessary and may extend. This period shall be in accordance with the conditions it deems appropriate and its decision in this regard shall be final unless the parties agree otherwise.

3. If the Court issues a decision to terminate the arbitral proceedings, either party may file its case with the court originally competent to hear it.

Decision on Preliminary Matters Article 43

If, during the arbitration proceedings, a matter which is outside the jurisdiction of the arbitral tribunal or challenged by forgery is presented in a paper submitted to it or criminal proceedings have been taken for its forgery or for any other crime, the arbitral tribunal may continue to consider the subject matter of the dispute if it considers that the decision in this matter or in the forgery of the paper or in the act The other penalty shall not be necessary for adjudication of the dispute, otherwise it shall suspend the proceedings until a final judgment is issued in this respect. This shall result in the suspension of the date set for the award of the arbitral award and shall be counted again from the day following the date of informing the arbitral tribunal of the disappearance of the reason for the time.

Article (44)

Subject to the provisions of Article (47) of this Law, the Arbitral Tribunal shall announce the award to all parties by handing each of them an original copy or a copy signed by the Arbitral Tribunal within (15) fifteen days from the date of the judgment.

Article (45)

1. The arbitral proceedings shall end with the issuance of the judgment ending the entire dispute by the arbitral tribunal.

2. The arbitral tribunal shall terminate the proceedings in any of the following cases:

If the parties agree to terminate the arbitration procedures in accordance with the provisions of this law.

(B) If the arbitrator leaves the arbitration dispute, unless the arbitral tribunal determines, at the request of the arbitrator, that it has a serious interest in continuing the proceedings until the dispute is resolved.

(C) If the arbitral tribunal considers for any other reason that the continuation of the arbitration is not feasible or impossible.

Arbitration Expenses Article (46)

1. Unless otherwise provided in the agreement of the parties, the arbitral tribunal shall assess the costs of the arbitration, including fees and expenses incurred by any member of the arbitral tribunal for the performance of its functions and expenses designated by the arbitral tribunal.

2. The arbitral tribunal may rule on all or part of the expenses provided for in item (1) of this Article.

3. No request may be made to the Court to reconsider the amount of expenses if there is agreement to determine them.

Failure to hand over judgment in case of non-payment of expenses Article (47)

1. Without prejudice to the right of the arbitrators to refer to the parties for their fees and expenses, the arbitral tribunal may refuse to hand over the final arbitration award to the parties in the event that the arbitration expenses are not fully paid.

2. If the arbitral tribunal refuses to hand over the award in accordance with the provisions of paragraph (1) of this Article, any of the parties may apply to the Court after the declaration of the other parties and the arbitral tribunal to oblige the arbitral tribunal to submit the award to the parties, after proving the payment of all fees and expenses requested by the Or those determined by the Court in accordance with Article 46 of this Law.

Confidentiality of Arbitrators' Provisions Article 48

The arbitrators' judgments shall be confidential and may not be published or part thereof except with the written consent of the parties. The publication of judgments dealing with the arbitral award shall not be considered a breach of this principle.

Article 49 Interpretation of the Arbitration Award

1. Once the arbitral award has been rendered, the arbitral tribunal shall not have any authority to adjudicate any of the matters dealt with in the arbitral award. The parties agree on other procedures or periods and the applicant for interpretation shall notify the other party of this request before submitting it to the arbitral tribunal

2. If the Arbitral Tribunal finds that the request for interpretation is justified, it shall render a ruling in writing within thirty days following the date of the submission of the application to the Tribunal and may extend this period for another 15 days if it deems it justified.

3. A judgment rendered in interpretation shall be deemed to be complementary to the arbitral award which shall be interpreted and its provisions shall apply

Correction of Material Errors by Arbitration Article (50)

1. The arbitral tribunal shall correct the written or mathematical errors in its judgment by a decision of its own motion or at the request of one of the parties after the announcement of the

other parties. The arbitral tribunal shall correct the judgment within (30) thirty days following the date of issuance of the judgment or submit the application for rectification as the case may.

2. The correction decision shall be issued in writing by the arbitral tribunal and announced to the parties within fifteen (15) days from the date of its issuance.

3. A judgment issued for correction shall be deemed to be complementary to the arbitration award and its provisions shall apply.

Additional Arbitration Rule Article (51)

1. Any party may request the arbitral tribunal within thirty (30) days following receipt of the arbitral award to issue an additional arbitral award in applications submitted during the proceedings and omitted by the arbitral award.

2. If the arbitral tribunal considers that the application referred to in item (1) of this article is justified, it shall render its judgment within (60) sixty days from the date of submitting the application.

3. An additional arbitral award shall be deemed to be complementary to the arbitration award and its provisions shall apply.

4. If the Authority does not issue an arbitration award in accordance with the provisions of this Article and Articles 49 and 50 of this Law, the Party concerned shall submit a request to the Court to do so.

Mandatory Force of Arbitration Article 52

The arbitral award rendered in accordance with the provisions of this law shall be binding on the parties. The court order may be authentic and shall have the same executive power as if it were a judicial ruling, but its execution requires a decision to be ratified by the court.

Article (53)

1. An objection to an arbitral award shall be admissible only by filing a nullity action before the court or during the hearing of the request for ratification of the award. The applicant shall prove any of the following reasons:

(A) the absence of an arbitration agreement, or that the agreement was invalid, or its duration was terminated in accordance with the law to which the parties were subject or in accordance with this law, in the absence of a reference to a particular law;

(B) At the time of the conclusion of the arbitration agreement, one of the parties was incompetent or incompetent in accordance with the law governing its eligibility.

(C) The person has no capacity to dispose of the disputed right in accordance with the law governing his or her eligibility as provided for in Article 4 of this Law.

D) If one of the parties to the arbitration is unable to present his defense because he or she has not made a valid declaration of the appointment of an arbitrator or of the arbitral proceedings or as a result of the arbitral tribunal breaching the grounds of litigation or any other cause beyond his control.

(E) If the arbitral award excludes the application of the law which the parties have agreed to apply to the subject matter of the dispute

F- If the arbitral tribunal is formed or an arbitrator is appointed in a manner contrary to the provisions of this law or to the agreement of the parties.

G- If the arbitration proceedings are invalid, we shall have an effect on the judgment or the award shall be issued after the expiry of the prescribed period.

If the arbitral award has decided on matters not covered by the arbitration agreement or exceeded the limits of this agreement, however, if the parts of the provision relating to matters subject to arbitration may be separated from those of non-arbitral matters, then the invalidity shall be null and void only in the latter parts.

2. The Court shall rule on the invalidity of the arbitral award on its own initiative if it finds any of the following:

(A) The subject matter of the dispute shall be one of the matters which may not be arbitrated.

B- Violation of the arbitration award to public order and public morals in the State.

Article (54)

1. The judgment rendered by the court in a nullity action shall be considered final and the appeal shall be accepted only by cassation.

2. A claim for nullity of the arbitral award shall not be heard after thirty (30) days following the date of the award of the award to the party requesting the nullity.

3. The award invalidating the arbitral award shall result in the removal of all or part of that award according to whether the annulment is wholly or partially invalid.

4. Unless otherwise agreed by the parties, the arbitration agreement shall remain in force in accordance with the provisions of this law after the annulment of the arbitral award, unless the annulment is based on the absence of the agreement itself, its termination, its invalidity or its inability to enforce it.

5. A claim of nullity shall not preclude the acceptance of a nullity claim.

6. The court which is required to overturn the arbitral award may suspend the annulment proceedings for a period not exceeding sixty (60) days if it deems it appropriate at the request of one of the parties in order to give the arbitral tribunal an opportunity to take any action or amendment in the form of the award that would remove the reasons. Revocation without affecting its content

Enforcement of Arbitration Award Article 55

1. Anyone wishing to execute an arbitration award shall submit the ratification of the award and order the execution thereof to the President of the Court, accompanied by the following:

Original or certified copy of the judgment.

Copy of the arbitration agreement.

(C) a translation certified by an accredited body into Arabic for arbitration award, if not rendered.

A copy of the minutes of filing the judgment in the court.

2. The President of the Court or his designee shall order the approval and execution of the arbitration award within a period of sixty (60) days from the date of submission of the request for ratification and execution thereof, unless he finds that there is one or more reasons for the invalidity of the arbitration award based on the proof of any of the cases mentioned. Article (1) of Article (53) of this law.

Suspension of Enforcement of Arbitration Article (56)

1. The filing of an action for nullity of the arbitral award shall not entail the suspension of execution of the judgment. However, the court hearing the nullity of the arbitral award may order a stay of execution upon the request of one of the parties if the request is based on serious reasons.

2. The Court shall decide on a stay of execution within fifteen (15) days from the date of the first specified hearing.

3. If the court decides to suspend the execution, it may order the applicant to submit a guarantee or financial guarantee and shall decide on the invalidity action within (60) sixty days from the date of issuance of this decision.

Appeal against the execution of the arbitration award Article 57

The court's decision ordering the execution of the arbitration award or refusing to execute it may be appealed to the competent court of appeal within thirty (30) days from the day following the announcement.

Chapter six

Final Provisions Charter of Arbitrators and their Lists Article 58

The Minister of Economy shall issue the Charter of Arbitrators in coordination with the arbitration institutions in the State.

2. The Minister of Justice or the head of the competent judicial authority shall draw up the lists of arbitrators from whom selection shall be made in accordance with the provisions of Article 11 of this Law.

Scope of the Temporal Application of the Law Article 59

The provisions of this law shall apply to any existing arbitration at the time of its application, even if it is based on a previous arbitration agreement provided that the procedures taken in accordance with the provisions of any previous legislation shall remain valid.

Abolition of Arbitration Articles in the Code of Civil Procedure Article (60)

- Articles (203) to (218) of the Federal Law No. (11) of 1992, referred to above, shall be repealed, provided that the procedures in accordance therewith shall remain valid.

2. Any provision contrary to the provisions of this Law shall be repealed.

Dissemination of the law and its provisions Article (61)

This Law shall be published in the Official Gazette and shall come into force one month after the day following its publication.

INDEX

MIX
Papier aus verantwortungsvollen Quellen
Paper from responsible sources
FSC® C105338

Printed by Books on Demand GmbH, Norderstedt / Germany